CHICAGO PUBLIC LIBRARY

R01007 95672

C0-AAQ-426

CHICAGO PUBLIC LIBRARY
SOCIAL SCIENCES AND HISTORY
400 S. STATE ST.   60605

THE CHICAGO PUBLIC LIBRARY

HV 8079 .C48 M36 1992x
McQueeney, Robert M.
Unpardonable sins

FORM 19

UNPARDONABLE SINS

CHICAGO PUBLIC LIBRARY
SOCIAL SCIENCES AND HISTORY
400 S. STATE ST.   60605

UNPARDONABLE SINS

A FATHER'S FIGHT FOR JUSTICE

Robert M. McQueeney
And Bob Vacon

NEW HORIZON PRESS
Far Hills, New Jersey

HV
8079
.C48
M36
1992x

Copyright © 1992 by Robert M. McQueeney and Bob Vacon

All rights reserved. No part of this book may be reproduced or transmitted in any form whatsoever, including electronic, mechanical, or any information storage or retrieval system, except as may be expressly permitted by the 1976 Copyright Act or in writing from the publisher. Requests for permission should be addressed to New Horizon Press, P.O. Box 669, Far Hills, New Jersey 07931.

Library of Congress Catalog Card Number: 91-68140

Robert M. McQueeney and Bob Vacon
  UNPARDONABLE SINS

ISBN 0-88282-068-0
New Horizon Press

1997 1996 1995 1994 1992 / 5 4 3 2 1

Manufactured in the United States of America

■ CONTENTS ■

R01007 95672

CHICAGO PUBLIC LIBRARY
SOCIAL SCIENCES AND HISTORY
400 S. STATE ST.   60605

v

Contents

■ AUTHORS' NOTE ■

This is the actual experience of a real person, Robert M. Mc-
Queeney. The personalities, events, actions and conversations
portrayed within the story have been reconstructed from extensive interviews and research, utilizing court documents, letters,
personal papers, press accounts and the memories of partici-
pants. In an effort to safeguard the privacy of certain individu-
als, the author has changed their names and the names of certain places and, in some cases, altered otherwise identifying
characteristics. Events involving the characters happened as described; only minor details have been altered.

■ ACKNOWLEDGEMENT ONE ■

To begin this acknowledgement, I would like to say a few words about my husband Bob.

Bob was a well-respected journalist at *The Hartford Courant*, who was given the opportunity to fulfill a life's dream to become a published author. Bob believed in Robert McQueeney's quest for justice. With Bob's sudden death we feared that Robert's story would never be told. If it wasn't for the people I am about to mention, this book would not have been completed.

First, to the News staff at *The Hartford Courant* for their encouragement and support. They convinced me to follow through with the book's completion. I am particularly grateful to Mike Waller, Editor of *The Hartford Courant*.

Most of all to Lyn Bixby, a veteran journalist at the *Courant* who not only worked with Bob for many years, but was also a close friend. He deserves heartfelt thanks for selflessly undertaking such an enormous and sometimes agonizing task in order to see a friend's dream come true. I am grateful for his intelligence, determination and insightful writing.

Thank you all, for making this legacy for Bob Vacon and Robert McQueeney a reality.

Susan Vacon

■ ACKNOWLEDGEMENT TWO ■

"Go, Giants!" were the last words Bob Vacon ever spoke to me. I am so very glad one of his last memories was New York's triumph over the Washington Redskins on that last Sunday football afternoon of his life. I miss him deeply.

Bob, as author, was the heart and conscience of this book. I am only the storyteller. His belief in me, right from our first contact, and his energy and passion drove this book to completion—even after his death.

After losing Bob, during the bleak moments when the fate of the book mixed with coping and grief, Lyn Bixby who completed the authorship offered me a piece of his life. *Unpardonable Sins* was rescued by his committment to justice and his love for Bob. I am so grateful to him and Bob's *Hartford Courant* family for their refusal to let his effort go unfinished.

Joan Dunphy, my publisher, like Bob, believed. Believed and was shaken by the travesty of my story. But, like too few, she had the courage to then act. I appreciate the rare opportunity she has afforded me.

A number of people stood by me during my horror. I wish there had been more. I cannot forget the support and friendship of my coworkers at MRC, most especially my boss and friend, John Agnew, and my "baby brother," Dave Brewer. My oldest pal, "Mitts" Samsel, his Pammie and my "Mom and Dad #2" stood fast, too.

My attorneys, Jon Schoenhorn, Hank Hurvitz and "Big John" Andreini were effective, professional and gave me the confidence and encouragement to keep my spirits up. My parents' deep, powerful love nourished us all. Selflessly, they pushed aside their own suffering to buoy me, make me laugh. As such, they acted in the only way they ever have—fully supportive and committed to go the distance. To be grandparents again is their only just reward.

My in-law family also never hesitated in their complete support, responding as my own blood, with compassion and strength.

And, if not for my wife, Jackie, and her granite constitution and unwaivering devotion, the trial and all its reverberations would have surely devastated me. With her patience and dedication, I have been able to repair much of my despair. And, she has given me Maddie—and the resolve to keep fighting and bring my "Beanie's" never-forgotten brother and sister back home.

Lastly, I must convey my single reason for publishing my story. This book will forever serve as a legacy of truth for "Keefe" and "Wendy." For you, this is a source of pure information about a time in your lives when mistakes, lies and sins were the rule. My hope is that, some day, this book will compel you to raise the questions you would not have asked as little children.

So, as long as one copy reaches your hands, my intentions are fulfilled.

Rob McQueeney

*"What is the Unpardonable Sin?" asked
the lime-burner. . . .
"It is a sin that grew within my own breast,"
replied Ethan Brand . . .
"The sin of an intellect that triumphed over
the sense of brotherhood with man . . ."*
     —Nathaniel Hawthorne

CHAPTER ONE

Frozen In Time

As the overcast sky began to darken to the east, Rob McQueeney pulled his small son's blue toboggan up the snowclad knoll. The hill was little more than a bump, about ten feet high and fifteen feet long—child's play for an adult, a challenge for a child. Rob reached the hilltop and let out a frosty sigh.

Even when Rob was in high school, he had dreamed of one day having a son. Now, he had one. His name was Keefe Michael. He was four years old. He looked exactly as Rob had once fantasized: blond, little potato nose, fair-skinned, not chunky like his equally fair-skinned, dark-haired, teddy bear-like father, but not skinny either.

Raising his hand, Rob signalled Keefe to come up. Then Rob glanced at Wendy, his nearly three-year-old daughter. From the sideline, Wendy was staring intently, first at her father, then at her brother, then back to Rob again. After a few icy spills and bumpy toboggan runs, she had decided it would be more fun—and a lot less wet—to watch. She looked so cute, Rob thought, in her snowsuit, mittened hands plunged deeply into her pockets like a tiny, blue Smurf.

Smiling to himself, Rob wiped some melting snow from his brown, close-cropped beard. The scene filled him with nostalgic pleasure. Like most fathers, he cherished the time he spent with his children. Like too many, a broken marriage now severely limited that time. Rob had become, much to his own shock, disillusionment and sadness, a weekend daddy.

1

When Keefe neared the top of the hill a few minutes later, taking those clomping, lurching steps that small children have always used to struggle up snow-covered hills, his call of "Daddy" abruptly broke Rob's reverie.

Keefe looked expectantly at his daddy. "One more ride down the hill, then we have to get home," Rob told him. "And this time, little man, you're going to go down by yourself. Okay?"

Rob answered his son's dubious look with a smile of encouragement and settled him into the toboggan. Gently, he handed Keefe the yellow, plastic rope, gave him a hug and some last-minute instructions before walking down the hill.

At the bottom, he turned to face his son. "C'mon, Keefe! You can do it . . . Don't worry; you won't fall . . . It'll be fun!"

Keefe wiggled his bottom back and forth, finally inching the plastic toboggan over the edge of the hill. As the toboggan slid down the slope, Keefe's animated face captured the story of every little boy doing something on his own for the first time. Part fear and part elation, it was the proud, wide-eyed look of children everywhere taking their first bicycle rides, climbing their first trees . . . or making their first solo toboggan rides. An ageless expression, yet as fresh as a child's curiosity. For Rob, it was a very special moment, frozen in time.

Keefe's eyebrows had arched above the snow-speckled rim of his New York Giants knit football cap. His eyes looked like twin full moons, so perfectly round that his pupils could have been blue marbles bobbing in a white lake. His mouth was wide open and his smile was squirreled away—banked for when the ride ended.

It quickly did. The toboggan hissed to a stop and Rob clapped his hands as he paraded over to his son.

"My little man made it down the hill. Keefe, you did it. Way to go! All right, little man!" Rob bent over to give Keefe a hug.

Wendy's hands were noiselessly clapping as she ran over, skipping with joy over her brother's performance and her father's excitement. She was screaming and giggling, though not exactly sure why. A few feet from the toboggan, she tripped and fell face-first into the snow, arms splayed out at her sides. But she sensed this wasn't the time to cry, so she boosted herself up, wiped the snow from her rosy face and threw herself into a hug of her father's legs.

McQueeney smiled down at her. Then Keefe got up from the toboggan and looked at his daddy. He was beaming, his face flushed with exertion and joy. He didn't say a word; he didn't have to.

McQueeney was filled with an exhilarating pride entirely out of proportion to such a simple achievement. He had never felt closer to his children, nor loved them more.

Instinctively, he felt that this Sunday afternoon, February 1, 1987, was a time he would cherish, a memory his mind would replay, again and again. When you only have your children for forty-eight hours a week, small things are important.

"Let's go, guys," he said, as Keefe pretended to fend off a hug from Wendy. He had reached that age when hugs from sisters were embarrassing, but still felt good. So, while he verbally protested, he snuggled close to her at the same time. Minutes later, the three, damp, chilly McQueeneys had gathered up their belongings and were in their small red Chevette, parked by the side of the building where McQueeney worked.

Feeling a bit nervous, Rob carefully calculated the time to drive the half-mile back to his home in the small, central Connecticut town of Plymouth. He was thinking about having to rush to get the kids bathed and fed and returned to their mother by seven p.m. Rob had been separated from his wife since the previous July and was seeking joint custody of his children. He tried to plan fun things, to have family routines for the kids, even in their limited time together. Vicki, his estranged wife, might be angry if he brought little kids home late. It was now past three-thirty in the afternoon and he had about a half-hour drive to Vicki's home. There was little time to waste.

It was nearly four by the time he had the children latched into their car seats for the ride to his rural, ranch-style home in Plymouth. Once there, McQueeney had the kids quickly strip to their underwear and told them to wait in front of a hot-air heater in the kitchen while he prepared their bath. The heater was a favorite place for Keefe and Wendy. They often sat in front of it, side by side in their pajamas, enjoying the warmth and thinking little-kid thoughts.

As McQueeney was filling the bathtub, the phone rang. It was Ruth McQueeney, Rob's mother, whom the children called Nana. After Rob chatted with her for a minute, Keefe asked to talk. Still excited, he screamed in the telephone.

"Hi, Nana. We been sleddin'. I went down the hill all by myself."

In the background, Ruth could hear Wendy insisting, "I did too. I did too." Ruth smiled into the phone as Keefe continued, "It was weally 'teep, but I did it. I didn't even fall. Daddy fell when he was on the sled. I didn't. But I got all wet. Even my toes."

Keefe's struggles with a still-new language delighted his father and grandmother. He couldn't quite say "really steep." McQueeney often had to catch himself, so Keefe wouldn't think he was laughing at him. It was just another normal phase of child development that McQueeney found enchanting.

"Put your sister on the phone, okay? Bye-bye, Keefe. Nana loves you."

"Bye, Nana."

Keefe handed the phone to Wendy. The receiver was too big for her, and she had to keep shifting it to talk in one end and listen in the other. She was a very tiny—and gorgeous—child, with radiant, blue eyes, sunshine hair and milky skin.

"Hi, Wendy. How's my little sweetpea? Did you have fun in the snow?"

"Nana, Nana! At my 'tool, the teacher says wash your hands and get a pot."

"Do you like your little cooking class at school, honey?"

"Yeah, Nana."

"Good girl. Nana loves you, sweetpea. Hope to see you next weekend. Put daddy back on the phone, okay, hon?"

"I love you! 'Bye!"

Rob said good-bye to his mother and went to turn off the bath water.

"C'mon you goofballs," he called. "Bath time."

"You're goofy," he chided, as Keefe slid to a halt on the tiled bathroom floor.

4

"You're doofy, Daddy," Keefe countered.

Wendy, as always, was a few steps behind Keefe. She sashayed into the bathroom where she and her brother squirmed out of their underwear. McQueeney, stripped to the waist, picked them up and put them in the bathtub. Wendy was easy, but he had to reach quickly for Keefe, who liked to try to get into the bathtub by himself.

They immediately grabbed their toy boats and whale-shaped sponges. McQueeney let them play for a few minutes before telling them to start washing. Then, he ducked into the kitchen to put a kettle on the stove for hot chocolate.

He was back at the tub a few seconds later. He picked up a face cloth and finished bathing Wendy as Keefe played with his toy tugboat. "Put your head back, piglet," Rob said, as he rinsed his daughter's hair. "Okay. You're done."

"You're doofy, Daddy," she responded—a delayed echo.

"I am, huh?" he said as he swung her out of the tub. He lifted her above his head and playfully shook her before putting her down on a couple of towels he had spread on the floor.

"Yeah, Daddy," she giggled.

Wendy loved to dry herself. She swayed to her feet and began struggling with a towel that was twice her size. In the course of her contortions, the towel would occasionally rub against her, randomly drying parts of her body.

"Okay, little man. Your turn."

After Keefe's shampoo, it was time for the face cloth. Behind the ears. The neck. Between the toes. All the places Keefe wouldn't think to wash.

Between the buttocks.

"Ow."

Keefe's complaint seemed more a whine of irritation than a cry of pain.

"Oh, come on, Keefe. What's the matter?"

"It hurts there," Keefe replied as his father rinsed the sore area with a cupful of tub water.

McQueeney thought the soapy water was stinging some hidden irritation, so he rinsed Keefe again with fresh faucet water. This time, Keefe didn't complain.

With the bath finished, McQueeney lifted Keefe out of the

tub. He still seemed uncomfortable as he started to dry himself. McQueeney thought he might have been chafed during the tobogganing. His clothes had been wet, and he certainly had bounced around a lot.

"Let Daddy take a look."

Wendy, who had dried more from evaporation than her towel, was all eyes.

McQueeney crouched down and tried to look between Keefe's buttocks. He couldn't see anything and Keefe was not helping much with his squirming.

"Keefe, bend over the toilet seat. And keep still, please."

Keefe bent over and his father spread apart his buttock cheeks. He saw an inflammation about the size of a quarter around Keefe's anus. It was a deep red, almost the color of blood. He couldn't see any blood, but it looked puffy—and painful.

"Wait there just a minute," he told his son. "I'm going to put some powder on it. Don't worry, it won't hurt. It's the same powder Daddy uses."

McQueeney returned to the bathroom and liberally sprinkled the medicated powder around Keefe's fanny. He dabbed the powder with a finger to spread it over the inflammation.

"Ow! You're hurting me, Daddy," Keefe complained. This time he seemed to be in real pain. McQueeney stopped spreading the powder with his finger and just sprinkled it on.

Wendy was totally absorbed in the goings-on, watching with great interest. Keefe seemed embarrassed by what was happening.

"Okay, you can get dressed. I'll get your hot chocolates ready."

While the kids were sipping their drinks, McQueeney cooked some hamburgers and french fries. He was beginning to be nervous again about being late. He didn't want Vicki to be able to hold *anything* against him at the custody hearing on Friday.

Keefe ate most of his meal, but Wendy, as usual, only pecked at hers. McQueeney worried about what happened when he wasn't there to coax and encourage his daughter. She was just a wisp, weighing twenty-two or twenty-three pounds, several pounds below the normal weight for her age.

It was six forty-five p.m. when they left the house. They would be about fifteen minutes late. He felt that familiar twinge of dread that came whenever he returned the kids to their mother. In addition to the obvious discomfort of leaving them, he always felt uncomfortable around Vicki's live-in boyfriend, Bruce Johnson. He thought Bruce was a macho jerk.

Halfway to Vicki's house in Goshen, Keefe started his traditional Sunday night whining about going back. McQueeney groaned to himself.

"I hate Bwuce," Keefe said. "Me too," piped in his little echo, Wendy.

"I don't wanna go back," Keefe implored. "I wanna stay wif you. You're all alone. Why can't I stay wif you?"

"Me, too, Daddy. I wanna stay wit' you," added Wendy.

Rob sighed. He wanted to tell his children that he agreed with them. He wanted to be their hero—their only hero. But if Vicki and Bruce eventually got married, McQueeney wanted everything to be as smooth as possible between the two families.

"I wish you could both stay with me, too," he told them. "You know I love you more than anything else in the world. But isn't it fun to come over to Daddy's on the weekends? Don't you like to do that? I sure like it. I can't wait until next weekend!"

"Yeah," Keefe sullenly replied. "Yeah," Wendy solemnly echoed.

"Good. Maybe if the snow's still around next weekend we can go tobogganing again. This time, maybe we can find an even bigger hill. And don't forget, we've still got to teach Wendy how to drive the toboggan."

"I can dwive, I can dwive!" she insisted.

"Well, we'll see about that next weekend, okay?"

Both kids were quiet the rest of the ride. McQueeney was disappointed the weekend was over, but thankful the visitations were going so smoothly. He had the kids every weekend and most holidays.

"Yeah, things could be a lot worse," he thought. Then, thinking about the objections to joint custody that Vicki had once again raised the previous week, he mentally crossed his fingers.

They arrived just after seven fifteen p.m. Keefe walked up the snow-covered steps leading to the door, followed by Rob, who carried the ever-dawdling Wendy. He felt a flash of irritation at the unshoveled sidewalk and steps and knocked on the sliding glass door. Vicki quickly appeared.

Vicki had a soft face, light brown hair, hazel-blue eyes and a quick smile, which brought out her dimples. She was a clinger, always touching people, always eager to show her affection. She was very proud of her lithe body and was meticulous about her appearance, never leaving the house until her makeup was perfect. With her bouncing manner, she was easy to like and had quickly become a favorite of McQueeney's mother.

McQueeney walked a few steps inside, stopping halfway into the dining room to put Wendy down. Both kids had nearly dozed off in the car, and Keefe seemed particularly tired. While Vicki was telling the children how happy she was to see them again, Rob glanced into the living room. He expected to see part of Bruce's legs as the six-foot-three-inch, two-hundred-and-twenty pound man reclined on the couch.

Sure enough, there were the feet. McQueeney grimaced. He was sure that Bruce was letting him know that he was there in case any trouble started. He was, after all, a deputy court sheriff—and *very* proud of it.

Wendy had caught her second wind and, after giving her mother a kiss, ran giggling into the living room. McQueeney was ashamed at the pang of jealousy he felt as his daughter scampered over to Bruce. He quickly turned to Vicki.

"By the way, we all had a blast today tobogganing. On the last ride, Keefe came down the hill all by himself. It was the best ride I've ever seen. I think we have a champion toboggan-driver here," he said with a sideways smile at Keefe. "It was a gigantic hill. And he was so brave."

Keefe stood morosely as Vicki told him how proud she was. He was either too tired, too sad or too angry to want to recount his adventure. He trudged a few steps away.

"Wendy had lots of fun, too," McQueeney continued. "You

should've seen her making this big fuss over Keefe." McQueeney paused, and then stepped toward Vicki, half-turning his back to Keefe.

"I don't want to embarrass Keefe," he told her in a low voice, "but when I gave him a bath tonight, he complained that his rear end hurt. I looked at it and there was a red inflammation around his anus, about the size of a quarter. I put some of that medicated powder on it. You should take a look at it, though."

He glanced over his left shoulder at Keefe. McQueeney forced back a choked-up feeling as he contrasted his son's dismal expression with the triumphant one he had worn as he tobogganed down the hill.

"Well, I have to get going now," McQueeney said. "I'm pretty tired, too."

"Wendy, your father is leaving," Vicki stiffly called. "Come say good-bye."

Wendy bounced into the room. She lifted her arms to her father and he picked her up, gave her a hug and a kiss and told her to be a good girl. "Daddy loves you, piggle-looney."

"I love you, Daddy. Bye!" And she skipped away.

Rob turned toward Keefe, who was standing a few feet to his left. The little boy's arms hung limply at his sides, his face forlorn and lost. Separation. Divorce. A shattered relationship. He didn't know the meaning of these words. But he knew how they felt. Daddy was leaving.

Rob crouched on one knee to whisper to his son, "I love you, little man. I'll call you Tuesday or Wednesday, as always, okay? Don't worry—it'll be here before you know it."

He gave his son a hug. It was not returned. Keefe looked like he was on the verge of tears. "Be a big boy. Take care of your sister." Rob stood up, turned to Vicki, and told her he would see her the following Friday night. He left quickly, not wanting her to see how shaken he was.

During the ride home, he remained troubled by his son's obvious sadness. He tried to force those thoughts out of his mind and began to replay the entire weekend. As always, he dissected everything that had happened, trying to decide if there were things he could have done better. He knew he still had to

9

work on his relationship with Wendy. She was born two weeks after he had lost his job, and he had spent much of the next two years concentrating on his engineering career. He was beginning to make up for that, but felt more had to be done.

By the time he arrived home, McQueeney felt better. The first day of February had been a good one. Maybe 1987 would be better than 1986.

On Tuesday, McQueeney telephoned his kids. Wendy was still pretty incoherent on the phone, so he spent most of the time talking with Keefe. He was glad to hear his son was in better spirits than he had been on Sunday night. Keefe chattered happily about staying home from his pre-school on Monday because of another snowstorm. Then, the sadness crept into his voice.

"Daddy, when can we go to our house again?"

It was a question Keefe always asked. He still thought of his father's Bemis Street home as his own.

Rob patiently reassured him. "I'll be picking you up on Friday night, unless there's another snowstorm," he said. "Maybe we can go sledding, and then visit Nana and Papa. How's that sound?"

On Thursday, McQueeney's lawyer, Henry Hurvitz, called to tell Rob that Friday's custody hearing had been postponed. When McQueeney asked why, Hurvitz told him that Vicki's lawyer said he had a conflict and couldn't make it.

On Friday afternoon, Vicki called McQueeney at work. "The four of us are stranded at Cape Cod. Bruce's truck has broken down," she said, sounding regretful. She agreed to call him the next day about any progress toward getting home.

Vicki was full of apologies when she called on Saturday. The part needed to fix the truck wasn't available and they would have to remain at Cape Cod all weekend. When McQueeney asked to speak to the kids, Vicki told him they were busy and couldn't come to the phone. She promised to make up for the inconvenience.

On Monday, McQueeney called Hurvitz to tell him that he had been unable to see the children that weekend. Hurvitz told him that he would immediately inform Vicki's lawyer that he would not tolerate any more missed visitations.

The next few days passed slowly. For McQueeney, they were a constant reminder of his enforced separation from the normal daily interchanges a father has with his children—those small, but meaningful, occasions that can never be recaptured.

McQueeney called his children several times on Tuesday and Wednesday. Each time, he heard Bruce's voice on an answering machine. No one seemed to be home.

The following Thursday, when Rob returned to work after lunch, there was a message to call Officer Mark Grodecki at the Plymouth Police Department.

"What's this about?" Rob asked Rita, the company secretary, absentmindedly.

"I don't know," she shrugged, equally complacent.

"Oh, they probably want me to buy some tickets to something," Rob smiled and returned to his desk to call Grodecki.

While waiting for Grodecki to get on the line, Rob toyed with a pencil, wondering what sort of pitch the police were going to make. He knew the owners of the small company were big supporters of the local police. He smiled absentmindedly again, as he listened to another of those beep tones, the ones that mean the call is being recorded.

A deep voice answered, "Officer Grodecki."

"Hello, this is Rob McQueeney. I had a message that you had called me. What can I do for you?"

There was a pause and a shuffling of papers.

"Oh, Mr. McQueeney. Thanks for calling. Can you come down to the station today? We'd like to talk to you about a complaint we have against you."

"A complaint!" Rob was floored. "What sort of complaint?" His thoughts skipped around. Had he bumped some car without realizing it? Or forgot to pay some traffic fine?

The officer's hesitant voice interrupted his thoughts, "I'm

11

sorry. I can't really go into this over the telephone. Can you come down here? We can talk about it then."

Rob pressed him, confused, "What's this all about?"

Again the officer hesitated, clearing his throat, "Well, our policy is not to say too much over the telephone." He paused again.

"But we have a complaint against you . . . for child abuse."

■CHAPTER TWO■

The Complaint

Unbelieving, Rob rubbed his eyes with one hand and gripped the telephone tighter.

"What?" His mind spun around, but got nowhere. "A complaint about *me*? Child abuse? What child? Who made the complaint? Who made the complaint?"

Silence answered his outburst. A few seconds later, Grodecki sighed and told him, "Your wife."

"Vicki! Vicki made this complaint! I can't understand this." Rob shook his head. "What do you mean? What sort of complaint is it? What's going on here?" His heart pounded. Had Vicki actually gone to the police and made a complaint? She obviously had . . . but why? And why was this policeman being so evasive?

Grodecki's voice softened, but remained businesslike. "Again, Mr. McQueeney, I would like to be able to tell you more, but I can't at this point. Not over the telephone. That's our policy. Why don't you just come down?"

McQueeney drew in a deep breath and slowly let it out, trying to clear his thoughts. This involved Vicki and his children, and he needed to know what was going on. This man could tell him. Of course, he would talk to him. "Okay. I'll be down later this afternoon."

Hanging up, McQueeney searched his mind to make sense of what he'd just been told. Obviously, something pretty serious was happening, but what? He groaned to himself, suddenly remembering the custody hearing that had been abruptly cancelled the previous Friday. He decided he'd better call his lawyer, Hank Hurvitz.

As the lawyer got on the line, Rob cleared his throat and tried to sound calm, "Hank? I just got the strangest call. Vicki has made some sort of child abuse complaint against me. The police want me to go down to the station and respond." He rushed on, "I told them I'd go down later this afternoon. Do you have any idea what's going on?"

Hank was vague. Very vague. In fact, he sounded just like the police. "I think you'd better come down to my office right away and we'll talk about it. I won't discuss this with you on the phone." Rob was stunned by his response. It seemed obvious that Hank knew more than he was saying. Why did everyone want him to come to their offices to talk? What was happening? Fear gripped him.

McQueeney replaced the telephone, leaned back in his chair, and looked at the ceiling. He thought about how serious Hurvitz sounded. He thought about how serious the police officer sounded.

He thought about his kids.

Rob's hand trembled as he dialed his father's number at work. This sounded bad—very bad. He didn't want to go to his lawyer's office alone. It was all somehow related to his children, and that made him extremely anxious.

"I just don't know what to expect, Dad," he said when he reached his father. "This is all so weird. I'm scared something really bad is happening. I mean, she complained to the *police*."

Within the hour, they were heading to Hurvitz's office thirty minutes away in Hartford. They spoke very little, each occupied with his own private speculations, neither wanting to add to the fears of the other.

McQueeney pounced as soon as Hurvitz came out to greet them.

"Hank, what the hell is going on?"

Hurvitz turned to Ray McQueeney. "Mr. McQueeney, I'd like you to wait out here while I talk to your son," the lawyer's voice betrayed his uneasiness. "I need to talk to Rob alone— *now*."

Ray started to protest and then stopped. He was irritated, but one look at Hurvitz's face convinced him to keep quiet. The lawyer's expression was worse than grim, it was *foreboding*. Ray took a deep breath, sat on a couch and absently fingered a year-old copy of *Sports Illustrated* while he tried to make some sense of it all.

After ushering Rob into his compact private office, Hank began to explain. "I wanted you here," he said, looking off in the distance. "I didn't want you driving after you hear what I'm going to tell you." He shifted his eyes back to Rob. "You'd better sit down."

"I can't," Rob said, wringing his hands and pacing the floor, impatient, agitated, bewildered. "Did you know Vicki made a complaint to the police. Why does Vicki think there's been some type of child abuse?" he blared at Hank, stopping in front of him. He was imagining Vicki's discovery of a bruise or scrape from one of his and the children's wrestling matches. "Did she find some bruises on the kids? Geez, kids get bruised, you know? Shit, remember when she complained after finding flea bites on the kids after we had gone camping? Christ! I mean, I play with the kids all the time. We wrestle, we jump on each other. Why would she go to the *police*? What's going on?"

Hurvitz put up his hand to stop McQueeney's runaway monologue.

"Rob . . ."

Hurvitz paused.

"The complaint is for *sexual* abuse."

McQueeney froze.

"What?"

Mouth agape, he replayed the words in his mind. He was sickened by the thought of sexually abusing Wendy. Christ, his daughter wasn't even three years old. She still needed help with her toilet routines. Was that it? Had he done something during potty training that Vicki had misconstrued? Or during a bath?

Hurvitz's next words exploded in his head.

"With Keefe."

"Keefe?" Rob gasped. *"Keefe?"*

He crumbled into a chair, vaguely aware of the stomach acid rising in his throat. He was being accused of molesting his "little man"? His dream-come-true little boy? Disbelief mixed with self-contempt, as though just hearing the accusation was enough to contaminate him—enough to cover him in filth.

Hank was still talking.

"Remember two weekends ago when you had the kids?"

"Yeah, yeah . . ."

"And do you remember giving Keefe a bath?"

"Yeah, yeah . . ."

"And he complained about his bottom hurting?"

Of course Rob remembered. He had put some powder on Keefe . . .

He looked up, astonished. The realization crashed into his brain. The red swelling around his son's anus. Suddenly, he understood. He was being accused of raping his son.

"Incest?" he screamed. "Me?"

What little self-control he had been grasping onto immediately disintegrated. He leaned on Hank's desk and buried his face in his hands as silent sobs shook his body. Tears crowded past his tightly shut eyes and landed on the thick glass that covered the mahogany desk top. For long moments, there was no sound in the room as he strangled in his agony.

Hank slowly walked out from behind his desk and briefly laid his hand on Rob's shoulder before leaving the room.

Alone, Rob slowly gained a semblance of physical control. When Hurvitz returned, the sobs were subdued, the initial visceral shock replaced by a miserable, disbelieving bewilderment. Rational thought was impossible. A maelstrom of images filled his mind as jumbled segments of thought crashed into and over each other.

The bath. The powder. The tobogganing. The custody hearing. The hurt he had felt when Vicki left him. The joy he had felt at Keefe's birth. The miserable look on Keefe's face that last Sunday night. The police officer's call. His parents. His friends.

His pulse pounded in his head. An unfathomable sense of loneliness enveloped him. The wretched unfairness kicked at his insides, churning his guts.

Hurvitz quietly sat down in his chair. "Look, Rob, I don't know how I would react if someone made the same accusation against me." He glanced at the moist rainbow smear near the corner of his desk, just behind a picture of his own children. Rob absently wiped away the tears that had fallen on the desk.

Rob finally spoke. It was a pathetic plea from a broken man.

"Hank, you *know* I didn't do this."

Hank nodded, his expression miserable. "We've been friends for a decade. Of course I do."

Hank then explained what he knew. Vicki had told her lawyer about the weekend, including the tobogganing, the bath and Keefe's inflamed anus. She said she was concerned that Rob may have sexually assaulted Keefe. Perhaps Wendy, too. The lawyer had called Hurvitz. Now, the police were involved.

Rob suddenly looked up. The solution seemed simple to him, "Officer Grodecki has invited me to talk, to respond to the complaint. Isn't that what I should do?"

Hank thought otherwise. "If the police call back, tell them to call me. I don't want you going down there. You'll be too upset."

Rob started arguing, "Look, I like to be straight up with people. It seems preposterous to me that I could be suspected of incest because a boy who had been tobogganing for two hours has a sore rear end."

"No," Hank replied. "There is nothing in the world you can gain by talking to the police. You'll be upset and they'll wonder why you're upset. If you get angry, they'll wonder why you're angry. If you're *not* angry, they'll wonder why you're *not* angry. If you're scared, they'll wonder why you're scared. If you're nervous—and you sure as shit will be nervous—they'll interpret that as something significant. Anything you said could be twisted, misinterpreted and used against you.

"The police are *not* your friends in a situation like this. They have a job to do. And that job is to close the books on this complaint—preferably with an arrest—so the complainant will be satisfied. You're being accused of a felony that could put you in prison for a long, long time. Listen to me. I'm your lawyer."

Rob's head snapped up when Hurvitz mentioned prison. He hadn't even thought about being arrested, let alone prison. The accusation was ridiculous. It couldn't possibly lead anywhere.

Incredulous, he asked, "Do you think the police are going to call again?"

The reply came from a bottomless well. "Probably."

Rob's next words were forced. "Do you think I'm going to be arrested?"

"I don't know, Rob. I'm not a criminal lawyer. My partner, Jon Schoenhorn, handles criminal cases, and I want you to talk to him about this. For now, though, you should just go home. I'd suggest you stay with your parents. This isn't a time for you to be alone. And don't contact Vicki, either. She isn't your friend now, any more than the police are. Rob, this is serious, serious shit."

Rob swayed to his feet. He felt utterly empty. Every emotion had been drained from him. He shuffled out of the office toward his father.

"What happened?" his father demanded, alarmed at how pale his usually robust son looked.

"Let's get out of here," Rob replied. There was a sense of urgency to the statement, as though he had to escape the scene of a gruesome accident. Without further words, they hurried out of the building.

At the car, Rob felt his father's light touch on his arm. "I'd better drive. Give me the keys."

Rob almost burst into tears. After the pummeling he had just taken, it seemed incredible that softness could still exist, that there were still people who loved him. A muffled sob escaped as he handed the keys to his father. He felt like a frightened little boy, unable to control events, relying on other people to take his hand and lead him home.

Raymond McQueeney is a taciturn man. A contract toolmaker, he usually does not say much, but he misses little of what goes on around him. He is a strong, gentle man, but the sight of his son, pale-faced and trembling, shook him badly. As soon as they were inside the car, he noticed Rob locking the door before slumping into his seat. He had never seen him do that before.

"What happened, son?"

Quickly, with few details, Rob told his father. "You figure it out yourself, dad. It's too hideous to say out loud." Rob dissolved into sobs and didn't say another word until they reached his parents' home fifteen minutes later.

"I think you should talk to the police," insisted his mother as soon as she heard the story. "You've *got* to. They don't know Vicki the way we do. You know how sweet and sincere she can seem, even when she's lying through her teeth. You know how she can turn on the tears whenever she wants. She fooled us for five years. She can fool them, too."

"I absolutely agree," his father said. "Right now, they only have Vicki's story. You have to give the police your story. You *have* to get it on the record."

Incest. Rob shuddered, anger flaring up within him. He had to make them understand, but he was frightened. In his heart he wanted more than anything to face the police and this filthy accusation. But his brain told him not to let some cop play amateur psychologist. He turned to his final arbitrator, his gut. "I'm not going to the police," he announced. He explained Hank's advice to his parents.

"But how are you going to let them know you didn't do it?" His mother objected. Rob looked at her miserably. He wanted the police and everyone else to know that he was incapable of doing such a horrid thing to any child, let alone to his own son.

His head swam. He wanted to do so much, was ready to do so much, but could do so little. Hurvitz had said the police were going to call again. What was going to happen? Was he going to be arrested? Was he going to jail? Were people going to read about him in the newspapers? When would he see Keefe and Wendy again? Did Vicki actually believe he did that to their son? Didn't she have five years of marriage to judge what kind of father he was?

He found the answer to the last two questions the next day, Friday the thirteenth. Rob had stayed home from work. All day, his emotions had been on a silent, raging roller coaster. Fear. Anger. Confusion. Resentment. Vicki's call came during a steep stretch of anger.

"The police said I'm supposed to get your side of the story," Vicki tonelessly offered.

"How *dare* you," Rob screamed into the phone. "How could you ever, *ever* think that I could do something like this. You *know* that I've always been a good father. You *know* how much I love my children." Rob could not hold his temper in this first confrontation with his accuser. "Damn you!" he yelled, before crashing down the telephone.

Still angry, he called Hurvitz.

"If she should call again, stay calm," Hurvitz told him in his most even, lawyerly voice. "If she insists, give her your side of the story. And, if she wants to talk, let her have her say. Then get back to me." He paused. "And, Rob, I mean it. Stay calm."

The phone rang ten minutes later.

"Are you ready to talk now?" Vicki calmly asked.

Rob struggled to contain his fury. Then, as coolly as he could, he defended his abilities as a father and began to recount what had happened on the last weekend. "I just can't believe that you would ever think this happened, especially after *I* was the one who told you about Keefe's inflammation in the first place, and *I* was the one who asked you to keep an eye on it." His voice was getting louder and his words more accusing. He was beginning to lose control. He paused to try to regain his composure.

Vicki, who had quietly listened to his ten-minute monologue, spoke for the first time. Her voice was expressionless. "Well, I have just one question for you."

"What?" Rob snapped.

Still calm, she asked, "Did your father ever do this to you?"

Rob's mouth flew open and his throat slammed shut as he recoiled from this unexpected angle of attack. Then the line went dead. Despair pinned him motionless.

The next few days were just as bad. Every muscle in Rob's body tightened, pulled to near-breaking point. He was constantly looking over his shoulder, waiting for the inevitable. Every time he drove into his neighborhood he looked for the police car in his driveway. He started at every ringing of the phone.

On Monday, Rob forced himself to go to work. Nobody at work knew what he was facing. It would be an escape. It would be better then sitting alone in his empty house, endlessly replaying these events.

And it was—until the police called again.

This time, it was Sergeant James Senetcen. He sounded gruffer than Grodecki. He told McQueeney that he could be interviewed either at the police station or at his home. Barely concealing the nervousness he felt, McQueeney told Senetcen that he had been advised not to talk to the police.

"My lawyer told me that I am not to talk to you unless he is present," Rob said. "If you like, we can set up a time, and my lawyer and I will meet you at the police station. Or, you can call my lawyer directly and set up an interview with him." He offered to provide the phone number.

"We don't call attorneys," Senetcen coldly responded. "And we don't talk to people with their attorneys present."

"Well, my attorney told me not to talk to you without him being there."

"So, you're not going to talk to us?" It sounded like an ultimatum. Rob's stomach lurched.

"Well . . . no."

The conversation ended. Rob hung up the phone and again felt utter despair. He had heard the contempt in the cop's voice. Any tick of the clock could find the police taking him away to jail. A spasm of terror cramped his heart. He was convinced that a cruiser would be waiting for him when he arrived home that evening.

But there was no cruiser in his driveway Monday night. For the next several nights, Rob sat in his darkened living room, staring out the picture window. There were no lights and no sounds in the house that had once been a home to the laughter of his children. Just Rob and Holly, his black, labrador-shepherd, sitting, watching, waiting and wondering what was creeping up on him. He would not retrieve his mail until darkness set in. It seemed somehow safer.

Every minute of every day, he was looking over his shoulder, waiting for the inevitable. He often pictured his arrest: there would be a knock on his back door and he would open it to the police. His neighbors would watch as he was taken away.

At work, he shrunk away from every telephone call. Each time he drove onto Bemis Street, he looked for the police car in his driveway. He braced himself each time he played back the messages on his answering machine.

But, as the days passed, Rob began to shake some of his dread. The authorities must be catching on to what was behind the accusation. Of course they were. They *had* to.

When nothing had happened by Sunday, he knew the insanity had passed. Much of his fear was replaced by a yearning to see his children again. He chastised himself for the agony he had put himself through. This had gone as far as it would go. Truth had won out. Calm, methodical reasoning had ended this absurdity.

The next day, Monday, February twenty-third, Rob was returning to work after having lunch with Ted, who handled most of the company's sales, and Dan, one of the co-owners. It had been eleven days since he had visited Hurvitz's office, and three weeks since he had spoken with his children. But his strength was returning, and, with it, came his usual optimism.

Rob had enjoyed the lunch; it was the first time he had ventured out socially since he had learned of the sexual assault accusation. He was relaxing in the back of Dan's new, silver luxury Buick, his left arm stretched across the wide back of the seat.

Rob wasn't thinking of anything in particular. Suddenly, he noticed a police car parked by the side of the road.

Rob's heart skipped a beat.

"No," he said half to himself. "Don't start imagining things."

"Something wrong?" his boss, Dan, asked absentmindedly.

"Hey, Rob, got a speeding ticket you forgot or something?" teased his colleague, Ted Andrews, glancing into the rearview mirror.

Rob cast a lingering glance over his left shoulder as Dan pulled the silver Buick into the driveway alongside the small, white office building.

The police car was following them, barely a foot behind their rear bumper.

Rob felt dizzy, faint. His heart kicked into his throat. He gasped, short of breath.

As they pulled into a parking space near the rear entrance to the building, the police car followed and parked broadside, inches from their car.

"I think this is for me," Rob murmured slowly.

"You're as white as a ghost," Ted, obviously concerned, leaned toward Rob.

"Are you all right?" Dan asked.

"All right," Rob answered mechanically.

When they got out of the car, the three men were face to face with two police officers. Rob stepped forward.

The cop with the dark glasses spoke first, "Are you Robert McQueeney?"

"Yes," Rob answered in a voice much calmer than he felt.

With that confirmation, the officer reached over and briefly touched McQueeney's right forearm. He was standing slightly to the side of McQueeney, bracketing Rob between himself and his partner.

The officer began reading from a piece of paper he was holding in his left hand.

"You are under arrest . . ."

The next words were lost in a spasm of formless, senseless noise that filled McQueeney's head. It was as though he was standing in the middle of a busy airport runway.

In a monotone, the officer continued.

"You have the right to remain . . ."

The horrible white noise struck again, a lightening-thunder combination that exploded inside McQueeney's brain. His knees buckled. The noise seemed to be spilling out of his ears, taking with it every ounce of his strength, of his very being.

The officer began to take the handcuffs off of his belt.

"Oh, no," McQueeney protested. "Do we really need those?"

"I don't know who you are," the officer snapped. "I'm not going to take any chances."

McQueeney weakly extended his hands as the officer cuffed

him. The cuffs were loose at the top and bottom of his wrists, but rubbed against the side . . . cold . . . foreign.

A sense of icy dread filled his gut.

The officer pushed his glasses up on his forehead and fixed his steel-blue gaze on Rob. "You are under arrest for first degree sexual assault and for risk of injury to a minor."

Dan and Ted stood transfixed as McQueeney was led away to the police cruiser. Finding his voice, Ted called out, "Is there anything I can do, Rob?"

"Call my parents. Tell them I'll be at the police station," Rob heard himself reply. As Ted began to ask what he should say to them, Rob added, "They know what's going on. Just say, 'It happened.' "

The police car passed McQueeney's Bemis Street home on the way to the station. Terrified, he stared, watching his home recede.

Five minutes later, they walked into the police station, passed the information desk and continued down a short hallway to an office beside the jail cells. Rob cringed.

Someone removed his handcuffs. He was rubbing his wrists when another officer came into the small office.

"Empty your pockets, please."

Rob dazedly complied. Driver's license. Credit cards. Change. Keys. A few bills. He didn't carry a wallet. Too bulky.

He handed over his coat.

"I need your belt, too, sir."

Stupefied, Rob looked up. The voice belonged to a different cop. He was silver-haired and seemed gentler than the two cops who had brought him in—almost sympathetic.

Still, the officer was taking his belt. Rob had never been in a jail. He didn't know they took your belt. He felt as though he was watching a bad movie.

A month before, Rob had dressed his little boy in New York Giants blue and taught him a cheer for the Super Bowl game. They had watched the game, together with McQueeney's parents. Three generations of McQueeneys. A special day. A month before that, McQueeney had taken a holiday picture of his children in front of the Christmas tree they had decorated together.

24

Keefe had unexpectedly put his arm around Wendy. Rob had been a proud father that night. Now he was going to jail for raping his son. The police believed it had happened. They had never heard his story. They thought he was guilty.

They took his belt. He couldn't get his mind off the belt. If he was scum enough to sexually assault a little boy, he was capable of hanging himself in a jail cell.

Then they took his shoelaces.

He was led into a cell, where he stood motionless for a few moments before sitting on the edge of a hard cot. He stared at the video camera just outside his cell. He stared at the still water in the stained toilet. For long minutes, he just stared.

He idly wondered whether someone could actually hang himself with the camera catching the action. He looked at the walls and was surprised they were clean. Must've just been painted—one of those off-white shades that really is no color at all. No graffiti to look at. How could there be? They took people's belts; who would be in there with a Cross pen, or a mechanical pencil? Rob's engineer's brain was idling.

They came to get him. He was fingerprinted. He stood for their pictures and was brought to an office to make a phone call. He called Hurvitz, who gave him explicit instructions not to talk to the police. He told Rob that his partner, the criminal lawyer, would meet Rob for his court arraignment the next morning.

His bond was set at $10,000.

He heard a commotion as his parents arrived. He was brought out to see them. He had to hold up his pants. He felt ashamed shuffling toward them in his socks. His mother was crying as she hugged him tight. He didn't notice that he was crying as well. He'd never seen his father's face so white. Abruptly, they took him away, bringing him into a small office where the bond commissioner was sitting.

Tall and hefty, the commissioner wore no expression. Just another day at the office for him. The man asked McQueeney some questions. It was as though Rob was applying for a loan.

Yes, McQueeney had graduated from high school. Yes, he had a fulltime job and a mortgage on his home. "Yes, *sir*." McQueeney was petrified. Hurvitz had told him this man could double his bond as easily as he could reduce it. McQueeney didn't think he could bear to spend the night in jail. He pushed the thought aside, as though he was clearing space on a cluttered desk.

The bond was lowered to $5,000. McQueeney was returned to his cell. An officer went to see his parents to tell them how much they would have to pay to get their son released.

Ray McQueeney started writing a check for $5,000.

Police don't accept checks.

Ruth took out a credit card.

Police don't accept credit cards.

McQueeney's parents were lost. They had no idea what to do, what was expected of them. Ray felt a helpless anger. Ruth began to sob wildly.

"How dare you do this." she shouted, her voice quivering with frustration and rage. "What do you mean you won't take our check? You took my son! How *dare* you! You've got Rob in some hole somewhere and he hasn't done anything. Why won't you let him out? What's the matter with you people?"

A thought kept repeating itself in Ray's mind: We're caught in the grip of the authorities and we can't do a thing about it. Nothing.

Ruth continued to protest and sob. She had been shaking since getting the telephone call about Rob's arrest. Now, she was *vibrating* with fear and anger. Ray led her away.

Ruth was still muttering to Ray when someone suggested calling a bail bondsman who would put up the $5,000 for $500 in cash. Ray found the name of the bondsman in a telephone book. It was a woman and she was located twenty miles away. They had less than $50 in cash between them and their bank was twenty-five miles away.

Rob heard bits of the argument. He could feel his parents' frantic frustration mix with his own fear of staying in a jail cell overnight. He asked if he could write a note. The silver-haired cop gave him a pen and paper and watched him as he wrote a note asking his parents to call Tom, a co-owner of the small company where Rob worked. Tom might be able to bring them the money.

Ruth called Tom, who quickly assured her he would be right over. She sat down again, very close to Ray. She could see other police officers calmly performing their duties and chatting with their colleagues.

"Look at them," she said miserably. "They don't care. My son is down in a hole somewhere and they're acting like nothing is wrong."

"Good guys, bad guys," Ray muttered, although the only "good guy" he had noticed was the silver-haired cop who had brought them the note from Rob.

Suddenly, a very large man walked through the door, followed by Ted, Rob's colleague. Ruth had never seen Tom, but Rob had described him as a "big, doughy man." She knew this had to be him. She sprang to her feet and Tom opened his arms. When he enveloped her, she felt as though she was sinking into a soft pillow. Immediately, she loved this rotund Italian. He told her not to worry, everything would work out. He gave her the $500 that would release her son. She hugged him again, her arms disappearing in folds of flesh. He hugged her back.

"How can I ever repay you?" she said with a sob. "You're so kind and wonderful to do this."

"Ruth, I've got a mother, too, and all I had to do was put her in your shoes," Tom replied. "I would want somebody to help her if she needed it."

Ted, who had quietly followed Tom through the door, was statue-like in a corner of the room, his mouth agape. He had wanted to be there to show his support of Rob, but he wasn't the type of person who said much.

Ruth hugged Tom good-bye. Ted, uncomfortable, mumbled some words of comfort, patted her shoulder and both men quickly left.

Four hours after arriving at the station, Rob walked out into the public lobby where his parents were huddled on a wooden bench. Ruth was sobbing uncontrollably as she reached for her son. The three of them held each other, rocking slightly.

The humiliation of being handcuffed in front of his friends was over. The waiting while his parents were stalemated by a system they knew nothing about was over.

27

He was out of jail. He was going home.

Rob McQueeney, accused child rapist.

It seemed that nothing could ever be worse than this moment, this day.

■CHAPTER THREE■

"Sweet Thing"

They had met on a sultry mid-August afternoon in 1981. It was one of those hazy, lazy New England days that brings out the backyard barbecues, the cold drinks and the idle gossip. McQueeney was twenty-six. He had just left work and didn't want to return to his empty house. He and his first wife, whom he had met and married while in college, had been divorced three months before. The marriage had been a casualty of youth and haste; the breakup had been amicable. McQueeney hadn't dated much since. Suddenly, today, he felt like some company. He headed toward New Britain, where his friend Tony Angelli lived.

Tony was pure Italian. The wiry, thirty-five-year-old Vietnam veteran had been born in Sicily and spent the first twenty years of his life in Italy. He had a big, black mustache, a temper to match and a healthy appetite for food and sex. He also had a young mate, Gina, who was very good at satisfying Tony's appetites, though not so good at deflecting his temper.

On this particular day, like so many others, Gina was at the stove, preparing food for Rob and Tony, who were sitting at the kitchen table drinking light beer and shots of peppermint schnapps. The kitchen was pleasantly cluttered with an assortment of small appliances, plants, spice containers and an occasional stray spark plug. Tony was McQueeney's unofficial mechanic, doing cheap, but good, under-the-table work on Rob's cars. Tony wanted his customers to like him. "Do good, they forget it; do better, they remember," was the favorite of his many sayings. McQueeney enjoyed this garrulous, colorful man.

Rob had just downed a shot of schnapps and was reaching for his beer when *she* walked in. His hand froze.

The faded blue jeans stuck to her taut body like a second skin. The fabric was clutching at her small, rounded buttocks, clearly revealing the outline of her tiny bikini panties. It was a young body on display—deservedly so.

Above the willowy hips were budding breasts casually covered by a small, pastel-tinged cotton top. And such an angelic face! Gorgeous brown hair framed her sweet features. Her hazel-blue eyes were at once sexy and guileless. Her dimples garnished the tiniest hint of a smile.

A stray strand of hair, moistened by the heat, fell across her forehead.

Rob's mouth dropped. The burning heat of the schnapps began to spread south from his stomach. He had to suppress a gasp.

The waiflike girl seemed oblivious to Rob's presence. She spoke briefly and quietly to Tony as Rob struggled to look nonchalant. Just as he was starting to swallow some beer, he heard Tony begin to introduce her. In an effort to be ready for the introduction, he swallowed much too quickly. He was attacked by a fit of coughing, followed by a loud hiccup. He recovered, laughed to himself and gave her his most winning, though still sheepish, smile.

Tony began again to make the introductions.

"Robby, I would like for you to meet Vicki."

The introductions were brief. Rob tried to think of something clever to say, but could only manage a dumb pleasantry about the weather. Then, as quickly as she had appeared, she turned to leave. Rob's eyes followed her as she walked out of the kitchen.

"Wow! Who was *that* fox?" he blurted at Tony as soon as she was gone.

"Ahh, you notice my little Vicki, eh? She is friend to Gina," Tony replied. "She such a little—how I should say this—naive, sweet thing. Her mother threw Vicki outta the house two years ago. Vicki was bouncing from friend to friend, stay two days here, three days there. Gina ask me, she tell me, 'Oh, Vicki, she's nice person. Can we help?' I see her, Robby. Those sad eyes. That's me, you know? I'm a sucker for that, you know what I mean?"

Rob started to reply, but Tony wasn't finished.

"I consider myself a man of the world, okay, but when I saw her, I say she just too damn sweet. I figure this girl, she gonna be out there, I guarantee you within about six months somebody's gonna spot her and they're gonna put her in the street working. So I say to Rosanne, bring her over the house, let her stay here. She can clean the house and help take care of the baby. I see with my eyes that she's a sweet person."

McQueeney nodded. She looked so untouched. It made Rob very nervous, but, he had to admit, it didn't diminish her desirability. Part of her allure came from what Rob perceived as a sweet vulnerability. She looked like a girl who wanted—and probably needed—someone to take care of her. She looked as though she would be happy to cuddle her way through life.

Rob knew he was being presumptuous to create this image of a girl he had barely met. But that, too, was part of her allure. There was a touch of mystery and intrigue about her. McQueeney loved mysteries.

Vicki also appealed to his love of the unconventional. She had been thrown out of her home. That piqued his curiosity, as well as his compassion. Rob liked to think of himself as a bit of an eccentric. His high school yearbook was filled with tributes to his willingness to do crazy things.

His friend turned warily paternalistic. Staring at Rob, Tony said, "Robby, you know I like you and respect you. I tell you, I am kind of like a father to Vicki. Vicki is a kind of weak person. She has trouble dealing with life. She always seems to be expecting the worst to happen. Look, I guess I just want to make sure some schmuck isn't going to take advantage of her."

Rob responded, "Well, I hope that doesn't mean you think I'm a schmuck." He paused before adding, "You know how terrible my romantic fortunes have been. She looks like she'd be good company. She's certainly—ahhh—not too difficult to look at. If something develops between us, that would be great. But I don't really expect that, and I certainly wouldn't push it. And I think you know me well enough to be able to trust me in that situation."

Tony smiled. He liked this McQueeney. An Irishman who thought like an Italian. He promised to ask Vicki what she thought of the idea.

Less than a week later, Vicki agreed to go out with Rob.

Rob, as usual, was punctual. He arrived at Tony's at precisely seven p.m., driving the big, black Oldsmobile 98 that he called Thunder. Vicki wasn't there. Tony shrugged and told Rob that she had gone to a party earlier in the day. She had said she'd be back by seven.

About ten minutes later, Vicki called to say that she was running a little late and would be there as soon as possible. Rob was instantly impressed that she had called. He thought it showed that she was considerate and mature. She wasn't just an airhead with a luscious body; she was a sweet, considerate girl —with a luscious body.

She arrived about twenty minutes later. For the next two hours they drove around the rolling central Connecticut countryside, talking.

Vicki told Rob about her mother, who had been divorced several times. "She liked to party a lot, and that meant I had to watch my little sister," Vicki said. "I watched her after school so Mom could work, and at night, so she could go to the bars. Sometimes, she didn't come home until I was getting ready for school the next morning."

Vicki grimaced. "I wanted to go out with my friends and do things," she said. "I didn't wanna have to watch my sister all the time. We were constantly fighting until I left. I lived with my boyfriend and his parents for awhile, and then we broke up and I stayed with a few other friends until I went to Rosanne and Tony's. I've been there for about six months. I think it might be time to move on."

A crazy idea popped into Rob's head, "You could come and work for me, be my housekeeper."

She looked up with those wide blue eyes and smiled. "You know, I've been wanting to get back to Bristol. My brother and sister live there, and it's hard for me to visit them from Tony's house in New Britain because I don't have a car."

Rob gulped, He was becoming a bit enchanted with Vicki. He was also impressed by the way she had seemed to cope with the tough hand she'd been dealt. The fact that he had such a wonderful childhood made his compassion for her rise. She didn't seem very intelligent or sophisticated, but Rob had been turned off by intelligent, independent-thinking women after his first wife had left him.

Rob had dropped out of Central Connecticut State College just a few credits short of graduation, insisting on getting a job so he could buy a house and Cheryl, his first wife, could continue her education. He had sublimated many of his own goals in an attempt to make her happy—and it hadn't worked. In a last-ditch effort to keep his marriage intact, he had vowed to change—to be whatever she wanted him to be. But Cheryl had wanted to be free to pursue her ideal. Their five-year marriage ended when the divorce she sought was granted on their wedding anniversary.

No, Rob was thoroughly disillusioned by challenging, complex women with strong ideas. He wanted a simple and sweet girl. Someone who would need him, not someone who would debate him.

Rob wheeled his Oldsmobile around and headed in the direction of Tony's house.

"So, it must have been tough breaking up with your boyfriend," he said. "Have you found anyone else?"

"Oh, no one, really," she said. "I've mostly just been going out with friends." She glanced at McQueeney as she said that. "I'm sort of like you, I guess. I'm just not ready for another relationship yet."

Rob was delighted that Vicki wasn't seeing anyone in particular. But he didn't want to spook her. In a perfectly businesslike manner, he said, "You know, think it over, really. If you decide to move in, there's plenty of room. You can have the upstairs bedroom and all the privacy you want. My bedroom's downstairs. I wanted to make it clear to you there isn't going to be any pressure there." He paused. "I don't want Tony coming after me."

By the time he dropped her off at Tony's a few minutes later, she had thanked him for the offer and accepted. A few days later, on Sunday, August thirtieth, she moved into the upstairs bedroom.

Rob had told Vicki Sunday night that he would stop in at lunchtime the next day to see how things were going. Monday was a wonderful late-summer's day—eighty degrees, with some billowy, white clouds lazing about the deep-blue sky. As McQueeney pulled into his driveway, he could hear music coming from his house. The windows were open and a gentle breeze was ruffling the curtains.

He drove into the carport and walked through the door into the kitchen. His dog Holly bounded up to greet him. Vicki was at the stove, stirring a pot of spaghetti sauce. She smiled as she said hello, her dimples dancing on each side of her full mouth. This is great, he thought. What a difference from coming home to an empty, shuttered house. This was the sort of life he wanted for himself. It wasn't just lust now; he *liked* this girl who had made a simple workday so special for him.

That night, they remained in the kitchen long after they had finished their meal. The stereo was on and they sipped red wine. When she began telling him how she had been sexually assaulted a year earlier, his eyes softened with compassion and he took one of her hands in both of his.

She told the story painfully and haltingly, with downcast eyes that often brimmed with tears.

"I needed a ride," she began. "And a neighbor—he was the father of one of my girlfriends—offered me one. We were going down Route 72 when he pulled over to the side, and, before I knew what was happening, he grabbed me and started feeling me.

"Oh, Rob, it was awful. I fought as much as I could, but he was punching and slapping me. He tore most of my clothes off and I knew he was going to rape me, but I managed to kick him away and I grabbed my clothes and ran out of the car."

She wiped her eyes and took a sip of wine.

"I went to the police to report it, but they were really rough. This cop—he's like forty years old—tells me they have to take pictures of the bruises and scratches that were all over me. I could just *feel* his eyes crawling over me.

"I couldn't do it," she said with a sob. "It was too hard. Too hard. The police said they wouldn't do anything unless I signed this paper saying I would testify in court. I would've had to tell the jury *everything*. It was just too awful a thing to talk about in front of strangers."

Vicki finished her glass of wine. "I feel so awful about it because I accepted the ride even though I *knew* he had tried the same thing with someone else in the neighborhood. And then, about a year later, someone told me that he went and assaulted somebody else. I mean, I wasn't looking for it, Rob; I swear I wasn't. I just wanted a ride.

"And then, when I didn't go through with the complaint, he did it to somebody else."

She started to weep. Rob remained quiet, letting his eyes convey his sympathy. When a minute or two had passed, and Vicki assured him that she was composed, Rob got up to open another bottle of wine. He laid a hand on Vicki's shoulder and she lifted her face to his. Her eyes were shining and there was a small, appreciative smile on her face.

"Thanks," she barely whispered.

"For what?"

"Just for listening, Rob. Just for, oh, I don't know. For being here. For letting me be here. For being so nice."

Rob could barely hear what she was saying. The tears were spilling off her chin.

"Vicki, you're a very beautiful, very special person," he said. "I'm glad you could talk about this with me. And I hope that whenever you need to talk about *anything*, you know that I'll be here to listen. I know I can't do anything to erase what's happened, and I'm sorry for that. But you can be sure that as long as you're in this house, nobody is going to hurt you. Ever." The talk—and the bond between them—became more intimate.

He brushed a tear from her cheek, smiled and took hold of her hands. "I have a rule in this house, Vicki: no pain allowed."

With that, Rob backed away, slowly dropping her hands. He turned to the counter and began opening the wine. Without a sound, Vicki rose from her seat and went to him. She took the bottle from his hand, placed it on the kitchen counter and looked up at him with wet, wide eyes.

With his back against the counter, McQueeney embraced her. She pressed herself against him. He pressed back, his hands roaming over her slender body.

They kissed. For long, delicious minutes, they held onto each other, touching and exploring, compassion giving way to passion and then to desire.

"Let's go to the bedroom," his husky voice ventured.

As they walked through the door, McQueeney felt a last-second prick of anxiety. Then it vanished.

They spent half the night making love. It was natural and easy with this undemanding young girl. McQueeney called in sick the next morning, and they spent half the morning making love. After lunch, Vicki moved her things—contained in two boxes and a grocery bag—into his bedroom.

Vicki was not a virgin. She had first become intimate when she was thirteen or fourteen years old, with the boy she had dated since she was ten. Since then, she had become very aware of her sensuality; it was in her eyes, her voice, her movements. It was deeper than flirting.

She seemed to love the closeness and the sweetness of giving herself to another person.

They were compatible bed partners. Rob had never been into wild sexual experimentation either. His sex life—with Cheryl and before her—had been sporadic and wholly unremarkable. During the first few months of his relationship with Vicki, though, their passion made them eager partners. They had a lot of sex.

But it wasn't long before they were having arguments, as well.

In early December, Rob was awakened when Vicki arrived home from a night out. These nights away from him were becoming more frequent. He frowned and looked at the clock beside the bed. It was one thirty a.m. A minute or two after he heard the front door close, Vicki was in the bathroom off the master bedroom. McQueeney knew what was coming next. The harsh sound of the toilet flushing hadn't yet subsided when she rustled beneath the covers and snuggled softly into her lover. She was naked. She kissed him on the cheek, took his hand and put it on her breast. With her other hand, Vicki groped between McQueeney's legs. "Rob?" she softly called. "Rob, are you awake?"

McQueeney groaned and rolled over. Vicki started rubbing her breasts against his back. "Rob, I'm horny. Let's do it."

McQueeney didn't answer.

"Rob? . . . Honey?"

McQueeney turned around and mumbled, "Vicki, it's almost two o'clock. I've got to get up for work in a few hours."

Vicki took his hand and guided it between her legs. With her hand on top of his, she began a slow, circular motion.

Rob was caught between his awakening desire, his annoyance at her absence and his urge to go back to sleep.

"Honey, rest up for tomorrow night," he abruptly said as he gave her a quick kiss. "We'll do it then."

When Rob returned home the next day, Vicki was peevish. She brushed him off as he went to hug her hello.

"When I'm in the mood, you don't want anything to do with me," Vicki said. "But, when you're in the mood, I'm supposed to respond?"

Rob swallowed a sharp retort and said, "C'mon, I'll open a bottle of wine and we'll talk about it."

Once seated at the kitchen table, Rob began talking. It was, in fact, a lecture.

"Vicki, you know I trust you. I'm not jealous that you go out at night. But I am worried about the sort of guys who might be attracted to you. And I'm worried about some of the girls you hang around with. I see Jennifer's name in the Bristol Press police blotter all the time. Why do you have to go out with people like that?"

Vicki protested that Jennifer just liked to party. "Sometimes, she gets a little carried away, with drugs and all, but I'm never around her when she does that," she said. "I mean, we smoke pot once in awhile, but who doesn't? She's really a nice girl. You'd know that if you came out with me and met her."

"Well, after working all day, I just don't feel much like partying," Rob said. "When I was your age, sure. But I'm not your age anymore. I've grown up. I prefer to stay at home. I mean, I don't mind if you go out once in a while, but you're really starting to go overboard. I mean, this is the first night all week you haven't been out. You should stay home more." He grimaced to himself. She was still a *schoolgirl*.

"All I'm saying is that I'd appreciate it if you were more considerate of me. I know we're not married, but it's the next-closest thing. You've got other responsibilities, now. With me. You should try to meet them."

Vicki stood up from the table. "And you should try to be just a little bit more sociable, Rob. You should come out with me once in a while, and do the things that I like to do. If you met some of my friends that you badmouth so much, maybe you'd find out they're not as bad as you think. I have to put up with your friends coming over here, why shouldn't you do the same for me?"

Rob started to argue that his friends were stable, hard-working people, not delinquents, but Vicki was already walking away. He shook his head. When is she going to grow up, he wondered.

Rob went to bed about an hour later. Vicki rolled over to face him. They kissed. Neither one of them suspected that their lives would be forever changed when they made love that night.

The following week, on Friday night, Rob stopped at a package store to buy a bottle of wine. He had had a rough week at work and fully intended to relax with Vicki at his side. He relished the thought.

When dinner was finished and Vicki had put away the dishes, Rob got up to get the corkscrew.

"Honey, how about you and me getting into some wine and soft music tonight?" he asked.

"Oh, Rob, I'm supposed to meet my friends at the Alley Cat tonight. They've got a good band there. Why don't you come along?"

"Ah, shit, Vicki, we had this argument last week. Do you have to go out *every* night? Why not stay home so we can talk? I want to be with you. I miss you."

"Rob, I'm bored here. I like going out. You can either come with me, or you can stay home again. Your choice."

"Fine," McQueeney snapped back. "Go out and booze it up with your sleazy friends. Great."

Vicki was already in the bathroom, putting on her makeup.

Vicki arrived home at three-thirty the next morning. That afternoon, Rob and Vicki visited his parents. It was a weekly tradition. While Rob was in the garage, helping his father restore his old Studebaker, Vicki sat and talked with Ruth.

Ruth had gradually grown to like, and then to love, the simple, sweet girl who seemed so affectionate and appreciative of their company. Ray, on the other hand, simply accepted Vicki as a fact of life—and hoped his intuition about her instability was wrong.

Vicki was always bringing Ruth and Ray a cake or a pie or something else she had made. She would never leave without hugging McQueeney's parents and telling them how much she loved them. She was amazingly easy to talk to, and she seemed to love confiding in Ruth, once telling her that her biggest dream was to be exactly like her and have a son who would turn out exactly like Rob.

That very day, Vicki asked Ruth how she had remained happily married for almost forty years. "Hon," Ruth said, "one of the secrets of a successful marriage is to never, never, *never* go to bed on a mad. Cancel the argument until the next day, but be sure to kiss each other goodnight. Give him a kiss, say, 'I love you and we'll talk in the morning.' Never go to bed, and never leave the house, mad at each other."

"It's as simple as that?" Vicki asked.

"Well, there's a few other things, I guess," Ruth said, proud that Vicki seemed interested in her advice. "I've always put my husband first, ahead of Rob and ahead of me. Ray gets the best piece of meat at the dinner table, he gets to choose the wine and he gets to make the decisions. That's just the way I am; it's the way I was brought up. I know that many women today think differently. And maybe Rob's upbringing has caused a few problems for you, I don't know. But I gotta tell you—it's worked for our marriage. Ray's happy, and I am, too."

39

Ruth smiled at Vicki. "You two planning to do something that we should know about, hon?"

Vicki giggled, as twin pink spots appeared on her cheeks.

With a twinkle in her eyes, Ruth added, "Oh, there is one other thing important to a good marriage. Never forget that once you're behind that bedroom door, anything goes. *Anything.* There is nothing bad about doing anything you feel like, as long as both of you want to do it."

Ruth had lost one child to a miscarriage and was physically unable to have any more children. She poured her love—enough for a dozen children—into Rob. Still, she had tried not to spoil him. He had to finish his homework—to Ruth's stringent standards—before he could go out to play. When he wanted a car, Rob had to work and save the money for it. When he wanted to drive it, he had to work some more so he could pay the insurance.

Ruth hadn't gotten along with Rob's first wife. She was too much of a women's libber for Ruth. And, like most mothers, she didn't think any woman was good enough for her son. Until Vicki came along.

In Vicki, Ruth believed Rob had found someone who wanted to bestow the same kind of attention and regard on him as Ruth did with Ray. It seemed to Ruth that Vicki wanted to please the man who had given her the calm, loving family life she had never had.

As the half-serious grunts and half-joking muttered curses drifted in from the garage, Ruth poured a glass of milk for Vicki.

"Oh, thank you, Ruth," Vicki said. "I really need this. I'm so hung over." She took a sip of the milk. "Don't tell Rob, but the cops stopped me last night for speeding. I was pretty sloshed, but I guess they didn't notice. All I got was a warning."

Ruth grimaced. "Vicki, why do you tell me these things?" she said, discouragedly. Despite how much she liked Vicki, Ruth was beginning to think there were warning signs. "You know I'm dead set against drinking and driving. Why do you do these things?"

Vicki got up from her seat, walked behind Ruth's chair, and draped her arms around her. "Oh, Ruth, it's not like I do them all the time. I don't really do anything wrong, you know that.

Please don't worry. I can take care of myself. If I have too much to drink again, I'll have someone else drive me home, how's that?" She paused. "And Ruth? Thanks for your advice. When I get married, all I want is a marriage as good as you and Ray have."

It was a sentiment Vicki repeated that night to Rob after they made love. It seemed to Rob a commitment to their relationship.

Two weeks later, on Christmas Eve, Rob gave Vicki a big, brightly-wrapped box that looked like it might contain a television set. She eagerly unwrapped it, only to find another, smaller box inside. She unwrapped that, only to be confronted with a still-smaller box.

Several progressively smaller boxes later, as Rob's camera hummed away, she found the heart-shaped diamond engagement ring.

"Oh, my god, this is the ring we saw at West Farms Mall a couple weeks ago!" she exclaimed as the tears streamed down her face. "I was going bonkers over it, and you bought it. It's so beautiful."

She reached over, brought Rob to her and gave him a long kiss.

"I didn't think we could afford this," she said, still sniffling.

"We can't," Rob said with a chuckle. "But we will. I *had* to get that ring."

There was no formal proposal from Rob. Just an underlying understanding that they would get married. That night, Vicki cried with happiness.

The next day, she cried again when McQueeney's parents gave her a pale blue winter coat as a present. She did not own a winter coat, and she burst into tears and exclamations of love when she saw it. She didn't take it off once that day. Nobody had ever made her feel so special, she said. Nobody had ever cared for her the way the McQueeneys did. She finally seemed to have a home and family.

When Vicki missed her period a few days later, she took a home pregnancy test. She was elated when it came out positive. She carefully wrapped the tiny bottle that signified her first pregnancy and secured it in a cabinet. She immediately stopped smoking and drinking. Vitamins and childbirth classes replaced nights out at the bars.

Her pregnancy completely turned their lives around. Rob was proud of her and ecstatic that she was pregnant. Vicki couldn't wait to have her first child—and McQueeney's parents were exultant at the thought of becoming grandparents.

They were married in April, when Vicki was four months pregnant. Rob wrote the ceremony, which was performed by a justice of the peace. Most of the twenty-five people who attended the simple ceremony in their home were Rob's friends and family.

One of the friends was Phil, a shy young man generous to a fault, who had once insisted that Rob take his watch as a gift, when Rob had remarked that he liked it. They had shared many mutual interests and good times during several years of close friendship.

A couple of months after the marriage, Rob and Vicki planned a clambake. Rob was counting on Phil to bring the clams. He never showed, and McQueeney never saw nor heard from him again.

A few months later, Ruth came across a list of Rob's friends that Vicki had given her to help organize a bachelors' party for Rob just before the wedding. Phil's name was on the list. Ruth had always thought it was strange that the friendship had ended so suddenly. She couldn't resist calling Phil.

After explaining who she was, she asked Phil what had happened to his friendship with Rob.

"I thought you knew," Phil replied. "Just after the wedding, Vicki called me and told me in no uncertain terms that I was not welcome in her house. She called me a fucking asshole —excuse me, Ruth, but that's what she said—and she said that Rob didn't have the guts to call me, but that he felt the same way. Neither of them wanted to see my—quote, unquote—'fucking face in their home again'."

Ruth was shocked. "Oh, you're not telling me the truth,

Phil. Vicki would never do that or even talk like that. Never. I don't think I should be talking to you anymore. Good-bye." She decided not to tell Rob about Phil's lies.

Vicki's pregnancy brought a calm, comfortable routine to the McQueeney household. They attended childbirth classes together, where Rob's dry wit would often break up the other couples. Rob was impressed with Vicki's commitment to her pregnancy, and was positive she was going to have a boy.

Vicki's contractions started in the afternoon of September third, 1982. After measuring the time between contractions, McQueeney called their obstetrician who told him to bring his wife to Bristol Hospital.

Vicki was admitted at seven p.m.—with her husband right beside her. Rob planned to remain in the birthing room throughout Vicki's labor, alternately giving her comfort and checking out the television set, which was carrying a pre-season football game between his beloved New York Giants and the Miami Dolphins.

Just after the final play in the 16–14 Giants defeat, Vicki began screaming in agony.

McQueeney was unprepared for the intensity of his wife's pain. He became faint and went into the bathroom to splash cold water on his face. Getting a grip on himself, he emerged a couple minutes later, and was able to stay by her side the rest of the long night.

At one forty-seven a.m. on September fourth, the obstetrician smiled and held up a seven pound, six-and-one-half-ounce, twenty-inch-long wrinkled, wet bundle. Keefe Michael McQueeney had arrived. Before he even saw Keefe, Rob knew that his dream had come true.

"You have your son," his wife said through her sobs.

Rob hugged her, as she started trying to pull tiny Keefe toward her.

"Wait a minute, we're still cleaning him up," the doctor said with a chuckle. "You can't have him until we cut the umbilical cord."

When the doctor lowered the towel-swathed Keefe onto Vicki's stomach, Rob put one hand on the baby and the other around Vicki's shoulder. He laid his head on Vicki's chest, and together they cried. At the age of seven minutes, Keefe looked exactly like the son Rob had pictured would one day be his.

When McQueeney went to the waiting room to share the good news, his mother mistook him for the doctor. He was still in the hospital gown and mask he had worn for the birth. Ruth burst into tears as soon as the masked "doctor" told her she had a healthy grandson.

"Where's my son?" she asked in a quivering voice. "Where's Rob?"

When Rob took off the mask and held out his arms, Ruth burst into fresh tears. A half-dozen family members flew into his embrace.

McQueeney always loved a stage.

"He didn't want to come out as long as the Giants were losing their game," McQueeney smilingly informed the group. "But as soon as the game was over, he was ready."

Rob paused to wipe his brow and the tears that had strayed onto his cheeks. "As you all know, I've wanted to have a son like this since I was a teenager. I even named him back then, borrowing 'Keefe' and 'Michael' from two of my many Irish ancestors. And I had this picture in my mind of what he would look like. Well, he's arrived, and he must've been made-to-order. He's perfect! Right now, he's lying on Vicki's stomach. Mother and son are doing well. The father I'm not so sure about."

With that, the sobs burst through, and there was another mass embrace.

While Rob's parents were driving home later that morning, Ruth turned to Ray and said, "Papa, you don't use that expression anymore."

Ray, puzzled, asked Ruth what she meant.

"You know how every so often after Rob and Vicki were married, you said you were waiting for the other shoe to drop. You don't say that anymore."

The new grandfather smiled, "Well, I guess it isn't gonna drop."

When Vicki and Keefe came home three days later, Rob lovingly placed Keefe in the middle of their queen-sized bed so he could start his twelfth roll of film. As he snapped away, Holly came over and mournfully rested her head on the side of the bed. You could almost see her wondering—with more than a little trepidation—what changes this new addition to the family would bring to her life.

Because their budget was so tight, Vicki started waitressing at two local nightclubs a couple of months after Keefe was born. They quickly settled into another routine, in which McQueeney would arrive home just in time to say good-bye to Vicki, who would leave for one of her jobs. McQueeney didn't mind, though. Keefe was keeping him busy changing diapers, giving baths and making up all sorts of sweet, cooing words of comfort.

Rob lovingly recorded Keefe's milestones, big and small. His first tooth showed up on February twenty-fourth, 1983. On March fifth, he said "Dada." He ate his first real vegetable on March ninth and went out to lunch with his parents for the first time on April first. His first bike ride—with his mother—was on March twenty-third. He started crawling on May second, and took his first two steps (One for each of us, Rob wrote), on May eighteenth. On June eighth, he said "Ma" and on June seventeenth, he had his first taste of real milk. The next day, he attended his first drive-in. He ate his first pizza crust on July fourth and his first Oreo cookie on August tenth. He spent his first night away from home on December third, when they all stayed at Rob's parents'. He ate his first peanut on December twenty-sixth.

Eighteen months after Keefe's arrival, Wendy was born on March 29, 1984. She came into the world two weeks after McQueeney had lost his job. For Rob, the timing was frightful and frightening, but he vowed not to give up nor to allow his family to suffer. He would find another job in quality control. He redoubled his efforts. By April he had found a position with a newly-formed technical group at a New Britain factory.

Again, McQueeney was enthralled with Wendy's birth. He wasn't disappointed that the baby was a girl. He had his son, and now he had a daughter. Two perfect dreams instead of one.

This time, McQueeney was prepared for the anguish of childbirth and was able to remain by Vicki's side throughout her labor and delivery. The miracle of watching a new life come into the world mixed perfectly with the pride he felt in having been a part of it. The tears he shed and the happiness he felt were as sincere as they had been at Keefe's birth.

About a month after Wendy's birth, McQueeney and Vicki resumed their previous routine. McQueeney would arrive home, Vicki would fill him in on the babies and, ten minutes later, would leave for one of her waitressing jobs. Their schedules put a strain on the marriage. One night, not long after Wendy was born, Vicki asked Rob if he would let her have the children if their marriage broke up.

"What are you talking about?" McQueeney asked. "I love you and you love me. At least, you say you do. Why would we break up our marriage?" He was astonished at her out-of-the-blue question.

"Well, people get divorced," she said, as she finished changing Wendy's diaper. "I'm not saying that'll happen to us, but, if it does, I think I should have the children."

"Are you making some kind of bad joke Vicki," Rob said, starting to become angry. "I wouldn't let you just walk off with the children. They're as much mine as they are yours. You know how important they are to me. I mean, you listened to me go on and on about the little boy I had dreamed about since I was in high school. And then, when it happens, and I have my son, you talk about taking him away and take my daughter too. C'mon, get real."

"You're forgetting one thing, Rob," Vicki responded. "I was the one who had these children. I have a right to them."

"Vicki, this is the craziest discussion we've ever had. For the life of me, I don't know why we're having it and, anyway, I don't think you're in any position to leave with the children," Rob said, his voice filling with hurt and irritation. "How could you afford to raise them? I hardly think the courts would consider a young barmaid who stays out to all hours to be a suitable single mother for two small children."

Vicki kept up the argument, telling her husband they were *her* children, and that a child's place was with its mother. Mc-

Queeney kept wondering why the hell she had brought the subject up in the first place.

Such rocky moments, however, did not seem of particular significance to McQueeney. Overall, life in his household was anything but extraordinary. They were a young couple doing the best they could, making the most of what money they had. He felt that, because of their mutual commitment, they were sacrificing their own relationship so the children could be raised at home instead of at a day-care center.

In the early spring of 1985, Rob took a position with a fledgling company that specialized in the custom design of measuring equipment. He would not only be inventing devices to inspect all sorts of automotive, military and consumer goods but have input in the company business plan—and its direction. The opportunity to learn advertising and marketing techniques in his field of expertise thrilled McQueeney. Such a chance to manage so many facets seemed endlessly challenging.

Immediately, Rob was working fifty to sixty hours per week. Days were swamped with familiar tasks—conceptualizing and drawing—and new actions, as well—telemarketing and budget plans. He was proud to have risen from his early machinist training to advance into the engineering world. He knew his grandfather, a twenty-five year veteran toolmaker at Pratt and Whitney Aircraft, would have been proud, too.

McQueeney hung a small picture of a confluence of ducks in his office. The caption read: DO SOMETHING—LEAD, FOLLOW OR GET OUT OF THE WAY.

As the new venture grew, sales trips became a demand. And to grow professionally, McQueeney enrolled in technical courses and became active in technical societies. He hated being away from Vicki and the kids so much, but he viewed it as a necessary investment in his career and their future.

On a pretty morning in May, while driving to work, he saw a "FOR SALE" sign in front of an adorable ranch just a half-mile from Rob's firm, on Bemis Street in Terryville on a huge, wooded lot. McQueeney screeched his battered Olds to a halt. Maybe such a move was in order for an up-and-coming executive.

Vicki instantly embraced the idea of moving into a larger,

more comfortable home. By November, the McQueeneys were settled in.

Money was even tighter than before. Vicki added a few extra hours of waitressing and started helping as a bartender.

When they did have a rare night together, Rob tried to talk Vicki into staying home so that they could be together, rather than going out. Vicki, however, still preferred her nights out. On one night that fall, she was at a bar with Pamm Samsel, the wife of Rob's closest friend, Brian. Pamm didn't really enjoy barhopping with Vicki. She, like Rob, had outgrown the bar scene. But she felt obligated to say yes on those occasions that Vicki asked her.

Vicki had just returned from the dance floor. She ordered another drink and turned to Pamm.

"You know, I have so much fun going out like this. Even when I'm working at the bar, it's like I'm not really working. I love it."

She paused to take a sip from her fresh drink. "I just wish Rob would come down to the bar once in awhile. I've begged him to come down so he could meet my friends, but he never, never does. I don't know what it is with him. He's always working at that stupid job. If he's not there, he's at night school, or studying, or reading, or watching the stupid Giants on television."

She took another sip of her drink and leaned closed to Pamm. "You know," she said conspiratorially, "if it wasn't for the kids, I would leave Rob. I really would."

Pamm was shocked, but thought that perhaps Vicki was just blowing off steam. They did have two kids: adorable kids. Pamm figured that meant that Vicki would stay with Rob. But it bothered her that Vicki would talk like that.

Just then, another of Vicki's friends asked her to dance. When she returned from the dance floor about fifteen minutes later, Pamm told her she was tired and wanted to leave.

"Okay," Vicki answered with a bright smile. "Just one more dance. I promised Barry a dance. Be right back."

As she waited for Vicki, Pamm decided not to tell anybody what Vicki had said about leaving Rob. It just wasn't the sort of news that you wanted to convey.

Still, there was another troubling revelation from Vicki that Pamm felt she had to confide. One night, a few weeks later, Vicki referred to her mother-in-law as a domineering, interfering bitch and said she would have nothing to do with her if she had her way. Pamm told her mother-in-law who was Ruth's close friend.

When the woman told Ruth, she was horrified. Ruth could not believe that the girl she loved as a daughter—the sweet girl who lovingly called her "Mom"—had said such things. A week went by and Ruth couldn't stand it any longer. She called Vicki.

After some pleasantries, Ruth got to the point.

"Vicki, I'm going to ask you something and I want you please to tell me the truth." Ruth's voice cracked as she began relaying what Pamm had said—without telling Vicki who had said it.

Vicki immediately started crying, "Oh, no, Mom. I never said anything like that. Oh, God, I love you, Mom. You know that. I don't know why anyone would ever say that I said those things. It's just not true. Please, believe me, Mom. I love you."

Ruth never mentioned the subject again, though the whole thing made her remember with an uncomfortable chill what Rob's friend Phil had said about Vicki, and how it had also seemed out of character with the sweet Vicki Ruth knew. Once again, she pushed it out of her mind and decided not to bother Rob with things people were making up about Vicki. She didn't want to spoil his happiness.

Even though everyone shielded Rob from Vicki's caustic remarks, as the days of summer wore on, Rob himself began to be concerned that he and Vicki were growing apart. Throughout July, he felt like they had become virtual strangers, barely saying hello and good-bye. Vicki continued working two jobs and he continued putting in extraordinarily long hours. Money remained tight as they struggled with the new mortgage. For weeks at a time, sex was nonexistent; neither had the time nor the energy for it.

Thursday, July thirty-first, was different.

Several days before, Rob and Vicki had decided to set aside Thursday night for themselves. Vicki would take the night off from work and they would bring the children to a sitter, who would take care of them until the following day. That would give Rob and Vicki the freedom to go out for a nice, intimate dinner, and then retire home early enough to have some long-delayed romance. It was a typical sentimental scenario scripted by McQueeney. He even readied some mood music on the stereo. And he deliberately planned each detail in advance so they could both look forward to it, savoring the anticipation.

On Wednesday, Rob took a tiny taste of the banquet he knew would be laid out for him the following night. Moments after he arrived home from work, Vicki was out the door and in her car, preparing to leave for one of her jobs.

Suddenly, though, McQueeney was aroused. "I love you, little fox," he said. He leaned in, took her face in his hands and kissed her, deeply and passionately. She returned the kiss with equal fervor.

When he pulled back, with a devilish grin on his face, he was a bit puzzled by her expression. She seemed caught off-guard and unsure how to react. There was a hint of a smile—the sort of expression that usually blossoms into a broad grin or a sly wink. But it did neither. She waved and was gone. McQueeney scratched his head and went into the house.

The next day, McQueeney arrived home a few minutes after five p.m. He was impatient with pleasurable anticipation. He took the single red rose he had bought off the car seat, and quickly strode to the door.

With her tail wagging, Holly greeted him.

Nobody else was home.

Puzzled, he looked around for a note.

"Ahh, here we go," he said to himself as he spied a piece of yellow notepaper on the kitchen table. She must have gone to the store to pick up a few last-minute things before dropping the kids off at her sister's.

He placed the rose on the table and picked up the note.

"The cat's outside . . . Vicki."

He felt a flicker of irritation. She always started her notes with "Honey" and ended them with "love and kisses." This was the sort of note you would leave for a plumber, not your husband.

He got a pen, wrote "What happened to 'love, Vicki?' " on the side of the note and circled it, with an arrow pointing to her signature.

He called his mother.

"Hey, Mom, were you talking to Vicki at all today?"

"No, Rob, but, you know, it's funny. I called her about eleven this morning and there was no answer. Why? Is anything wrong?"

"Oh, no, Mom," he quickly responded. "She's probably just doing a little grocery shopping. It's just weird because we had plans for tonight and I figured she'd be home. I'm sure she'll be right back."

He chatted for a few more minutes and then hung up the telephone. By now, it was almost five-thirty p.m. and he was starting to become aggravated. He hated when people were late. He changed into his jeans and went out to work on one of his beat-up old cars that had recently conked out. A half-hour later, he went back into the house, his anger more pronounced.

He called Vicki's sister. No answer. He called her mother. No answer there, either. Rob's carefully scripted night was falling apart. Where the hell was she? Why hadn't she left him a note, or called him? She couldn't have forgotten about this. Damn her. This was supposed to be a special night, a flawless night. Now, she had screwed it up.

By six-thirty, he was beginning to get frantic, as concern for his family's safety replaced anger. He went into the bathroom to wash up. Maybe she'd be home by the time he was finished. As he was drying his hands, he suddenly froze. A chill went down his spine. He was staring at the bathroom vanity. Vicki's make-up, nailpolish and hairdryer were gone.

"What the hell's going on?" he said aloud. Slowly, he walked over to her closet. All her clothes seemed to be there. Then he noticed that her work outfits were gone. He checked in the laundry room and they weren't there. In a panic, he raced into Keefe's room. It looked like everything was there. He went to Wendy's room and didn't find anything missing there, either.

He called another of Vicki's friends, a stewardess who lived a few towns to the west. No answer.

By now, it was a few minutes past seven. He called the Plymouth Police Department.

After breathlessly reciting what had happened, McQueeney felt his heart drop when the officer told him there was nothing they could do. She had not been missing for the twenty-four hours that is required before he could file a missing persons report.

"Well, can you at least keep an eye out for her car?" he worriedly asked. "It's a 1977 Ford Grenada, a really weird color, sort of a rusty orangy brown. Can you let me know if you see the car?" After the officer assured him they would watch out for the car, Rob let out an agonized sigh.

Shoulders slumped, he trudged back to Keefe's room and began to look more closely. His little boy's pajamas were missing. In a daze, he crossed the hall and went into Wendy's room. Her pajamas were also gone. He sat down and cried.

An hour later, he called his parents again. His mother answered. Rob told her that he was going crazy just sitting in the house waiting. It was now almost ten p.m. and he had no idea where his family was. He told his mother he would drive around for awhile, looking for Vicki.

"I'll call you in the morning, Mom."

"Good luck, hon. I'm sure it will work out."

"I don't need luck, Mom. I need my wife."

Rob didn't want to be alone, so he brought Holly. They rode around for more than an hour, checking out the homes of various friends and relatives. By midnight, McQueeney had come full circle, ending up where he had first looked—at Vicki's mother's house. There were no lights on. There was no answer when he knocked. He went back to his car, parked in the driveway, and got in. Exhausted, he rested his head against the steering wheel. Holly rested her head on his lap. They both fell asleep.

He was awakened by the slamming of a car door. His eyes flew open and he quickly raised his head to see who had made the noise. It was a neighbor getting into his car, probably going to work. He looked at his watch; it was seven a.m.

He let Holly out so she could relieve herself. He was stiff and sore and emotionally drained as he drove back to his house.

He called Vicki's father, who was living in North Carolina. He was surprised at McQueeney's call and told him he didn't know anything about Vicki's whereabouts. He promised to call if he learned anything.

At eight a.m., McQueeney called in sick. He forced himself to remain composed.

At about ten, he was again on the telephone with his mother. As he stood in the kitchen doorway, he could see part of his driveway and a large part of Bemis Street out the big bay window in the living room.

He saw a white Cadillac slowly traveling west on Bemis Street. Just before his driveway, the car slowed to a near stop. It turned into the driveway.

"I'll call you right back, Mom. There's somebody here."

It seemed that every sheriff McQueeney had ever seen drove a Cadillac. He knew this was a sheriff.

Dreamlike, he walked out to the car. He expected a huge, menacing man to get out. Instead, a petite woman in her fifties popped out the door.

"Are you Robert McQueeney?"

"Yes." he said agitatedly. "Please, tell me what's happened."

She calmly handed him a sheaf of papers and a pen and pointed to a dotted line. He signed his name and limply stood there as she left. He opened the papers. It was a divorce summons. He clutched them in his fist and began walking back to the house.

It felt like his entire body was shaking. He had passionately loved his wife and the life they were building with their children. He had thought their marriage would be forever. Now, they were gone. He was going to be divorced a second time.

Perching on a barstool by the kitchen's center island, he unfolded the papers. Tears so filled his eyes, he could barely read the words. He felt as though he was starting to fall out of his body. It was the worst feeling he had ever experienced in his life—up to that point.

He decided to call Henry Hurvitz, his lawyer. He had trouble dialing the numbers. He felt clumsy, as though his brain couldn't quite control his fingers. Finally, he got a secretary on the line.

Hurvitz was on vacation and wouldn't be back for more than a week.

He hung up and stared at the papers. He wasn't conscious of any thought or physical feeling. There were no more tears. He just stared. As he was sitting there, an idea suddenly blew into his brain. He opened the divorce summons and looked to see who was representing Vicki. It was John P. Clifford, Jr. His phone number was on the summons, which had been drawn up in the lawyer's office. He called.

"Gersten and Gersten law offices," a woman's voice answered.

McQueeney asked to talk to Attorney Clifford.

"May I ask who's calling and what this regards?"

McQueeney told her.

"Is Attorney Clifford your attorney?"

"No, he's my wife's attorney."

In a voice that made it clear that this sort of thing just wasn't done, the woman asked McQueeney why he would possibly want to talk to his wife's attorney. He should be talking to his own attorney.

"Well, I've just been served these divorce papers and I need to know what's going on." McQueeney's voice was pleading. He was losing control. "I can't reach my attorney."

"Just a minute, please." About thirty seconds later, she returned. "I'm sorry. I can't put you in touch with Attorney Clifford. You really need to get in touch with your own lawyer."

He couldn't stop the tears from bursting out. Moments later, Clifford was on the phone.

"Why can't you talk to your own attorney?" he asked McQueeney.

"He's on vacation and he won't be back for over a week," Rob said.

"Well, I really can't tell you anything, Mr. McQueeney,"

Clifford replied. "I understand your situation, but you really do have to go through your own attorney."

"Is this really happening?"

"I'm afraid it is."

"Where are they? Can you tell me where they are? I have no idea where my children are."

"I'm very sorry, but I can't give you that information. I just can't. I'm sorry, Mr. McQueeney, but I really do have to go."

Rob interrupted him, "Can I ask you just one question. Do *you* know where they are?

Clifford, surprised, asked McQueeney what he meant.

"I just want to know that there's *somebody* who knows where they are," Rob implored.

"Yes, I know where they are."

Rob thanked him and put down the phone. He laid his head on the small table and cried.

CHAPTER FOUR

Clutching At Hope

From the time Vicki left, through the following four days, Rob had no idea where his wife and children were living. He did not learn of their whereabouts until Vicki's attorney, John Clifford, told her that she *had* to tell McQueeney where his children were. Finally Vicki called Rob.

For the next two weeks, Rob had to be satisfied with telephone conversations with his kids. But, by mid-August, an informal visitation was worked out by Hurvitz and Clifford. It had been easy for the two lawyers to reach agreement on the visitation and child support. They assumed the rest of the divorce would proceed just as smoothly.

Rob spent the entire month of August trying to win Vicki back. He sent her flowers. He wrote her long letters. He called her and accepted all the blame for the broken relationship. His thoughts were centered on Vicki rather than his children. She had been the one to leave, not them. She was the one that he couldn't figure out. If she came back, so would they. He begged Vicki for another chance.

He even wrote her a poem.

> *Trying to deal,*
> *Trying to cope.*
> *Still in love,*
> *Clutching hope.*
> *Feeling desperate.*

Possess the knack
To change your heart,
To win you back. ‾

At first, Vicki gave McQueeney every reason to continue clutching hope. "I just need time to think things out," she told him more than once. "I need some space. Please, don't bother me now. Maybe we can work things out later, even get back together. But for now, please just leave me alone."

She insisted she was not involved with another man, and McQueeney believed her—even after several of Vicki's family members told him otherwise.

But, in the fall of 1986, Vicki and Bruce Johnson moved in together. At the same time, she quit her waitressing jobs.

Vicki had met Bruce when he stopped by for late-night suppers after he closed the indoor shooting range he owned. Bruce was divorced and eight years older than Vicki. He didn't have any children.

On first meeting Bruce, most people immediately noticed his extraordinarily strong self-image. His behavior suggested he was a man in control of events—though his babyish face suggested he was anything but macho. He did, however, seem to know how to get things done. And he had money.

Vicki had occasionally talked to McQueeney about Bruce. A few months before she left Rob, Vicki had told Ray about Bruce's offers to teach her how to shoot a pistol and to give her a job at The Pistol Shot.

"It sounds to me as though he might want something more than just a new student," Ray responded.

"Maybe you're right!" Vicki said, with a laugh. Ray wondered at the time why Vicki didn't come to him if she wanted to learn to shoot. Ray had taken numerous trophies at local and national matches over the years—shooting everything from pistols to high-powered rifles. It made Ray, who never entirely trusted Vicki, wonder yet again if there was another shoe that was going to drop.

Rob, though, assumed Vicki and Bruce were just friends. It wasn't until a few weeks before she moved in with Bruce that

McQueeney finally believed that she was romantically involved with him.

The realization that there was another man in his wife's life forced McQueeney to admit to himself that he would not be getting back with her. Just as he started to accept the separation as permanent, Vicki called him. It was a Wednesday morning in early October, and she wanted Rob to meet her for lunch. She sounded upset.

They met at McDonald's. Rob was thrilled to see his kids— he smiled as he saw a wide-eyed Wendy watch Keefe climb into the big cheeseburger. After they ate, the children busied themselves on the playground outside while they talked.

For half-an-hour, Vicki made small talk about the children. As she droned on, McQueeney became more and more confused. Finally, he couldn't stand it any longer. "You sounded so upset on the phone, Vicki. Is anything wrong? Is there anything you want to talk about?"

A torrent of tears was her answer.

Though he pressed her, Vicki still wouldn't say what was bothering her. "I don't know; things just aren't going well," she said. "I don't know what it is, really. I just feel so confused. Things aren't the way I thought they'd be, I guess."

Rob hoped the fling was over. He slid into the bench seat beside her and put his arm gently around her shoulder.

"I don't care what's happened in the past," he told her. "I want you to know I still love you and I want us to get back together. I always thought we had a good, strong family. Vicki, I know it's going to take a lot of talking and a lot of work before we can patch up our relationship, but I'm willing to do anything to save our marriage and I hope you are too."

He paused. Vicki was looking down at her folded hands atop the table. She didn't say anything.

"Vicki, I know you need to think about it," Rob continued. "But the door is open. If you're going to walk through it with me, I know it's got to be done slowly and carefully, but please remember I love you and the children very much."

They said good-bye. Vicki gathered the children and left in Bruce's truck. Rob remained behind for a few minutes, trying to gather his thoughts.

The next day, Vicki called to ask if she could come to pick up some of her clothes from the house. McQueeney thought that she had finally decided to talk to him, to tell him what was bothering her. His heart skipped a beat. Maybe they would start to mend their relationship.

That night, as he was waiting for her, he concluded that Vicki must have had a major fight with Bruce. Maybe the green grass that she had strayed for had started to turn brown. He started pacing, anxious for her arrival. He wanted more than anything to resurrect his marriage.

He felt a sharp pang of disappointment when the truck pulled into his driveway with Bruce behind the wheel. When he let Vicki in the house, she muttered a hello and brushed by him on the way to the bedroom they had shared for so long. She remained silent as she started gathering her clothes from the closet. Rob left her alone for a few minutes and then joined her.

"Do you think you're going to want to talk about things?"

"No," she answered abruptly. "There's nothing to talk about."

He tried to prod her, as gently as his impatience would allow. She refused to talk.

"Well, what was all that yesterday?" he asked, in an irritated, whining tone he immediately wished he could take back. He took a breath and said, frustratedly, "What were the tears for? Why were you so anxious to meet me for lunch?"

Her words were razor sharp. "That was all bullshit, Rob. Just bullshit. Drop it, OK?"

McQueeney, hurt and furious, grabbed her by the arm.

"What the hell do you mean, 'bullshit?' What are you trying to do to me?"

She jerked her arm away from him. "You do that again and I'll call the police." She turned away and continued to gather her clothes.

McQueeney, burning mad, walked out of the room, down the hall and into the living room. He paced back and forth, trying to decide what to do. Still running on emotion, he turned and went back to Vicki. He took hold of her arm again and begged her to come back. When she said nothing, he asked her again why she was doing this to him. Stonefaced, she pulled away from him, spun around and strode into the kitchen. She picked up the phone and started to dial.

McQueeney bolted after her, took the phone and slammed it down. "OK," he yelled. "Just get your stuff. Get your damn stuff and get the hell out of here."

As she was walking toward Bruce's truck she stopped and turned to face McQueeney. Rob was standing at the front door, hands on his hips, barely able to control the angry words he wanted to scream at her.

She felt no need to control her words. "You know, Rob, there *is* something that I want to tell you," she said in a sarcastic tone. "You're a lousy fuck, you know that? You're the worst fuck I've *ever* had." She paused as McQueeney stared at her, flinching. "But, boy, am I making up for that now. Bruce is so-o-o-o good. He's ten times the man you'll ever be. And he's not just better . . . he's bigger. *Much* bigger."

With a spiteful laugh, she turned and got into the truck. As they wheeled out of the driveway, she stuck her arm out of the window and gave him the finger.

McQueeney sat on his front step for a long time, her words ringing in his ears. "Damn you," he muttered to himself. "And damn me for being such a fool." An hour earlier, he had been hoping for a reconciliation. He had allowed himself to be taken in. Filled with anger and frustration, he got up and went into the kitchen to pour himself a bourbon.

The drink calmed him. Vicki couldn't possibly remain so filled with hate. She had probably been putting on a show for Bruce. Jesus, his children had already been through so much. Hell, *he* had already been through too much. They all deserved better. "Well," he thought, "I have to forget about her. I have to do without her. I still have my weekends with the kids.

"She can't take that away from me."

■ CHAPTER FIVE ■

"Daddy, Did You Lose the Moon?"

A week after Rob's confrontation with Vicki, McQueeney was still replaying her ugly words to him, still wondering why she hated him so much.

He, Keefe and Wendy were in his little red Chevette, on their way to visit his parents in Newington. The sun had just set and they were travelling south on Newington Road in West Hartford. Keefe and Wendy were secure in their carseats—Keefe directly behind his father and Wendy in the passenger side of the backseat.

McQueeney was fond of spontaneously making up little games to play with his children. When they were driving along Route 72 at night, he would ask the children "who turned out the lights?" whenever they went through an underpass that blocked the bright lights of the street lamps. They were silly, meaningless games. But they helped entertain the children and kept Rob's mind occupied.

That night, the moon was full, hanging low in the dusky eastern sky. It was blinking in and out of view as they drove past the oak and maple trees that lined the road.

"I see the moo-oon," Rob said in a sing-song voice that invited a response.

"I see the moon, too!" Keefe obliged. He was always ready to join in a game.

"I don't see it, Daddy. Show me where. Where?" Wendy

was more hesitant. She wouldn't play until she understood the game.

A row of trees blocked out the moon for a few seconds.

"There it is," Rob pointed as it winked back into view.

"I see it!" Keefe immediately responded, leaning forward in his car seat.

After three or four such exchanges, Rob was suddenly buffeted by a gust of emotion. A melancholy self-pity pinched his heart. He couldn't believe his family had been ripped apart. His children were being brave, but how long would they be able to hold onto their innocence? Why had this happened to him? The catch in his throat kept him from speaking, just as the moon reappeared.

After several seconds, he heard Keefe's voice, soft and concerned: "Daddy, did you lose the moon?"

It was a few seconds before Rob recovered sufficiently to answer his son. "Oh, yes," he said, forcing a normal voice. "I see the moon. There it is."

Neither of the children saw the single tear that trickled below the rim of his eyeglasses. Nor did they notice Rob wipe it away, just as the moon disappeared behind a distant hill. It was the last they saw of the moon that night.

■CHAPTER SIX■

Ghostbusters

When Vicki took the children, Rob suddenly realized how much he missed their everyday presence. He loved watching Keefe develop his own personality as he scaled each little step of childhood on his way to becoming an independent person. And there was Wendy, doggedly following each footstep of her big brother. It wouldn't be long before she began to set out on her own course.

But, as a weekend daddy, Rob was more an observer than a participant. He had always been a stricter parent than Vicki, who tended to baby the children. When they had all been together, he could see the positive impact he had on the children, and it had been gratifying. Now, though, he had been demoted from first-string to benchwarmer daddy.

He missed both kids equally, but it was Wendy's absence that he most mourned. He had never spent enough time with her, and the knowledge gnawed at him. He knew it would be difficult to make up for that when he only saw her two days a week.

That's one reason why he worked so hard and gave so much of himself on the weekends. He was not going to relax in front of the television while his children were with him. He would wring as much as he could from every minute of every weekend. He took them camping, to country fairs, to the beach, to Teddy Bear shows and puppet shows. His life revolved around the children. He was very nearly obsessive about it, being driven partly by guilt and partly by determination.

Rob generally picked up the children on Friday night after work. During the fall, while Keefe was attending the pre-school's morning session, the children would remain with him until Monday morning, when he would meet Vicki at Keefe's pre-school. Vicki would take Wendy out for breakfast or to visit her sister, while Keefe was in school. She would then return to the school at eleven twenty-five a.m. to pick up Keefe.

During the winter, when Keefe was going to the afternoon session, McQueeney brought the children back to their mother on Sunday night. The system had been working smoothly, and the children seemed to be adjusting to their new routines.

When he wasn't bringing them to a special outing or to visit his parents, Rob was turning his house into a playground. The cavernous living room with the cathedral ceiling had been left nearly empty by Vicki, who had taken most of the furniture. It was almost like having an indoor backyard. Rob and the children spent a lot of time on the living room floor, wrestling, teasing each other and playing countless games.

There was a lot of physical contact. They had devised three ways to "get" one another. You could go for the other person's "neckie meat," his "leggie meat," or his "butt meat." A gentle pinch or squeeze always provoked a giggle and instant retaliation.

The children's routine at Rob's home almost never varied.

After breakfast, the children would do their appointed chores.

"Keefe, it's time to fetch the wastebaskets," Rob would say. "And don't forget the one in the bathroom." Keefe would bring the small wastebaskets to his father, who would empty them into a big garbage bag.

"Your turn, Wendy," he would say, prompting his daughter to return the wastebaskets to their original locations. "Make sure you put them right-side up!" he would remind the giggling girl.

Both children knew they had to pick up their clothes and toys. No new game could start until the pieces for the old game were put away.

For some reason that will remain forever hidden from adult minds, Wendy and Keefe's favorite chore was helping their father with the dishwasher. After Rob loaded the dishes, he would shake the soap powder into the little semicircular door.

"Lemme pact the powder!" Keefe would exclaim.

"No, I wanna pack the powder," Wendy would complain.

The referee would have to rule. "Alright, this time Keefe can pack the soap powder and you can lock the door. Ok, Wendy?"

For their efforts, Rob paid Keefe a quarter and Wendy a dime—a practice that prompted some of Rob's friends to give him grief about perpetuating an unequal and sexist wage scale. Rob countered that Keefe had the seniority, the experience and the more difficult chores. "Besides," he would tell them, "if they thought the wages were unfair, they could always petition the Labor Department. They must be happy. They've never asked for union representation."

When the chores were finished, he and the children would play with building blocks, fantasy figures and other toys. For an hour at a time, they would play the He-Man game, with dozens of mutant heroes and villains spread over the floor. There would be castles and space-age vehicles and other accessories. Wendy would bring over her Care Bears and her cloud car and they would incorporate all the disparate figures into a mammoth battle between good and evil. The children would invariably play the good guys, seeking to rescue one of their pals from the clutches of the dastardly Skeletor, or some other villain played by Rob. They would thrash the figures against each other, as Rob and Keefe dictated the story line.

"I saved the world!" Keefe would proclaim at the end of the game. "I beat you, Daddy, I beat you."

Sometimes, when Rob was chasing one of Keefe's good guys, Keefe would pick him up and run away. "Hey, he can't fly," Rob would complain.

"Yes, he can!" Keefe would reply.

"Oh, no, he can't," Rob would say. "It says so in the book of mutant superhero rules. Wanna bet?"

Keefe would be momentarily distracted, only to find his father wielding Skeletor.

"Gotcha!"

At which point Wendy would zoom by, giggling as her Care Bear flew off in the cloud car. "Can't catch me, can't catch me," she would chant. "I can fly. I can fly."

Often, when there was a lull in their games, Rob would suddenly begin to walk toward Keefe or Wendy in slow, hulking steps, his arms outstretched and a menacing look on his face. He didn't have to announce who he was; the children knew that the Marshmallow Man—the monster that had stalked the city streets at the end of the *Ghostbusters* movie—was after them. They would instantly shriek and race away, warning the world, "Run! It's the Marshmallow Man!"

Despite his lumbering steps, Rob would inevitably catch up to an obliging Keefe, who always wound up falling to the floor and curling up in a little giggling ball. Sometimes, as he was lying there, Keefe would suddenly spring to his feet and shoot his father with his invisible finger-and-thumb ray gun. Rob would either collapse to the floor with a chorus of gurgling sounds, or pinwheel about the room, as though he was a deflating balloon. The children would be in hysterics—until Marshmallow Man slowly regained life to once again pursue his shrieking targets.

Other times, Keefe would either forget to use the ray gun, or Rob would tell him that the gun wasn't working. Then, Rob would go down on his hands and knees, caging Keefe and cackling in what he thought might be the Marshmallow Man's voice. He would slowly lower himself, gently squashing the giggling, squirming boy beneath him. As this was going on, Wendy, who always ran into the kitchen when danger was approaching, would sometimes come to Keefe's rescue, jumping on Rob and using her Care-Bears' magic powers to rescue her big brother.

Depending on his mood, the Marshmallow Man would either succumb to Wendy's efforts, or would swoosh her into the cage and squash her as well. When he did that, Wendy and Keefe—with those instincts that every child has—would writhe and shudder to a noisy death.

Ghostbusters was Keefe's favorite movie and he loved it when his father became the hulking, stalking Marshmallow Man. He and his father had watched the movie several times on cable television. He knew the song's refrain and the characters by heart. He ate Ghostbusters cereal for breakfast.

Keefe never watched *Ghostbusters* by himself, though. It was fine when his father was there. But some parts of the movie scared him a little. It was fun to play with Daddy, but, once in a while, the movie seemed just a little too real to him. Especially the bodiless flying ghosts and the huge Marshmallow Man tromping through the streets.

Another routine that never varied was the stories that Rob would read the children at bedtime. Keefe always wanted the Flintstones; Wendy opted for the Care Bears. Rob would read Wendy's story first; she was usually asleep by the time he reached the end.

After carrying Wendy to bed, he would read the Flintstones' story. This always proved to be a little more challenging than when he read to Wendy. Keefe knew almost all of the book by heart, and whenever Rob deviated from the dialogue of Fred, Wilma, Betty or Barney, Keefe would glance up, "Uhn-uh, Daddy."

"That's called ad libbing, Keefe," Rob would explain with a smile. "It's what daddys do when they've read the same book five thousand times and they don't want to lose their sanity. It's like when . . ."

"You're not saying it right," Keefe would interrupt. "Say it right, Daddy. Don't want no 'libbing. Say it right."

When the book was finished, it was time for bed. Keefe almost always insisted on one of two rituals when his father tucked him in. His favorite was to ask Rob to lie with him and call off the names of the Star Wars characters that adorned the bedroom curtains. Keefe wanted to be sure that all the characters were accounted for. Rob would call out, "I see Darth Vader," and Keefe would answer, "I see Dart Bader, too."

Once in awhile, instead of "reading the curtains," Keefe would ask his daddy to say a few words to the three "buddies" he slept with. Keefe had a stuffed Huckleberry Hound that Rob had had when he was a child. Keefe called him "Bo-berry." He also had a Baby Bear puppet, and a little, blue, stuffed bear that had come with a flower arrangement someone had given them when Keefe was born. That was Blue Bear. After a brief conversation with the three buddies, Keefe, satisfied that all was well with the world, would go to sleep.

During the week, Rob filled his time by reading horror novels, attending wine tastings to learn more about his new hobby, and working as an executive committee member of the local Society of Manufacturing Engineers. He also spent a lot of time with his parents, and at Chef's, a restaurant and bar where he would often go to eat and have a drink after work. As if he were in the television sitcom, he became like a real-life Norm, who entered *his* "Cheers" to a chorus of friendly recognition. Anything to escape the empty house.

One Saturday night in late October, Rob got a call from his best friend, Brian Samsel, who had extra tickets to the Hartford Whalers hockey game. He accepted the invitation, and called his mother to ask if she could watch the kids. As soon as he had spoken the words out loud, though, Rob felt a rush of guilt.

"Oh, Mom, never mind. I don't think I should go."

His mother instantly recognized what was happening. "Oh, Rob, you ought to go. You haven't been out in such a long time. Me and Papa would love to see the kids, you know that. Go ahead with Bri. It'll give Papa and me a chance to play with the kids."

McQueeney went—the only time he ever left his children during a visitation. When the game was over, he declined an invitation from Brian to go out and hurried back to his parents' house.

Although his professional life was going well, his social life was in neutral. Rob tried to lose weight, be more positive, and think out the future. Then, in late November, he began seeing his first wife, Cheryl.

Their lives had been on remarkable parallels since their breakup. She had re-married and given birth to two boys. But her new marriage was a disaster. She had too many bruises and black eyes from a husband who too often was drugged-out. She was now in the process of trying to start a new life.

Rob and Cheryl found themselves sharing their problems and consoling each other. But neither of them was ready for another entanglement—particularly with a former spouse. As friends, though, they got along well. Their children played together, often assuming the roles of various *Ghostbusters* characters—giving Rob a break from his Marshmallow Man routine.

Once, as they sat on a bench watching their children scampering about in Hartford's Elizabeth Park, Cheryl turned to face Rob.

"You know, Rob, leaving you was a mistake," she said. "I should have tried harder to make the marriage work. I guess I didn't appreciate it at the time, but you're a good man, Rob. You really are."

But Cheryl also noticed a disturbing change in her former husband. He was not as easy-going and fun-loving as he had been. He seemed filled with stress and tension. But she couldn't fault his treatment of the children.

Rob had the children for every major holiday, since Bruce and Vicki preferred to spend those times with each other. He and the kids went camping for Labor Day weekend. They all made a Halloween dummy stuffed with leaves and then went out trick-or-treating. Wendy wore a Wuzzle costume and Keefe went as Rambo.

During the Christmas season, Rob brought Keefe and Wendy to meet Santa Claus, and, later, they helped decorate Rob's Christmas tree. Rob was moved nearly to tears when he had them pose for pictures and Keefe suddenly put his arm around his little sister. A year ago, Keefe would have died before he hugged his sister. Now, he was starting to act like a protective big brother.

Rob had constantly tried to instill in them a sense of sharing and love for each other. When they played their mutant superhero games, Rob always made sure to include a few lessons about loyalty, love and sharing. They weren't perfect kids; he often had to yell at them or send them to their "quiet corner" when they misbehaved. But, at least, he assured himself, their childhood wasn't being ruined by the broken marriage.

Early in the New Year, Rob was cooking dinner for his children and his parents. When he had the time and he put his mind to it, Rob was a good cook. As he hovered over the stove, Wendy began saying, "Daddy, Daddy, Daddy." Rob responded, "Wendy, Wendy, Wendy." Wendy looked up at her father and, with a big smile, said, "Guess what?"

"What?"

"I miss you."

A few minutes later, Wendy was in the bathroom, practicing her toilet routine, which still needed some work. Her tiny, squeaky voice drifted into the kitchen.

"Daddy?"

Rob looked at his parents and rolled his eyes. What was she having trouble with now? Ruth began to get up to help her granddaughter.

"What, honey?" Rob asked.

"I miss you."

Ruth sat back down and laughed.

"I miss you too, piglet."

Keefe then marched over, wanting some attention for himself.

"Hey, Nana, wanna hear me sing the song?" Keefe asked.

"Oh, what song is that, hon?"

"The song from *Ghostbusters*!"

"Sure, let's hear it."

"Nahnahnahnanah . . . Ghotebusters!" he shouted.

Wendy scurried into the kitchen. "Nahnahnah . . . Ghotebusters!" she squeaked.

Rob enjoyed Sunday, January 25. His New York Giants had made it to the Super Bowl for the first time ever. To celebrate, he hosted a Super Bowl party, inviting his parents and closest friends. Wendy had been sick that weekend and remained with her mother. Rob and Keefe prepared for the party, getting the food ready and decorating the house with blue and white streamers and Giants' banners and posters.

The doorbell rang three times, as McQueeney's parents, Brian and Pamm Samsel and Ted Andrews came by for the party. McQueeney had the big television in the living room, a portable television in the kitchen and a small, battery-operated television in the bathroom. Nobody would have to miss even one play.

A coffee table in the living room was covered with old Giants memorabilia. One magazine had Y. A. Tittle on the cover; he was the Giants quarterback in the early 1960s. Little plastic containers were spread throughout the living room. Inside each was a bit of brown grass. It had come from the end zones at the Yale Bowl, where Rob and Brian had watched several Giants games years ago.

Keefe was dressed in a number 56 Giants' jersey—representing the team's star linebacker, Lawrence Taylor—and clutched a small, blue football throughout the game. He and his father exchanged high-fives and demonstrated the Go-Giants cheer Rob had taught him. With each Giants touchdown, Keefe would run around the living room, arms upraised in the official signal for a score, screaming "TOUCHDOWN!" When the Giants won, McQueeney reveled in the victory of their team. Three generations of McQueeneys had shared the victory of his team and the companionship of each other. It was his best day since Vicki had left him six months before.

The following weekend got off to a slow start. There was a snowstorm on Friday night that prevented Rob from going to Goshen to pick up the children. Instead, he went for them at mid-morning on Saturday.

When they returned home, they settled into the familiar routine of their games. They played He-Man for a while, and then Keefe announced that it was time for a picnic. They put away their figurines and accessories and brought out a small blanket, toy plates, cups and utensils and proceeded to set up an elaborate picnic in the living room.

"Daddy, ya want some hot dogs?" Keefe asked.

"Sure, little man. Heap 'em on my plate."

"Daddy, d'ya wanna have some 'tato chips?"

"Oh, thank you, Wendy. I was waiting for those."

"Daddy, someone wants to talk to you," Keefe said, handing over the toy telephone."

"Hello?" Rob said into the plastic receiver. "Oh, I'm sorry. Just a minute." Rob put his hand over the plastic receiver and told Keefe, "This one's for you."

"Is it Nana?" Keefe eagerly asked.

"Yup. She called to tell you how good the picnic smells. She says she can smell the food way over there and wants to compliment you on it."

With a serious look on his face, Keefe accepted the phone. He listened intently for a few moments. "Thanks, Nana. Bye."

After the imaginary meal was finished and the dishes put away, Keefe and Wendy brought out their coloring books, eager to do new pictures to go under the magnets on the refrigerator door. But, before they had a chance to spread their crayons and books on the floor, they were confronted by the Marshmallow Man.

Amid squeals of delight, Wendy took off for the kitchen and Keefe began walking backward down the hall toward his room. He fired the invisible ray gun, but the Marshmallow Man kept coming. Eventually, he was caged and was about to be squashed when Wendy came in and shot the Marshmallow Man with her own invisible gun. Rob, surprised that Wendy would think to do that, rewarded her with his deflating balloon act. When the children returned to their coloring, Rob stretched out near them and finished another chapter of Stephen King's, *The Stand.*

After dinner, Rob read to the children. He carried Wendy to bed and lay with Keefe to call off the Star Wars characters on the curtains. When each of the characters was accounted for, the lights went out.

There was one goal for the next day: tobogganing. Rob made up what he called "Daddy's mix" for breakfast—a curious blend of raisins, broken granola bars, Kix, Cheerios and Ghostbusters' cereal. After their chores were done, Rob gave each child a zip-lock bag filled with the leftover daddy's mix. They were allowed to snack on it until ten a.m.

The kids saved most of the mix until nine thirty, when "The Wind in the Willows" came on the Disney Channel. It was the one television program they always watched on the weekends. Rob was never sure who enjoyed it more—him or the children. Just a few months ago he had been the one to introduce the characters as they appeared on the screen. Now, Keefe had taken over, providing his daddy and little sister with tidbits of commentary about Toad and all the others.

"There's Rat's boat!" Keefe called out. A second later, Wendy echoed him. "Shhh, Wendy, I wanna listen," Keefe reprimanded her.

After a hot lunch—Spaghettios out of a can—they went tobogganing at the rural industrial park where Rob worked. The squeals and laughter of his kids that day have never stopped echoing in Rob's ears. Nor has there been any fading of the snapshot image in his mind of Keefe's face as he bravely conquered the little hill.

Rob still cherishes these little echoes and images. He feels nobody can ever take them away from him. He believes, has to believe, that even if he loses everything else, he will not lose these.

■CHAPTER SEVEN■

"I Want My Husband Arrested."

As McQueeney tried to be the best father he could in the limited periods accorded to him, he was unaware of how the inexorable process leading to his arrest had been set in motion. Later, when he knew how it had happened, he would spend endless hours agonizing over how people could have *let* it happen. For now, though, there was no target to aim at. And, of course, nothing to aim *with*.

When McQueeney telephoned his son on the Tuesday after they had gone tobogganing, he did not know that, a few hours before, Vicki had been on the phone herself, telling a worker at the Langley Center's sexual abuse program that she was worried about what was happening to Keefe and Wendy when they were with their father.

Bruce Johnson, who was now her live-in lover, already had contacted a friend of his, Philip Mercer, who was executive director of the Langley Center. Hearing Bruce's explanation, Mercer suggested that they bring the little boy in as a possible victim of sexual abuse. The center was expecting Vicki's call.

After hearing Vicki's claims, the center labeled the situation an emergency.

Two days later, on the morning of Thursday, February 5, Vicki brought her two children to the center's Parent Abuse/ Child Evaluation and Treatment (PACE-T) program. They met with Barbara Barrett, a fifty-one-year-old social worker who handled most of the cases involving young children, and her boss, David Marshall, a psychologist and director of the program.

Vicki started describing her fears.

Marshall suggested having Keefe examined as soon as possible. He felt the doctor might be able to find some type of injury to his rectum.

He suggested a further session with Barrett. Vicki made an appointment for the following Tuesday. Then, she called to make an appointment with her pediatrician. When Vicki told the doctor's secretary that the Langley Center had advised her to see a pediatrician concerning a possible case of child sexual abuse, Vicki was told to come in that afternoon.

After getting something to eat, Vicki dropped Keefe off at his pre-school about noon. As always, Susan Blackwell, the teacher, was happy to see him. She liked Keefe, and had been encouraged by his recent improvement at school. He was beginning to participate now, and was even willing to raise his hand to answer questions.

Keefe had arrived in September as a shy, withdrawn child, but had recently started coming out of his shell. Susan thought Rob probably had a lot to do with that. McQueeney was one of the few fathers who came into the school as a volunteer helper. Susan had remarked that she liked the way he acted with the kids, and the children obviously loved having him around.

It seemed obvious to her that Keefe and his daddy had a strong, loving relationship. McQueeney was always asking about Keefe's progress—in contrast to Vicki, who never seemed to question how her little boy was doing in school.

It always pained Susan to see these vulnerable, confused, aching products of broken marriages. She hoped that Keefe would continue making progress, and privately wished that Keefe's father could somehow gain primary custody of the child.

At three p.m., Vicki and Wendy picked up Keefe from the school. They went straight to the pediatrician.

Dr. Ranjit Pandit arched his eyebrows as he glanced at the medical records for Keefe McQueeney. At the bottom was the most recent entry, referring to that day's visit: "Rectal exam requested by Langley Center—question of abuse by father."

The forty-one-year-old doctor from India slowly shook his head and headed out to Vicki and Keefe.

Vicki told the doctor that she had brought Keefe to the Langley Center earlier, where they said she should have him examined.

In the room, Keefe didn't want to remove his clothes. He kicked and screamed for a few minutes before allowing his mother to take his clothes off. He remained sullen as he submitted to the examination.

After examining Keefe's anus and surrounding tissue, Dr. Pandit wrote on Keefe's medical record: "No evidence of any rectal injury or inflammation around anus, no visible external injuries." The little boy's bottom looked absolutely normal. Whatever had been bothering him before was now completely cleared up.

"I do not see anything now, but, you know, you do not all the time see an injury," he carefully told Vicki. "You say this thing, if it happened, was four, five days ago. I would make sure to take him back to the Langley Center. I mean, really, you should, you know, follow this up."

Vicki nodded and commented that the inflammation around his anus had cleared up. She went on to say she was bringing Keefe back to the center the next week.

Pandit informed her that he had to report his examination to the State Department of Children and Youth Services, It was required by law that the doctor report these suspicions of sexual abuse.

Dr. Pandit was to observe later that the law had its good point—a doctor, teacher or other so-called "mandated reporter" could go to jail for failing to report even the slightest suspicion of child abuse. It was good to err on the side of caution in these cases. It was very important to protect the children.

But the law also meant that he was obligated to report a suspicion of child abuse even though that suspicion was not his. His examination did not prove that Keefe hadn't been abused. However, the injury might have healed, or there may have been little penetration and thus no injury at all. But he would be making this report solely on the basis of Vicki's suspicions, even though he had no way to judge their accuracy. Good or bad, the law was clear.

The next day, Friday, Vicki brought the children to the Young Parents' Program at the Bristol Girls' Club, where they were taking cooking and swimming lessons. While the children busied themselves in cooking class—where Wendy happily washed her hands and got a pot—Vicki told the head of the Young Parents' Program about her suspicions. Afterward she decided to call the State Department of Children and Youth Services to issue her own complaint against McQueeney. She told a woman with DCYS the same things she had told the Langley Center.

The woman suggested filing a report with the police.

Vicki complied.

First, she called McQueeney to tell him that she, Bruce and the two children were stranded at Cape Cod. Shortly after that conversation, Vicki went to the Plymouth Police Department.

At one thirty p.m., Vicki sat down with Officer Grodecki. She told Grodecki that, after the visit to Dr. Pandit, Keefe had started to open up to her, and had started providing details about how his father was hurting him. Vicki then recited a list of things that she said Keefe had told her the previous evening.

"Keefe said he liked to play the 'Marshmallow Man' game when he was with his father on the weekends. He said that his daddy got on top of him, covered his mouth with one hand and used his other hand to stick his finger as far as he could into Keefe's heinie. He told me that this hurts very much, but that his father had told him that if he screamed he would have to stay in his room for the entire weekend. And then he said that when the game was over, he and his daddy had to go to the bathroom to wash their hands because they were so dirty."

Grodecki, who had been a patrolman for the Plymouth Police Department for thirteen years, immediately filled out a family violence offense report—complaint number CR-80-87—and contacted the State Department of Children and Youth Services. On the report, he listed sexual assault and risk of injury as the offenses.

It was the next day, Saturday, when Vicki called McQueeney to apologetically tell him that the part needed to repair

Bruce's truck wasn't available. They could not make it back to Connecticut that weekend, but she would be sure to make up for the inconvenience she had caused.

On Sunday, police contacted Vicki and asked her to give them a written statement when she had the chance.

Two days later, Vicki gave police her statement. It appeared that the details of the sexual abuse had crystallized in her mind. Vicki began to remember things that Keefe had told her, starting with the night of February 1, when McQueeney had dropped the children off after they had been tobogganing. Her statement left no doubt about what had happened.

Vicki reported that her husband had told her about Keefe's inflamed anus when he dropped the children off on that Sunday night. She also said that when McQueeney was about to leave, he knelt down to talk to Keefe.

"Keefe came close to his father and started crying, saying to his father, 'You hurt me, you hurt me,' her written statement says. "That night, while I was giving Keefe his bath, I noticed his bottom was red. I asked Keefe about the games he played with his father. Keefe said one of the games was 'Marshmallow Man.' Keefe said Marshmallow Man jumps on little kids, covers their mouths. He squashes them. They have to stay very still. If they move or talk they have to stay in the house the whole next day."

Vicki's statement continued: "The night after Keefe went to the doctor's, Keefe told me how he plays with his father. When they play Marshmallow Man, they go to sleep on the couch. He and his father don't have any clothes on. He has to lay still and be quiet. His father rubs him and tells him how much he loves him. Keefe said his father put his finger in his heinie real far and it hurts. Keefe said after they are done playing Marshmallow Man it's very messy. Keefe said his father covers him up with a sheet, brings him in the bathroom, cleans him up very well. Keefe said it's sandy. And then puts his PJ's on and goes back to the couch and goes to sleep. Keefe said his father washes the sheets on the couch every day.

"I have asked Keefe to play 'Marshmallow Man' with me. Keefe said you wouldn't like that and that it took a long time and you're very, very tired afterward."

Vicki's statements implied that McQueeney had forced his son to perform oral sex on him, and that McQueeney used to ejaculate onto his son's face: "I started asking Keefe about what he did while he visits with his father. I asked Keefe what he hated to do the most and Keefe said 'eat.' I asked Keefe why he hated to eat food at his father's; that he liked food. Keefe said 'not food, silly.' Sunday night, February 8, I had a stiff neck and put some Ben Gay on my neck. Keefe came by and asked what smelled. I told him my neck was sore and I had slept on it the wrong way. Keefe said 'Once I was with my father, I turned my neck and he missed and wet me on my shoulder.'"

She concluded her statement: "I want my husband, Robert McQueeney, arrested for assaulting my son Keefe, and I am willing to testify in court to the above statement."

On the same day, Vicki brought Keefe back to Barrett at the Langley Center. Once again, Keefe did not indicate in any way that his father had harmed him or acted in any sexual or inappropriate manner. He again played with the Play-Doh and the toy stove.

"This is just like the one we play with at our house . . . I mean Daddy's house," he told the blond-haired therapist. "Me and Wendy cook up stuff for Daddy."

As he fiddled with some pots and pans, he looked at Barrett. "Our stove is better 'cause there's a phone on it and we can call Nana anytime we want. Some times Daddy will answer the phone and say it's for me. Nana calls us and we call her."

Barrett told Vicki that she wasn't surprised by Keefe's reluctance to talk. He needed more time, that's all. Vicki immediately scheduled another session for Thursday, February 19, nine days away. This time she made the appointment for both children.

McQueeney had received his first call from the police on Thursday, February 12, two days after Vicki had given them her written statement. It was the next day that Vicki had called McQueeney to ask him whether his father had ever sexually abused him. The following Monday, McQueeney got the second call from Sergeant Senetcen. The dread he had felt at the time was justified; the police were almost ready to apply for an arrest warrant. They needed just one more piece of evidence.

After seeing the children on February 19, Barrett, at Vicki's request, wrote this report for the police:

"On February 19, 1987, Keefe was seen by me in a play session where he demonstrated a game he called the 'jumping game.' Using the anatomically correct dolls, he identified the adult male doll as his father and the small boy doll as himself. The dolls wore only shorts and the boy doll was placed on a chair lying face down. The chair was identified as father's couch where Keefe sleeps when visiting his father. Keefe took the male doll and began jumping on the baby doll with his penis in the boy doll's anus. Keefe described this as the 'jumping game' he plays with his dad.

"Keefe's younger sister, Wendy, age 2.5, reported having snuck out of her bed and into the living room where she observed her father and Keefe 'bumping heinies.' Wendy and Keefe both stated that father sent Wendy back to bed and that father has never played this game with Wendy.

"The children have also reported a game called 'Marshmallow Man.' Keefe indicated that father wets on his tummy and shoulder when playing the 'Marshmallow Man.'

"Keefe reported that these incidents have happened two times, however father said 'he was going to do it every two days.' Keefe stated 'When he stopped, I was so pooped. He was going to put my PJ's on and put me to bed.'

"It is my professional opinion from the information provided by Keefe and from his demonstration with the dolls that Keefe has been sexually molested."

Later that day, Bruce Johnson picked up the report from the center and brought it to the police station, where he had police make an additional copy to bring home to Vicki.

Also at Vicki's request, Barrett videotaped the February 19 session with Keefe and Wendy and gave it to the police. The videotape showed Keefe briefly banging two dolls together.

The next day, Friday, Grodecki applied for an arrest warrant against Robert McQueeney for the crimes of first-degree sexual assault and risk of injury to a minor child. The application for the warrant relied entirely on the comments made by Vicki and the report and videotape done by Barrett.

The children had to be protected. The criminal justice system moved quickly. On Monday morning, February 23, the application for the warrant was approved by an assistant state's attorney and a superior court judge. Later that day, McQueeney was arrested.

From then on, it would be up to McQueeney to defend his innocence. It would be up to McQueeney to fight for even the most minimal contact with his children. And, for a long time, it would be up to McQueeney to figure out how all this had happened—and why Vicki was doing this to him and his children.

■CHAPTER EIGHT■

"Robert, Did You Do It?"

Shortly after the bail bondswoman posted the $5,000 bond, Officer Paul Beals unlocked the cell door. Rob stepped out, grabbed the small pile of belongings waiting for him on the floor by his cell and slunk away with a beaten, hesitant gait. Suddenly, he realized he had forgotten to put on his belt or his shoelaces. He didn't stop to do these mundane things, but shuffled along, hurrying to meet his parents. He had to get out of the building—and away from the dirty, shameful things it represented. He collapsed in an exhausted, humiliated heap in the back seat of his parents' car.

It was his mother Ruth who remembered the dog, the cat and the suit. They stopped briefly at McQueeney's house to feed the pets, and to pick up Rob's only suit. It seemed important to wear a suit when he appeared in court the next morning.

Little was said during the half-hour drive to his parents' home in Newington. Ray kept thinking of how helpless they all were. He was more afraid than angry. The anger would come later.

Ruth was totally shaken by her experiences in the police station. As she sat in numbed silence, a loathsome thought started to form in her jumbled mind. As they neared home, it began gnawing at her insides. Each time she tried to push it away, it came back.

When they arrived at the white, eight-room, colonial-style house, Ray followed the narrow driveway down the side of the house and around to the back. Rob irrationally wondered whether his parents' neighbors were peeking out their windows as the three of them got out of the car and walked through the dark and into the house.

They had just removed their coats and were standing by the dining room table when Ruth could no longer deny the insistent voice inside her.

Rob had started to hang his coat on a highbacked chair when Ruth stepped over to her son and cradled his face in her hands. She was sobbing as she looked up into Rob's eyes. "Rob, I gotta ask you something. It hurts me so much to say this. But somebody's gonna ask you, and I wanna be the first. I love you, Rob. Whoever asks you next might not."

Rob, with slumped shoulders and lifeless eyes, leaned on the edge of the table and looked at her. To Ruth, he seemed like an obscenely pathetic imitation of her son. "What?" he asked listlessly.

Ruth paused, staring at him, as she felt her heart breaking. The tears in her eyes were making her son's image shimmer. She blinked and took a breath.

"Robert, did you do it? Did you touch your son? Did you do anything to Keefe?" In an instant, she was swamped by two terrible emotions. She was horrified by what she had just asked her own son—and panic-stricken at what she might hear.

What would happen if the answer was not the one she needed to have? Oh God, what would she do if Rob simply crumpled into tears? Could she go on living, thinking that her son had molested Keefe? Oh, dear, sweet Jesus what had she done? Her thoughts, like a great breaking wave, took only moments to crash through her mind.

Rob looked at his mother as though she had calmly drawn a gun and shot him. His wounded eyes told her all she wanted to know. His reply was soft, but straightforward: "Oh my God, Mom, no."

Ruth forced out her next words. "I had to ask you, Rob, I had to. As much as I love you, things can happen, you know? I had to do it, Rob. Please, please, don't hate me for it. I just didn't . . ." Before she could finish the sentence, she burst into great heaving sobs. She pulled her son toward her and Ray joined them in a tight embrace. They stayed that way, quietly weeping, for several minutes.

Later, as Ruth and Ray were preparing drinks at the kitchen table, she began to berate herself. The despairing look that Rob gave her was a look no mother should ever have to see from her son.

"I'm sure Rob will hate me for the rest of my life," she sobbed to her husband. "Look at everything that's just happened to him and now look what I've done. I'm his mother. I shouldn't have *had* to ask."

"Ruth, it's alright," Ray said, patting her shoulder. "Rob understands. We all understand."

Several hours later, long after dinner had been served and the kitchen table set for the next morning, Ruth and Ray were lying in bed. She was still agonizing over what she had done. "It isn't that I thought he might have done it; I just needed to hear him say he didn't." Her husband clasped her in his arms silently.

"You know my relationship with Rob has always been more than a mother-son relationship. We were best friends. We often get into terrible arguments because we're so much alike. Sensitive and stubborn. But our love has never, ever wavered. I don't think I could take it if something happened to that. I can't believe what Vicki has done, what misery she has brought into our lives. I curse her. I curse myself."

She got up and went to the bathroom, where she cried as she had never cried before. She cried until there were no tears left, and then she cried some more. When she finally made her way back to bed, Ray patted her cheek.

"Oh, Papa, was I wrong?" she miserably asked the man to whom she had been married for thirty-nine years. "Was I wrong in asking him? Papa, I had to ask him. I had to hear it from him. Was that wrong? Does he hate me now?"

"Ruth, let me hold you," he said, placing her head on his shoulder protectively, supporting her as he had for four decades. "I understand why you asked the question," he said, speaking slowly. "I think it's very normal that you wanted to know if anything happened. It's . . . well . . . it's human nature, that's all. It's okay to have that few seconds of doubt flash in your mind, Ruth. That doesn't mean you don't trust Rob, or that you think he might have done it. You know, if you hadn't asked him, I think that at some point I would have."

Ray paused as his hand found hers. "But I think we both knew what the answer would be."

Ruth had never loved her husband as much as she did in that instant. His words were a balm to her aching conscience. Still, she did not sleep that night.

Early the next morning, the three of them drove to the Bristol courthouse. Rob was wearing the gray, double-breasted suit he had picked up for fifteen dollars in a thrift shop. It was a good suit, except for the fit. The right arm was shorter than the left, and when he tried to compensate for it by slightly tilting his shoulders, he looked like a decrepit old man. In other circumstances, they would have shared a laugh over it.

They arrived at Bristol Superior Court early. Rob's arraignment was set for ten a.m., and Hurvitz's partner, Jon Schoenhorn, was supposed to meet them there. Schoenhorn was the law firm's trial attorney.

At about nine-thirty a.m., a dark haired slender man with a drooping black mustache wearing a natty three-piece suit strode into the lobby just outside the courtroom. McQueeney recognized Schoenhorn from the few times their paths had crossed at the law firm's offices, but he didn't move from the bench he was sharing with his parents until Schoenhorn walked over.

Schoenhorn introduced himself to the three McQueeneys before turning to Rob. "Let's go over here and talk," he said, gesturing to an empty bench a few feet away.

Schoenhorn pulled out the contract he had drawn up for Rob. It was a standard contract for retaining a lawyer, with a few paragraphs of legal jargon and two blank spaces for the amount of the retainer and the per diem charge should the case go to trial. Schoenhorn had filled in the blank spaces; all he needed was McQueeney's signature. He passed Rob the contract and a pen.

Rob barely contained his shock when he saw how Schoenhorn had filled in the blanks. He was requiring a $5,000 retainer and $400 per day if the case went to trial.

"I'm going to have to talk to my parents," he said, returning the contract and pen to Schoenhorn.

"Why? Don't you have the money?" Schoenhorn asked.

"No, I don't have that kind of money," McQueeney stiffly replied. "I'm going to have to get it from my father."

They had started walking over to his parents when Rob turned to Schoenhorn and asked him to wait. Rob continued on, sat down, and told them how much money it was going to cost.

"But *why*?" his mother plaintively asked. "You didn't do anything. Why all this money when you didn't do anything?" Her voice was breaking, as it often did when she was angry or confused.

"We have very little choice in the matter, Mom. I have to have an attorney right away and this is probably what's normal in a case like this."

"We'll find a way," Ray said.

"Of course, we'll find a way," Ruth's voice echoed.

At that moment, they looked up to see Schoenhorn sauntering over to them. They told him they would formulate a payment plan later that day.

"No, you have to sign this right now, or I can't represent you," he curtly replied. "And you don't have much time," he added. "The judge will be here in a couple of minutes. I'm not going into the courtroom until I get the retainer."

Ray and Ruth weren't sure what to expect from a criminal lawyer, but they thought they would get more compassion than Schoenhorn seemed to be exhibiting.

"What a miserable son of a bitch," Ray murmured. He briefly considered calling Schoenhorn's bluff. He didn't think the lawyer would drive all the way back to Hartford empty-handed. Even if he did, Ray figured all he had to do was tell the judge what had happened and everything would proceed normally. "Who am I kidding?" he suddenly said. "I'm a greenhorn at this. I don't know anything about courts and lawyers. What if I did something that ended up hurting Rob?"

He looked searchingly at Ruth. "Write him a check."

Ruth started to fish in her purse for the checkbook. She figured Schoenhorn would be happy with a few hundred dollars deposit and they could pay the rest in a week or so.

"How much?" she asked.

"Five thousand dollars."

"I beg your pardon?"

"Five thousand dollars," Schoenhorn impatiently repeated. "That's what the contract says."

"Where do you think I'm going to get five thousand dollars?" Ruth protested.

Schoenhorn's reply was curt and to the point: "If you can't give me five thousand dollars, I can't represent him."

The thirty-two-year-old lawyer's face was grim. As a criminal attorney, he had to represent people accused of murder, but sex crimes, as far as he was concerned, were the worst. Not only did he worry about the implications of such a crime, but he knew the defense, in such cases, had to accuse the victim of lying, consenting to the act, or being mistaken in the identification of the assailant.

In this case, there was no question of the little boy giving his consent or mistaking his attacker. That meant he would have to either attack Keefe as a liar, or attack his mother for manipulating Keefe to advance some hidden agenda. Either way, it would be a messy case. He did not know whether McQueeney had committed the crime; he made it a point never to ask his clients about their guilt or innocence. But he hated to think about grilling a little boy who may or may not have been the victim of a horrendous personal assault, or of questioning the motives of someone who may simply have been trying to protect a vulnerable child. Schoenhorn wished he was somewhere—anywhere—else.

"We can give you a check, but we're going to have to post-date it," Ray broke in. "It'll take a week or two for me to get the money. I'll have to cash in a real estate trust fund I've been saving for my retirement."

Schoenhorn didn't look pleased, but he accepted the postdated check. As he was folding it to put in his wallet, he said, "You know, normally I charge a $10,000 retainer for a Class A felony, which is what your son is facing." His voice softened. "I know $5,000 sounds like a lot of money to you, but it really isn't. Not for this, anyway."

None of the McQueeneys knew the going rate for a Class A felony. They didn't even know what a Class A felony was, beyond the fact that Rob had been charged with one. But Ruth and Ray knew their son was in trouble, serious trouble, and they had to help him.

The appearance at Bristol Superior Court was brief. In less than a minute, the judge had routinely transferred the case to Hartford Superior Court. On the way back to his parents' house, Rob tried to reassure them that Schoenhorn was only doing his job.

"I know neither of you like him, but it's not necessary to like him," Rob said. "His only job is to represent me to the best of his ability. Let's not worry about anything else."

They were silent for a while as Ray drove through the Bristol streets. As they were leaving the town, McQueeney asked his parents to stop at a pharmacy so he could get a copy of the local newspaper. One of McQueeney's fears was that his friends, co-workers and relatives would read in the newspapers that he had been arrested for sexually molesting his son. He had to find out if the story was there. He dashed into the newsstand, grabbed up the paper and, embarrassed, paid the cashier, wondering if she had read the paper.

Despite the cold weather, his forehead was shiny with sweat as he climbed into his parents' car and quickly opened *The Bristol Press*. He scanned page after page. Then he found it, a small item on page twelve, near the lower left-hand corner of the newspaper:

MAN CHARGED WITH
SEXUAL ASSAULT

PLYMOUTH—A Terryville man was arrested for sexual assault and risk of injury to a minor Monday, according to police.

Police arrested Robert McQueeney, 31, of 44 Bemis St. in Terryville at about 2 p.m. Monday on a Bristol Superior Court warrant, police said. McQueeney was charged with 1st degree sexual assault and risk of injury to a minor, police said.

Police said the arrest stemmed from an investigation of an incident that occurred on or about Jan. 31, police said. McQueeney was released on a $5,000 surety bond and is scheduled to appear in court today.

Rob felt like he'd been punched in the stomach. Trembling, he handed the newspaper to his mother as he fought the gorge rising in his throat. A few minutes later, she passed the paper back and he read the story again. His forehead burned with shame. He forced himself to take a deep breath before he read it a third time. And then a fourth. By the time they had arrived at his parents' house, he was able to talk about it.

"Well, if there's anything at all to be thankful for, I guess it's the fact that they didn't say anything about Keefe," he told his parents. "It could have been worse. I don't know what I would have done if it said that I was accused of raping my own son—or any child, for that matter."

"I'm not so thankful," Ray mused thoughtfully. "I'm horrified that Rob's name has been publicly connected to a sexual crime. I wonder," he said grimly, "how many of Rob's friends will suddenly fall out of touch with him. I hate all this."

"I'm still relieved it wasn't a bigger story," Rob said slowly. "At least, it didn't detail the accusations." Still, he could not stop the aching, sick feeling in his stomach. It was the same feeling he'd had dozens of times since he'd been arrested less than twenty-four hours before. It always snuck up on him . . . before it kicked him in the groin.

"Oh Christ," he moaned, suddenly burying his head in his hands. He was an accused *child molester*.

After spending Tuesday night at his parents' house, McQueeney returned to his own home. He spent the next three nights imagining that people were pushing aside their curtains to peer at his house. He wondered what they were thinking about him as they sat in their cozy, secure homes with their children around them. In his more rational moments, he still believed that Vicki had simply made a horrible mistake. He did not consider the possibility that she or anyone else had orchestrated his arrest. He yearned to get into court, tell the truth, and get the charges dismissed, so he could see his kids again and get his life back to normal.

Somehow, he couldn't shake the feeling that he *was* guilty —not of a particular crime, but of *something*. It didn't matter that he had done nothing. What mattered was being arrested in front of his friends and then having the cops take his belt and his shoelaces before locking him in a jail cell. It was the humiliation more than anything else that produced that dirty, smothering feeling of guilt. At the same time, *because* he had done nothing wrong, he was denied the rehabilitative powers of remorse. He could not feel remorseful, any more than he could confess. There was no way to purge himself of this amorphous guilt.

More than anything, he was afraid. His fear was that of a blind man trying to negotiate a room in which somebody keeps moving the furniture. He didn't know what he might trip over next. He didn't know what to be scared of; he only knew he was petrified.

He kept returning to the newspaper item about his arrest. He read it dozens of times. In his mind, he bent the words and twisted them and turned them inside-out.

Alone, his nights were similar, but worse than they were just before his arrest. He sat in the complete darkness and nursed a bourbon, looking out his front window, wondering what would come next. Each hour brought a new possibility to his mind. Filthy graffiti in his driveway? Christ, what was going to happen to him?

He hit bottom on Wednesday night, forty-eight hours after his arrest. He had been sitting on the couch. Every light was off. In a daze, he slowly got up from the couch and shuffled to the center of the living room. As he stared out the window, his mind began to bend toward madness. He backed into the corner of the room. As he leaned against the walls, he began to slowly slide toward the floor. He was sobbing before he made it halfway down. By the time he reached the floor he was wailing. He sat there for what seemed hours, huddled in the corner, until his wails softened to whimpers.

About eight-thirty the next morning, Rob called Susan

Blackwell, Keefe's preschool teacher. He wanted to ask for a meeting to review Keefe's progress at school.

But there was something else he had to ask first.

"Susan, I hope you don't believe I did it."

Susan, who had a four-year-old daughter, responded without hesitation. "No, I don't."

Then, she told McQueeney how her husband had taken Tuesday morning's newspaper to work with him, and had called her at home when he saw the item about the arrest. He had recognized the name because Susan had often spoken of Rob McQueeney, one of those rare fathers who volunteered in her classroom.

"I immediately told my husband that I knew it couldn't be true," she told McQueeney. "I mean, I know you told me you were having a great deal of difficulty with your wife during the divorce, but that story about the arrest was a complete shock! I told my husband it's ridiculous. I could see that by the way you are with the four-year-olds in our class. You really have a nice way with children, Rob. They love it when you come in to volunteer. And it's absolutely clear to me that Keefe loves you. No, Rob, you don't have to worry about what *I* think. I *know* you didn't do it."

McQueeney felt only a dull appreciation. How many times would he be asking people that question? How many times would people profess to believe him, only to be harboring private doubts? McQueeney wasn't questioning Susan's sincerity; he was worried about the reactions of untold others in his very uncertain future.

"Did any of the parents or other teachers say anything about this?" he asked.

"Nobody has said anything at all to me," she replied. "And don't worry about that. I'm not going to discuss this with anyone else."

"Rob, are you okay?" the twenty-eight-year-old teacher asked. "You sound so defeated. Like someone walking along the edge of a cliff, who doesn't much care if a stiff breeze happens along."

Susan quickly agreed to meet McQueeney the next day.

That was the least she could do, although she couldn't help feeling uncomfortable about it. She didn't want to get caught in the middle of this situation.

Susan had just started to say good-bye when McQueeney asked if she could do one thing for him.

"I haven't been able to see or talk to Keefe for over three weeks," McQueeney said, fighting to keep the trembling out of his voice. "I have no idea how all of this has affected him. I wanted to know if you could give him a message from me. Could you tell him that his Daddy loves him and hopes that he's alright?"

McQueeney was relieved when Susan quickly agreed to convey the message. He thanked her and promptly said good-bye.

With his spirits somewhat buoyed by the phone call, McQueeney decided to try to return to work. He called in at ten-thirty to say that he would be in around noon. About an hour later, he had finished his shower and was getting ready to leave when that out-of-control feeling he had had the night before began returning. With a wrenching effort, he forced himself to concentrate on getting to the telephone and dialing the number for work. He spoke to Tom—the rotund fellow who had given his parents the money for his bail.

"Tom. I don't think I'm going to be able to make it to work today," he began. He couldn't say another word, as sobs overcame him. He collapsed into a rocking chair.

A short while later, Tom and Ted, one of the people who had been with him when he was arrested, knocked on his door. "Rob," Ted said, "we're concerned about you."

Rob let them in. Both men knew the charges McQueeney was facing, but didn't know the details.

"What's really going on?" Tom asked.

The innocuous question brought Rob's painful emotions to the surface again. McQueeney was able to speak six words before he collapsed again in his rocking chair. "They said that I raped Keefe."

As he sat there, barely able to speak, Tom and Ted came and stood on either side of him. Each of them put a hand on his shoulder. After a few minutes, McQueeney sat up and told them he would be alright. They could go.

Silently, not knowing what else to do, they both complied.

Susan Blackwell was relieved that the telephone conversation with McQueeney had ended when it did. She had a full day in front of her and there were some things she still had to do to get her classroom ready for the nine a.m. start of school. To make matters even more complicated, this was the day—of all days—that Rob's estranged wife Vicki had picked to bring in her boyfriend Bruce to talk to the kids about his job. It was part of Susan's Career Day program, in which people, usually parents of her students, came in to describe their various jobs to the children.

Two weeks earlier, Vicki had asked Susan if she could bring in Bruce, as a deputy court sheriff, to participate in the program. Susan had reluctantly agreed. She now wished she hadn't. She had never met Bruce, and didn't know what to expect—or, given the recent turmoil, if they would show at all. With a sigh of trepidation, the teacher, in a pensive mood, started walking back to her classroom.

As she opened her classroom door, she realized that she now knew why Keefe had missed the last several days of class. "God, what a thing for a child to cope with," she thought. "The divorce was bad enough, and now he's got to deal with his father being arrested—on a complaint made by his mother."

She shook her head and tried to check her anger. She had to appear impartial when Vicki and Bruce arrived. Her principal had cautioned her against taking sides when speaking with either of the parents—and she'd already strayed from that course. The principal, who didn't know McQueeney, had also made it clear that both parents had the right to see Keefe unless the school received legal documents specifying otherwise. So far, he said, the school had received no such documents.

As she thought about what was happening, her anger flared again. Keefe's attendance sheet was filled with erasures and crossouts, because Vicki often brought him fifteen to twenty minutes late—after the attendance had been taken and he had been marked absent.

As Susan rearranged the tables and chairs in the classroom, she made a pact with herself to stay neutral. "I'll have to try not to think about Keefe," she thought. "He's such a cute little boy, and he was really starting to come out of his shell. And now this."

A few minutes after school started, Susan was summoned out of her room by a tall, dark-haired man, dressed in a sheriff's uniform, standing in the hallway. It was Bruce Johnson. Vicki and Keefe were standing a few feet away. An instant after she had passed through the classroom door, Bruce reached behind her and firmly closed it. With his handcuffs and billyclub hanging off his belt, he glanced up and down the hallway. He folded his arms across his chest, leaned against the wall and addressed Susan.

"I'm Bruce Johnson, the deputy court sheriff," he began. "Now, I'm sure, Mrs. Blackwell, that you're aware of what has happened. Robert McQueeney, the father of Keefe, has been arrested on a warrant charging him with first-degree sexual assault and risk of injury to a minor. The state is accusing him of sexually abusing Keefe."

Susan just stood there, nodding awkwardly, saying nothing.

Bruce continued, "The boy has been placed under the protection of the state's attorney and I am here in his stead. In my capacity as a court sheriff, I'm going to make sure that Robert McQueeney is nowhere near here today." His eyes narrowed. "And *you're* going to make sure that Keefe is at no time left unattended and therefore vulnerable to a kidnapping attempt."

Susan held up her hand. "Listen, this is not a jail, this is a classroom," she snapped. "These are four-year-olds, not second-graders, and they are never let out of the room unattended. I wouldn't even be out here in the hall, except that I have a teacher's aide with the children. You don't have anything to worry about. Keefe will be perfectly safe." She paused to catch her breath. "Besides, I hardly think Rob is going to swoop in here like Batman and snatch his child away."

Bruce appeared unfazed. "Well, you never know, Mrs.

Blackwell, you never know. I intend to stay here all day to make sure that that doesn't happen."

Bruce glanced at Keefe, who was quietly standing by Vicki. "By the way," Bruce added, "this will be Keefe's last day of school. Will you please make the necessary arrangements for his withdrawal, prepare his records and gather his things?"

Susan flashed Bruce a grim look, but didn't answer him. Then, Bruce said, "Thank you, Mrs. Blackwell. If you're ready, I'll go in and address the children."

Neither Keefe nor Vicki had said a word. Sighing, Susan opened the classroom door and led the trio inside. Vicki and Keefe sat on the classroom floor with the other children as Susan introduced Bruce Johnson, the deputy court sheriff.

To her amazement, Bruce walked to the far end of the room where there was a raised platform, about six inches higher than the classroom floor. He stepped up on the platform and started talking to the sitting children. Every other adult who had participated in the career day had sat down, either on a chair, or on the platform this man was standing upon.

When Rob visited the classroom, he would get down on his hands and knees, to play with the children and their toys. He talked to them as though they were his equal. This guy was just too much. Susan made a show of leaving her seat and sitting among the children, hoping Bruce would take the hint. He didn't.

As he continued speaking, Susan became increasingly angry at Bruce and at herself, for allowing him to come in. She had assumed he would talk about how policemen and other law enforcement officials were children's friends: people they could go to if they were lost or needed help. Instead, he had told the children about his billyclub, his handcuffs and how to subdue a troublesome prisoner. Now, he was giving them a seminar on how to transport violent criminals between the jails and the courts.

Then, he started talking about jail cells. Susan glanced around the room and saw frowns and worried looks on the faces of several of the children. Their faces were tilted up at a ridiculous angle so they could see Bruce. She had had enough. She interrupted Bruce in mid-sentence.

"Now, children, things like jail and sheriffs and billyclubs are only for adults who do bad things," she said. "They have nothing to do with little children. If you hit your brother, this man is not going to take you to jail. Are you, Mr. Johnson?"

Bruce primly smiled. "Of course not. If they do that in a few years, maybe, but not now."

His talk lasted only about ten minutes, but it seemed much longer. When he asked if there were any questions, two boys asked him about guns. He seemed to enjoy talking about them. Susan shuddered.

As Bruce was talking about guns, Susan glanced over at Keefe, who was sitting by his mother. Keefe hadn't said a word to Bruce or Vicki. When Bruce finished his talk, he stepped off his stage and went over to Vicki. After whispering something in her ear, he left the room.

During the rest of the morning, Bruce wandered in and out of the classroom, peering out windows and walking around the school. When the class was dismissed, he told Vicki to hold back Keefe while he checked to make sure it was safe.

In between greeting parents and saying good-bye to her students, Susan watched as Bruce checked the cars in the parking lot and then walked behind every tree and bush on the school grounds where McQueeney might be hiding.

Vicki did not know that the teacher had spoken to Rob that morning, so she could not know that Rob had asked her to deliver a message to Keefe. But it seemed as though Vicki was going out of her way to make sure that Keefe was never alone with Susan, even for a moment.

Just then Bruce returned from his sweep of the schoolgrounds. He looked at Susan and then at Vicki. "It's safe for Keefe to leave the school," he said gravely. Susan shook her head disgustedly.

Keefe hadn't spoken to Susan during the entire morning. Now, as the little boy started to walk away with the two grownups, Susan softly called to him. Keefe stopped and looked back, his tiny fingers entwined around his mother's.

"I won't be seeing you anymore, Keefe. I'm going to miss you." Susan paused to give him a chance to respond. Keefe stared at his feet. "You be a good boy, OK?" Susan started to step forward to give him a hug good-bye. Before she could, Vicki and Bruce began to maneuver Keefe away toward the parking lot.

The next day, Rob went to see Susan. She was shaken by his appearance.

"Rob, it's only been about a month since I saw you, but you look awful! You look like you've aged ten years." There was no life in his walk, and, even more frightening, no life in his eyes. She didn't know that he had drunk himself to sleep the night before, and cried himself to sleep the night before that.

Rob and Susan each sat in a tiny, toy-like chair next to a table in the empty classroom. They had about thirty minutes before the afternoon session would begin. It was the first time Rob had spoken in detail about what had happened to him with anyone other than his parents or his lawyers.

In a subdued voice, Rob told her about the tobogganing weekend and Keefe's sore rear end. About the phone calls from the police and his arrest. There were sporadic pauses as he struggled to maintain his composure.

"But why would she believe this happened?" Susan finally asked. "It sounds to me like it probably had something to do with his toilet hygiene habits. You know, Rob, I've been around children for years, both as a parent and as a professional. I'm what the state calls a 'mandated reporter,' which means that, under the law, I am required to report even the slightest suspicion of child abuse. In the six months Keefe has been in my class, he has *never* exhibited *any* sign that he was being abused. You know, I've *known* children who were sexually abused. I've been their teacher. It's ridiculous to think that anything happened to Keefe."

Susan then went over Keefe's progress report, telling Mc-Queeney that he was a bright youngster who had just started to get over his shyness. She was about to tell him that he had been withdrawn from school the previous day when McQueeney interrupted her. He was starving for information. He wanted to know *everything* about Keefe. Too many other people had given him too little information during the past three weeks. He pressed Susan: "Was there *anything* at all out of the ordinary?" he asked. "Anything at all that Vicki might have interpreted as a sign of abuse?"

Susan emphatically shook her head. "Not at all. No mood swings, no fear of adults, no precocious sex play, nothing out of the ordinary when he went to the toilet, no suggestion of abnormal submissiveness or aggression, nothing. Absolutely nothing. I mean, if anything, it's just the opposite. He's made real progress since September, Rob. That's why this was such a shock to me. His recent behavior is directly opposite that of an abused child."

Rob let out a deep breath. Finally, a professional was giving him information. Better yet, this was someone close to his son, who had seen Keefe a few days after Rob had supposedly raped him. She was required by law to report even a suspicion of abuse. She'd seen nothing. She didn't think it had happened. She believed in him when so many others had not.

Then, Susan told Rob that Keefe had been withdrawn from school the previous day—and described how Bruce had made a complete idiot out of himself. She was surprised that Rob was not sharing her anger at Bruce. In fact, he impatiently interrupted her story. He had a more important question to ask.

"Did you get a chance to talk to Keefe? Did you get a chance to give him the message? What did he say? Is he alright?" The words had run together in his rush to get them out. His eagerness made it all the harder for Susan to answer.

"I tried, Rob. I really did. But Vicki was on top of Keefe all morning. I couldn't get him alone for even a few seconds. And I didn't want to give him the message while Vicki was there. Frankly, I don't think she would have handled it very well if she heard me tell Keefe his daddy wanted him to know he loved him. I'm sure she would have caused a scene."

McQueeney couldn't hide his disappointment. It was time to go. With an effort, he extracted himself from the tiny wooden chair and extended his hand. Susan clasped it gently in both of hers.

"I really do hope everything works out," she said. "Not just for your sake, but for Keefe's as well. I don't think Vicki understands the effect this is going to have on him, never mind what it's doing to you. I don't think there's anything that can ruin a person's life more quickly or more completely than this. It's just so terrible."

"Yeah, I know," Rob responded. "Believe me, I know." He paused for a moment, a faraway look in his eyes. "Well, I want to thank you for meeting with me and sharing the information you have. If it means anything, you've made me feel a little better. There was a time there that I didn't think anyone other than my parents believed in me."

Back home, McQueeney sat down and tried to digest what Susan had told him, and to make sense of everything that had happened to him in the last few weeks. He thought he was getting better. This time, it took a whole quarter-hour before the tears came.

His mother called a couple of hours later. Rob had cried himself to sleep in the middle of the afternoon, and the jangling phone frightened him. He couldn't stop shaking. He cried when he told his mother about the meeting with Susan. And then he got upset at himself for crying so much. Ruth, frightened at how her son sounded, suggested that she come to keep him company. Rob again declined, telling his mother he just needed some sleep. He promised to call her in the morning.

McQueeney was never so happy to see his parents than when they knocked on his door the next morning. Ray stayed for a cup of coffee before leaving.

Hours upon hours passed during the weekend without a word being spoken. Mother and son shared their grief and their love through small gestures; a hug here, a touch there.

In the dark, McQueeney found some solace . . . but no escape. While Ruth tossed and turned on the living room couch, McQueeney fitfully slept on the floor beside her, curled up, fetal position, inside a sleeping bag. His cat slept beside him. Several times during the night, Ruth stepped off the couch, knelt beside her son and gave him a hug. She knew he was awake because he returned each hug.

McQueeney did not have the strength—either physical or psychological—to move even a few steps from the living room to his bedroom. The sleeping bag became his womb. He pulled it partially over his face. But it didn't really matter. The misery of reality wouldn't go away.

He sweated and still he covered himself. He sweated and still he shivered.

The house was cold. With all his legal expenses, Mc-Queeney couldn't afford to heat it to a comfortable temperature. He'd closed off his own bedroom and his children's rooms, where everything remained as it had been on that last tobogganing weekend. The decorations for the Giants Super Bowl victory party still hung from the ceilings. Some of the blue and white crepe paper had started to sag, but Rob couldn't bring himself to take it down. Keefe had helped him put the decorations up; Keefe would help him take them down. When he entered the room, Rob's head would occasionally brush against the faded crepe paper; it seemed somehow a symbol of hope.

The weekend passed like a ticking time bomb. The very air seemed to weigh on them with a great oppressive malevolence. The mail went uncollected. The newspaper went unread. The television went unwatched. As a concession to his mother, Rob left a dim light on in the kitchen. For long stretches, one or the other would sit crosslegged on the floor and pet Holly. Ruth's heart hurt each time she looked at her son. His eyes had a glazed, injured expression to them. She could only imagine what he must be thinking.

McQueeney was imagining what it would be like to be on trial for raping his four-year-old son. In his worse imaginings, he pictured imprisonment. He felt powerless, as though he was being carried away on a fantastic rolling wave of blind contempt. He had been accused of something hideous. People would think he did it. When he read about people being arrested for crimes like this, he always assumed they were guilty. He always wondered how someone could be that cruel, that sick, and that out of touch with reality.

At nine-thirty Sunday morning, Rob turned on the television to watch one of his favorite shows, "The Wind in the Willows." A few seconds after the theme song started, he snapped it off. He was hearing Keefe's voice and Wendy's giggles.

Ruth left on Monday and Rob returned to his office. He lost himself in his work for hours at a stretch. But then he had to go home. Everything was different there. If someone had entered his house at night and asked him what he was doing, sitting alone in the dark, he would have calmly replied "watching." It made perfect sense to him. He had to guard against further attacks. If something else was going to hit him, he wanted to see it coming.

Later that week, he met with Schoenhorn to begin preliminary work on the case. Schoenhorn told Rob that he was facing up to forty years in prison. Before that had even sunk in, he asked Rob if he wanted to go all the way in fighting the charges, or be willing to accept some sort of deal from the prosecutor's office.

"You have to at least consider how far you want to let this go," Schoenhorn said. "You not only have exposure to forty years in prison, but, if this goes all the way to trial, you'll be facing considerable financial expense . . . maybe tens of thousands of dollars, and no guarantee you'll be acquitted."

McQueeney didn't hesitate. "I won't accept anything short of their dropping the case," he said. "I want a complete dismissal of the charges. I won't accept a *nolle* and I won't plead guilty to *anything*." He paused. "I'll find the money somehow."

Schoenhorn was surprised at his adamancy. "Well, Rob, that's fine. But I've got to tell you that if they offer a *nolle* on this case, we should take it. That would end up being just like a dismissal. The only difference is that the state reserves the right to reopen the case. If they don't do that within thirteen months —and they rarely do—then the charges are dismissed."

"I don't care," McQueeney responded. "A *nolle* leaves a question mark there. I don't want any question mark. I want a dismissal . . . with no strings attached."

Schoenhorn sighed. He had been a practicing attorney for five years. In his experience, the initial reaction of his clients had often been just like McQueeney's. Later on, as the financial and psychological costs mounted, they often moderated their views. Especially if it looked like the case would go to trial. He didn't think things would go that far, but, hell, anything could happen.

On March 12, McQueeney went out socially for the first time since his arrest. He had become a borderline agoraphobic;

101

he avoided leaving home for anything other than his job. When he arrived at work, he stayed there, making excuses to avoid going out to lunch. He would shake when the phone rang or he saw a pair of headlights heading down Bemis Street in front of his home.

But March 12 was special enough to puncture that near-phobia; it was his thirty-second birthday. He went to lunch with Ted Andrews—who had been with him when he was arrested. Ted also was born on March 12, exactly one year before Mc-Queeney. They went to Chef's—McQueeney's favorite restaurant and pub. The converted New England barn with its authentic exposed beams and barnboard walls was a favorite stop for truckers because of its wide crescent shaped driveway.

As Ted and Rob were having a drink in the bar to celebrate their birthdays, a toddler came careening in from the dining room, bouncing his rolling walker off tables and chairs. He was about six months old.

"Ted, look at this baby!" McQueeney exclaimed. "Where did this baby come from? Who is this baby? I've never seen a baby roll himself into a bar like that," he laughed heartily. "Have you?"

Ted languidly turned to look at the baby. "Hmm. That is kind of strange." He turned back to his drink. Babies weren't high on Ted's list of interests.

Rob's spirits rose. "Ted, this is so weird. He looks just like Keefe did. Whose baby is this? I wanna talk to this baby."

Rob went on and on about the baby, while Ted politely listened. Finally, Rob ordered another Bloody Mary and asked the bartender who the baby belonged to.

"Oh, that's Lorie's baby," she said, frowning slightly. "She's one of the waitresses in the dining room. She brings him in a lot. Poor girl, her boyfriend left her when he found out she was pregnant. She's bringing him up by herself."

Rob was enthralled. To him, the toddler looked and acted like Keefe. He *had* to find out more about this baby. He *had* to meet his mother. He asked the woman behind the bar if Lorie could possibly come by for a couple of minutes. He told her that the baby looked almost exactly like his own son had looked at that age. The woman looked at Rob, as though sizing him up.

"Well, I can give her the message, but I'll tell you right now that this is the busiest time of the day for her. It would be better if you come back some other time. She brings Joshua in here quite a lot, so I'm sure you'll see him again."

Rob looked at Ted, and Ted took a long sip from his drink. "We really should be getting back," Ted said. "Why don't you try to come in some other day?"

McQueeney decided Ted was right. They paid their bill and walked toward the door. Before he closed it behind him, McQueeney allowed himself one more backward glance at Joshua. He was such an adorable little boy.

A month went by before McQueeney got up enough nerve to talk to the waitress named Lorie. He was alone at Chef's, sitting in the bar after finishing his lunch. He was drinking another celery-less Bloody Mary. The time seemed right. And he was in the mood.

"Hey, waitress!" he jokingly called to her. "With the money I spend here, you guys could put up a whole new addition to this little hole. But can't you give me a little piece of celery?"

Lorie expressionlessly glanced at Rob and disappeared into the back room. She emerged a minute later, carrying a tree-sized stalk of celery on her shoulder. She looked like a baseball player walking up to the plate as she approached McQueeney. Without a word, she deposited the celery in his glass.

McQueeney had to grab his drink before it toppled over from the weight of the stalk.

"Could I have a bigger glass, please? Or, maybe a pitcher?"

She laughed. And they talked.

McQueeney told her about his surprise at seeing a baby roll into the bar.

"Oh, yeah, Joshua," she replied. "I bring him in here when I can't get a babysitter for him." She glanced around. "I just hope his habit of rolling into bars doesn't become a permanent thing."

McQueeney told her how Joshua reminded him of his own son. He asked how old he was.

"Oh, he's about seven months old now. He was born on September 4th."

McQueeney's mouth dropped open as he stared at Lorie.

"You're kidding! That's Keefe's birthday!" He paused for a moment, to let his amazement subside. He had been sitting in a bar on his birthday, with a friend who had the same birthday as him, and he'd seen a little boy who looked like Keefe. Now he finds out this little boy has the same birthday as Keefe. McQueeney didn't believe in fate, or symbolism, but this seemed too coincidental to ignore.

"Do you wanna go out sometime?" he asked. Even as he said it, he wasn't sure whether he was asking out Lorie . . . or her son. He supposed it was a bit of both.

Their first date was a backyard barbecue at Rob's house the following weekend. Lorie brought Joshua and McQueeney happily entertained them both. Lorie cautioned Rob that she had just gotten over a rough relationship and that all she wanted was to have a good time and be friends. Lorie was the first woman he had asked out since Vicki had left him nine months earlier.

Lorie was a notch above plain-looking, with short, sandy brown hair and a medium build. She rarely smiled and seemed very demanding.

But that didn't matter to Rob. He was drawn to Lorie because it seemed that she needed somebody. He wanted to nurture her, to give a helping hand to this woman who was raising her baby alone.

Much of his attraction was, of course, Joshua. He was a cute, cuddly little boy who helped replace what Rob had just lost. During their five-month relationship, Rob spent a great deal of time babysitting Joshua, often falling asleep on the couch with the little boy cradled in his arms.

On their third date, Rob gave Lorie a brief of the accusations he was facing. Even though he only talked for five minutes, he was crying by the time he finished. Lorie calmly accepted it. "I don't believe it happened," she said. "I believe you."

But it wasn't her words that Rob so much appreciated; it was her willingness to entrust Joshua to him. Rob felt very fatherly toward the little boy. He gave him baths and read stories that the infant couldn't possibly understand. But, more than anything, he cuddled him. It didn't end the sense of loss he felt for his own children—but it helped.

As time went on, Rob washed the dishes, cleaned the house, and babysat while Lorie went out with her girlfriends. He spent an enormous amount of time, energy and money on Lorie and her son. Once in a while, he would wonder to himself what he was getting out of the relationship? Their relationship was completely nonsexual. She thought of him as a good friend and babysitter. Nothing more. Still, he reveled in the feeling that he was needed.

Of course, the real reason that this uneven relationship lasted for five months was Joshua. He made Rob feel like a daddy again. On Father's Day, Lorie got him a gift and a card—and signed them from Keefe and Wendy. She also gave him a small gift from Joshua. When he got them, McQueeney's heart soared.

Inevitably the relationship ended. Shortly after they stopped seeing each other, Rob was sitting in his house thinking of the incredible sequence of coincidences that had filled his life during the past few months.

On March 12, just about the time he had been casting that last backward glance at Joshua before leaving Chef's restaurant, Vicki was being questioned by Rob's two lawyers. What she told them in that sworn disposition had started to cast a barely perceptible glow on how Rob had arrived in his current situation. There was still much more darkness than light. But they had at least started to cut through the underbrush and begin making their way through the maze. Rob kept wondering what awaited him at the end.

Mercifully, he couldn't even guess.

■CHAPTER NINE■

Vicki Speaks

Jon Schoenhorn had an advantage in defending the criminal charges against McQueeney. Because McQueeney was getting divorced, Schoenhorn was able to ask the principal witnesses in the divorce case questions—under oath—that also were important to the criminal case.

The question and answer sessions—called depositions—were conducted jointly by Schoenhorn and Hurvitz. The two lawyers were only supposed to ask about issues related to the divorce. But they figured they would push the questioning as far as they could, until someone challenged them.

Schoenhorn's first target was Vicki. He wanted to talk to her as quickly as possible to find out what he was dealing with. He summoned her to his office on March 12, less than three weeks after McQueeney's arrest.

Vicki looked like a fresh, young cheerleader as she took a seat at a long table in a conference room at Hurvitz, Hershinson and Schoenhorn. Her lawyer, John P. Clifford Jr., was at her side.

Hurvitz began the questioning as a stenographer quietly recorded the proceedings. After some preliminary queries, he asked Vicki why she had left McQueeney with no warning.

"Well," she answered. "I didn't want to be there when he was served with the papers."

"Why not?" Hurvitz asked.

"Because he would have fought with me on it."

"What do you mean by fight?"

"I have talked to him about getting divorced in the past and, no, no, no. And I asked him to work things out and he says things are great, things are great. But they're not. And I'd talk to him and he says 'I'll try and try and I'll try and change,' but he never does. We have talked for many, many years. 'Let's stop, let's go back, let's talk about things.' "

Hurvitz asked what sorts of things needed to be worked out. Vicki instantly brought up their sex life. She said her husband masturbated in front of her.

"So these were sexual things that you fought about?"

"Being together."

"And what do you mean by being together?"

"We didn't get along," said Vicki, getting annoyed. "He didn't get along with anybody. He had his six friends and that was his life."

"What other things did you fight about?"

"None that I can remember, just not getting along."

"Now, you said that you didn't want to be there when he was served with the [divorce] papers because you fought?" Hurvitz asked.

"I was afraid of him," she said, her tone exasperated.

"What do you mean by 'afraid?' "

"He scared me. I didn't understand what he was doing."

"What didn't you understand?" Hurvitz patiently asked.

"How can someone jerk off in front of you?" she snapped. "You think it's normal?" Tears started running down her cheeks.

Clifford lifted his hand and called a brief recess to allow Vicki to compose herself. When they resumed, Hurvitz patiently, but persistently pursued his questioning.

He asked Vicki why she had left her mother's house.

"We didn't get along," Vicki responded.

Hurvitz leaned back. There was that answer again.

"Why didn't you get along?" he continued.

"Difference in opinions toward life."

"Can you tell me about those differences in opinion?"

"Some," she answered.

Hurvitz asked if they were major differences.

"Some of them."

It had become clear that Hurvitz was going to have to ask about three times as many questions as he had anticipated.

He stifled a sigh. "What were they?"

"Not getting along."

Hurvitz continued to pursue that line of questioning for quite a while without getting anywhere.

Then, he asked if she had ever been sexually molested.

"I was attacked once."

"When was that?"

"I was about 15."

"About 15. Was it somebody you knew?"

"Yes, my next-door neighbor."

"How old was the next-door neighbor?"

"About 40."

"Did you report this to the police?"

"Yeah."

"And what happened?"

"I didn't go through with it," she said with a sigh. "They told me there was a lot of work involved. They drilled me on it. It was hard."

"What do you mean 'hard?' "

"One, I wasn't living at home. And then it happened in the past where I had known he had done it to other people and they said usually they get off for it. So I figured it would be better to just forget about it. I was young. I didn't want to go through something like that by myself. And he didn't go inside me. I got away."

Hurvitz asked her why she quit working after moving in with Bruce Johnson.

"Bruce and I talked and at the present time it was better that I stay home with the kids," she said. "The kids were having a rough time with the divorce and understanding it and it wasn't right to leave them with a babysitter or something and we talked about it and for their best interest it was better that I stayed home."

"During the time of the divorce you've been claiming sole custody of the children," Hurvitz continued. "Why did you feel that you should have sole custody?"

"I think I have higher views on life than Rob."

"What do you mean?"

"If I asked Rob if they could go to a private school, I think he'd object to it and I'd rather have it that I pay for it and send them to it. Because I was checking into a private school."

"And what other reasons?"

"Better education, I feel."

"Did you, back in November, have any problems with Rob as a parent?"

"Yes I did," she said emphatically.

"What were those problems?"

"The kids would come home with bruises on them after the weekend."

"What kind of bruises?"

"Keefe would have a gash under his eye, a bruise on his back. I had problems, a few other incidents. Potty training went rough. I had to teach them how to do it."

"What other bruises?"

"None that I can remember, just his back and his eye," she said, straining to remember anything else. Then her face brightened. "Another time they had flea bites."

Hurvitz asked why she wanted sole custody as opposed to joint custody of the children.

"Basically I wanted them in private school and such . . . and I wanted them to go to church and Robert didn't want to," she said. "He told me he would have brought them after Christmas. He never did."

"Do you go to church?"

She paused for a moment. "No, I don't. But I want my kids to. And Rob is an atheist, and I think they should learn different views on religion, not just not go and not learn anything."

"Who suggested that you have sole custody?"

"Who suggested?"

"Yes."

"Nobody suggested that I have sole custody," she bristled.

"Did you talk to Bruce about your divorce?"

"Sometimes." Her voice softened.

"Did Bruce suggest Mr. Clifford's law offices?"

"Yes, I think so."

A few minutes later, she said Johnson also suggested she go to the Langley Center because he knew the director there.

She said she took Keefe to the center because of what happened the last weekend that Rob had them.

After delving into that subject Hurvitz questioned her about Dr. Pandit's examination of Keefe. She said the center suggested she take Keefe to the pediatrician. After the rectal examination, Vicki said Keefe came up with more stories.

"What kind of stories?" asked Hurvitz.

"More about the bad guy," Vicki said, looking like she might break down again. "He told me his father shoved his finger up his rectum way up to here [Vicki indicated an area between her wrist and her elbow] until it hurt and he started crying."

"When did he tell you that?"

"The night he came home from Pandit," she said after a moment. "He said that to me and he was afraid and shaken up by Pandit's visit and he started telling more and more."

Hurvitz changed the subject, asking whether she wanted Rob arrested or was glad he was arrested. She answered no to both questions.

Hurvitz asked what happened when she called the State Department of Children and Youth Services. She said a woman told her not to let Rob see the kids.

"Did she tell you what might happen to you if you did allow him?" asked Hurvitz.

"I'd get arrested."

"Pardon?" He gulped.

"I would get arrested."

"So therefore, based on that, you haven't been allowing him to see the children?"

"After what Keefe told me," she said, "I wouldn't let him."

A few minutes later, Schoenhorn took over from Hurvitz after assuring Clifford his questions would all be related to the divorce case.

Schoenhorn was pensive. His first impression of Vicki had been that she came across as sweet and innocent, almost childlike. And he felt that the way she had broken down, would draw the sympathy of a jury if the case ever got to trial. Still, there was a disturbing undercurrent here. Schoenhorn wanted to find out more about Johnson.

"Did Bruce give a statement to the police?" asked Schoenhorn.

"No, he didn't."

"Was he asked to?"

"No, I don't think so."

"Did the police officer, Officer Grodecki, ask him to come down?"

"No, he didn't."

"Did the DCYS worker?"

"No."

"Did anyone at the Langley Center?"

"I don't think so."

As the interview went on Schoenhorn questioned Vicki in depth about the last weekend, about Keefe's sore bottom, about Keefe's stories, about the movie *Ghostbusters*, and about Barbara Barrett, the social worker at Langley Center. Then Schoenhorn got back to Rob. He asked whether Vicki ever saw Rob hit the children.

"He spanked them," she said.

"He just spanked them on the butt?"

"I don't remember," she frowned. "He spanked them."

"Did you ever see him punch them?"

"No."

"Smack them in the face?"

"Not that I remember."

"Pull their hair?"

"I don't remember."

"Bang them against a wall or something?"

"When he is mad," she said, "he has a temper."

"What does he do when he gets a temper?"

"He screamed his head off," Vicki answered.

"But he doesn't get physical?"

"I don't think so," she said. "I can't remember."

Then Schoenhorn asked how Vicki had obtained a copy of the confidential Feb. 19 report by Barbara Barrett—the one that was sent to the police saying Keefe had been sexually molested.

"Bruce gave me a copy of it," she responded.

"Bruce gave you a copy?" repeated a surprised Schoenhorn.

"Bruce brought it to the police," Vicki answered simply.

"Let me back up a step," Schoenhorn paused. "How did Bruce get this report?"

"He picked it up from Barbara," said Vicki.

"Did you give Bruce specific permission to pick this up?"

"Yes. I asked him if he could bring it to the police station."

"Did you look at it first?"

"No, I didn't."

"Did Barbara call you and tell you she had a report for you?"

"Yes."

"Did she tell you it was for you or for the police?"

"She said it was for the police."

"Did she say why she wanted you to pick it up and bring it to the police?"

"Not that I can remember," responded Vicki.

Schoenhorn told Vicki what Barrett thought had happened with the children.

"She said they were definitely molested. Keefe tells her more stories than he tells me and I don't want to know the stories."

"You told Barbara you didn't want to know the stories?"

"Yes."

"Why?"

"Because I don't think I can handle it right now, OK?" Vicki again started crying and the lawyers called a short recess.

When they resumed, Schoenhorn asked, "Have you ever seen Rob act inappropriately with either of the children?"

"I don't know what you mean by 'inappropriately,' " Vicki answered.

"In a way that a father should not act with the children, with his own children?"

"Not that I remember, no."

"By your reaction, I take it, you believed Barbara Barrett's opinion?"

"She is a specialist in it," said Vicki, sniffling. "I think she knows what she is talking about."

112

■CHAPTER TEN■

Grandparents Cry, Too

June 25, four months after her son was arrested, Ruth Mc-Queeney was talking to her brother, George.

"I never knew the law could be so unfair," she protested. "And I'm not just talking about Rob's arrest. God knows, that was bad enough. But what about us? They took our grandchildren from us. How can they do that? We aren't even *accused* of anything. We lost the most precious gift in our lives and there's nothing we can do about it."

That's when George told Ruth of something called "The Grandparents Act."

"I don't know too much about it," he said, "but I know it's supposed to help out people who are in situations like yours. You should talk to a lawyer about it."

Two days later, on June 27, Ruth and Ray were in the office of John M. Andreini, who had been recommended by Rob's attorneys.

"My son has been accused of this terrible crime," Ruth began. "We don't believe he could possibly have done it. We would like to help him as much as we can, and show him our support. But we also believe that we've been deprived. Can you do anything to help us?"

After questioning Ruth about the details of the accusation, the big, bearded lawyer leaned back in his chair and smiled.

"This is a piece of cake," he said. "Which days do you want to see them?"

"Oh, come on," Ruth replied. "It can't be *that* easy, can it?"

"Sure," Andreini replied, reaching for the telephone. "You didn't do anything. You weren't involved in the alleged incident, nothing is alleged to have happened in your house, or while you were present. There's no connection at all where the court would consider the children at risk in visiting the grandparents. It'll be no problem."

"But will it hurt Rob with the criminal case?" Ruth asked.

"No, I don't think it will affect that in any way," Andreini said. "But, you *must* realize that there is no way that you can allow Rob to be present when the children are there. If you are granted visitation with the kids, then only you can be there. Don't ever try to give Rob access to them while they're with you." Ruth and Ray assured Andreini they would not do so.

Andreini called Vicki's lawyer, John Clifford, and told him that he was going to file a motion to give the grandparents visitation.

The motion was filed five days later, on July 2. Due to various court delays, it was not considered until September 16. But it was worth the wait. The court ordered that supervised visitation begin the following week, and continue every Wednesday thereafter.

The order, in part, read: "Further visitation to be expanded or restricted in accordance with Dr. Ledder's evaluation at the first visitation session."

In August, Rob's visits with the children were reinstated. Now it was September 23, and Ray and Ruth McQueeney were finally going to see their grandchildren.

Not one day had gone by without Ruth thinking of Keefe and Wendy. She buried herself in volunteer work at the Newington Senior Citizens Center, delivering meals to the elderly and calling bingo games. But it wasn't nearly enough. She was aching to hear the laughter of her grandchildren, their squeaky voices. She wanted to feel their hugs. She wanted to dig into the big box of toys at her home that hadn't been touched since January.

Although Ruth knew only too well how badly the visitations had been going between Rob and the children, she was deter-

114

mined to re-establish a relationship with them. All it would take, she felt, was love and patience.

In fact, she thought, hadn't she already overcome one obstacle? Several months ago, after Andreini had filed the motion for grandparents visitation, Vicki had gone to see Richard Dyer, the lawyer representing the children.

"Why, all of a sudden, do they want to see the kids?" Vicki had angrily asked Dyer. "They never had anything to do with them before. They never even saw them."

When Ruth heard about that, she and Ray marched into Dyer's office, her arms loaded with hundreds of photographs and dozens of greeting cards. Rob had saved every card his parents had sent; Ruth had saved the cards the children had sent.

"Look at these and judge for yourself, Mr. Dyer," she said. "I hardly think that we could have taken all these pictures of the children in one or two visits. After you look at the pictures and read the cards, ask yourself if that sounds like grandparents who aren't involved with their children.

"And when you're finished, *you* tell *me* whether Vicki is being truthful, or whether we're being truthful."

After meeting the grandparents and reviewing their photographs and greeting cards, Dyer felt he knew who was telling the truth. He was impressed by the grandparents' desire to see their grandchildren, and the quality of the relationship they had had with them. He thought Ray and Ruth had played an important role in their grandchildren's lives.

When Dyer told Ruth of his decision, it had bolstered her strong belief that truth always won out in the end. That was one reason she was so optimistic about the visit with the children. She had happily chattered to her husband during the drive to Ledder's office, filled with eagerness to see her grandchildren.

But now, as she held onto Ray's hand and waited for the children to be brought into the room, she made a little confession to her husband.

"Papa?" she whispered. "I'm scared."

Vicki walked into Robb Ledder's office at 3:30 p.m. Wendy was already crying. As she put her daughter down, Vicki told

Ledder, "I expect this visit to last fifteen or twenty minutes. After that, I've got to bring the children home."

"Vicki, the children are supposed to visit with their grandparents for an hour and then with their father for an hour," Ledder said. "That was the arrangement. That's what the court ordered."

"Well, it's just not going to happen," Vicki breezily replied. "I've got to leave long before that."

"We'll talk about that later," Ledder said. "Come on. The grandparents are waiting."

"Let's go, children," Vicki said. "You've got to go see your grandparents."

Wendy wouldn't budge. Keefe was frowning.

"Come on, I'll get you an ice cream cone after the visit," Vicki said. "I'm sorry, but you've got to do this."

Vicki picked up Wendy, who was still crying, and started walking toward the room where Ray and Ruth were waiting. When she reached the door to the room, Vicki put her daughter down and left. Ledder walked into the room, squeezing past the children who remained standing by the doorway.

"Hi, sweet-pea! Hi, Keefe!" Ruth called to them. "Boy, it's sure been a long time since you've been over to Nana and Papa's house, hasn't it? We've missed you both so much."

"We sure have," Ray said. "It just hasn't been the same without you guys around. It's real nice to see you again."

The two children remained motionless. Keefe was holding his squirt gun and frowning. Wendy continued to sob.

"Sweetheart, why the sad face?" Ruth asked. "Why don't you come close to us. It's hard to talk when you're so far away."

There was no response.

"Keefe, Nana loves you," Ruth said, in a near-pleading tone.

"You hurt our feelings," Keefe answered. "You love Rob and he hurt our feelings."

Ruth started to ask Keefe why he didn't like his father when Ledder gently interrupted, suggesting they talk about something else.

"How is school going, sweetheart?" Ruth asked Keefe.

No answer.

"I love you, Keefe. Why don't you and Wendy come in here a little closer?"

After about fifteen minutes of coaxing, the children shyly came in.

"Ohh, Sweet-pea, I heard you hurt yourself on the swing-set at school, honey."

"Yeah, Nana. I was walkin' by and got kicked. I fell down and got a big, bad boo-boo."

"Oh, can Nana see?" Ruth asked as she stretched her arm toward Wendy's strapped shoulder.

Wendy cringed and turned away from Ruth. Ruth quickly turned toward Ray, so the children couldn't see her tears. But a moment later, Ruth heard Wendy say, "Nana, Nana. My mommy says that I can take the strap off next week. I can play on the swings again, too!"

Ruth quickly wiped her eyes and turned back to Wendy. "Oh, sweet-pea, Nana loves you so much. Can Nana have a hug if she's very careful not to hurt your shoulder?"

"No," Wendy replied. "But you know what? I'm learnin' to spell in school. My teacher says I'm good, too!"

"Oh, that's wonderful, Wendy," Ruth said with a smile. Turning to Keefe, she asked, "How about you, sweetheart? I love you. Can Nana get a hug?"

"Rob's bad and he's going to jail," Keefe responded. "You're not nice because you like Rob. I've got a gun and I'm going to kill Rob. Our daddy has a gun, too, and he runs a jail. It's *his* jail. Rob's going to go to daddy's jail."

"But why does your father have to go to jail?" Ruth asked.

"Because he hurt me. He hurt my feelings."

Her eyes again filled with tears and Ruth turned away. She sat on the couch next to Ray. Ray put his hand on her knee and whispered, "Oh my God, he's such a mixed up little boy." Ruth looked at her husband and at that moment saw how these months had aged him; he seemed an old, old man. She would have collapsed right then, if it hadn't been for her determination to break through to the children.

After taking a few minutes to compose herself, Ruth stood up from the couch. "I love you, sweetheart. Nana and Papa want you to know that we both love you very much."

Keefe's eyes filled with tears. But he didn't cry. And he didn't answer her.

As the tears streamed down her face, Ruth looked at Keefe. "Would you do Nana a big favor? It's been a lot of days and I haven't had a hug. Would you come over and hug Nana?"

Keefe seemed confused. His eyes were still filled with tears. But he didn't move. Ledder walked over to Keefe and asked him if he wanted to hug his Nana. When Keefe didn't respond, Ledder took his hand and gently led him the few steps over to Ruth.

Sobbing now, Ruth bent down on one knee and wrapped her arms around her grandson. "I love you so much, Keefe," she whispered. Keefe accepted the hug, but did not return it. His arms remained limp at his sides. One hand still held the water pistol.

"Would you give Papa a hug, too?" she asked after a few seconds. "Papa would really like a hug."

Ray walked over to Keefe and, with a little effort, kept his composure. He bent over and hugged the little boy. It was like hugging a mannequin.

But the hugs seemed to relax Keefe. He walked over to one of the chairs and, for the first time, sat down.

"Would you like to go over to Nana and Papa's house to visit them?" Ledder asked.

"Oh, no," Keefe immediately replied. "Mommy would never bring us there, because Rob would be there. He'd be there and he'd take us."

"Yeah," Wendy agreed. "He'd take us."

"Oh, sweethearts, you wouldn't have to worry about that," Ruth said. "Nana and Papa would be the only ones there. We want you to come over and visit *us* because we miss you so much. How about it? Wouldn't you like to see us again, Keefe?"

Keefe responded with a shrug of his shoulders.

"Do you remember the big toy box at Nana and Papa's house that we used to pull out whenever you came over?" Ruth asked Keefe.

Keefe again shrugged his shoulders.

"I 'member, I 'member," Wendy said with a wide smile.

"Wouldn't you two like to come over and play with some of those toys again?"

But before either child had a chance to answer, Vicki was calling to Ledder from the hallway. The session was supposed to continue for another fifteen minutes.

After motioning for the children to remain behind, Ledder walked out to Vicki. "What's going on?" Vicki impatiently asked. "I told you we only had fifteen or twenty minutes. Why are they still in there?"

Ledder remained calm. "The children still have some time left with Mr. and Mrs. McQueeney, and they are scheduled to have a one-hour visitation with their father after that," he said. "Vicki, this was supposed to have been all pre-arranged and set."

"I'm sorry, but I have to leave," Vicki responded. "Bruce has to get back to work and he's my only transportation."

Ledder suggested, "Well, how about if I drive the children home after their visitations are over?"

"No," Vicki told the church therapist. "I don't feel safe with someone I don't know driving the children home."

"Well, how about if I drive *you* and the children home?"

"No," Vicki said, seeming to be bored by the question. "I also don't feel safe with someone I really don't know driving me home."

Ledder turned on his heels and went back to tell the children they had to leave with their mother. The three of them quickly walked out the building and climbed into the truck. Bruce drove them home.

Rob arrived about five minutes later. He was furious when he learned that Vicki had already taken the children. He called Hurvitz and instructed him to file a contempt-of-court motion against Vicki. His parents then called Andreini and told him to file the same charge against Vicki.

In a report written the next day, Ledder concluded:

"After initial hesitancies the grandparents and the children were able to begin to re-establish their previous bond. The grandparents seem capable of developing a relationship which is unique and separate from their son's. The children, though not enthusiastic, were not overly negative and rejecting of their grandparents. With time, this relationship could be developed and nurtured to be mutually satisfying to all parties involved.

"At this point, it is my opinion that further supervised visitations with the grandparents are not necessary."

At the October 20 court hearing on the motions for contempt of court by McQueeney, his parents and Vicki, Andreini told Judge Freed: "Your Honor, I do represent the grandparents, and I stressed from my very first meeting with them that there could be no way of bootstrapping the father's visitation rights through theirs. And they urged on me, Your Honor, they *implored* me that they wanted to see these children.

"And I discussed with Mr. Clifford whether or not they needed to take the stand to tell the court about their relationship with their grandchildren, and he said 'absolutely not,' it would not be necessary. Through no fault of their own, they're being deprived of any relationship at all with these children, based on Ms. Barrett's recommendations.

"I suggest, Your Honor, as innocent as the children are, I represent the next-innocent parties on this, the grandparents. All they want is one Sunday visitation for an afternoon. Your Honor, that's all we're looking for right now."

But the judge rejected Andreini's arguments and Ledder's recommendations, and sided with Barrett, who wanted all visitation with the grandparents halted. When Judge Freed issued his ruling, Andreini was incredulous—and crushed. The only rationalization he could think of for the ruling was that Judge Freed had relied heavily on Barbara Barrett as the expert who was most qualified to know what was in the children's best interests. Andreini also observed that Barrett knew quite well how to testify in court, having done so dozens of times. She deflected all questions that could have generated an uncomplimentary picture of Vicki. On the other hand, this had been the first time Ledder had testified in court. His inexperience had made him seem awkward.

Andreini was also upset because the crowded court calendar had forced Judge Freed to rush the hearing. And, although he didn't blame Judge Freed, he still thought the ruling was unjust.

Andreini didn't want to turn away from the judge's bench and walk back through the spectator section of the court. But he knew he had to face his clients. With slumped shoulders, the lawyer that Ruth called "Big John" walked over to the Mc-Queeneys and conveyed the sad news. Ruth hugged the West Point graduate and Ray shook his hand. They both thanked him for his efforts and left.

During the silent ride home, Ruth's thoughts turned to the September 23 visitation with the children. When Vicki had cut the session short, Ray and Ruth had walked out of the room just in time to see Wendy and Keefe's backs as they were being led out of the building by their mother.

Ruth did not know that it would be two years before they would see their grandchildren again. And, when that time came, Ray and Ruth McQueeney would learn all over again that they had underestimated the amount of pain that could come their way.

■ CHAPTER ELEVEN ■

Splashed With Venom

Six months and three days had passed since Rob last saw his children. It was now August. The court had finally reinstated his weekly visiting rights, although with restrictions. In just a few minutes, Wendy and Keefe would be joining him.

McQueeney was pacing around a room in a church that served as the Pastoral Counseling Center of West Hartford. Robert Ledder, a marriage and family therapist, was about to bring Keefe and Wendy down a hallway and into the room. Ledder was to be the chaperone. His job was to observe McQueeney and his children during the one hour that had been allotted them.

Rob was nervous, but optimistic. In the interim, he had again revised his thinking about Vicki and decided she had simply made a terrible mistake. Time was on his side. He figured the supervised visitation would continue for a few months—until the case against him was thrown out of court and his life returned to normal.

Rob had spent hours the previous night preparing for this first meeting with his children. He had made an outline of things he wanted to accomplish and ways to do them. Most of all, he wanted his children to think of him as the same old daddy they had always known.

To do that, Rob had brought two blank photo albums and a couple of dozen photographs he had taken of the children at various special events. Each week, he planned to ask Keefe and

Wendy to pick out two photographs to put in the albums he would give them.

Rob had purposely worn a T-shirt he had bought at a Teddy Bear Fair he had attended with his children the previous fall. As he waited impatiently, he wondered what Wendy and Keefe had been told by their mother. Intellectually, he expected the kids to be tentative and maybe even a little frightened of him. But, deep in his heart, Rob felt that, as soon as the children walked into the room, their faces would light up and the three of them would come together in the biggest, best hug any of them had ever known.

He could feel his heart quicken as he heard the footsteps start down the hallway. His children were coming to him. Just a few seconds more. The indistinct murmur of voices was getting clearer.

He heard Wendy quietly sobbing, asking for her Mommy. His optimism evaporated. He braced himself as Ledder and the children came through the door.

Ledder was carrying the tearful Wendy. Keefe was slouching and shuffling beside him, ready to burst into tears. McQueeney's children were in pain. Rob dumped his checklist of goals and "action items." He needed to stop the hurt.

"Hi, Keefe!" Rob said in his most cheerful voice. "Boy, it's been a long time, huh? I really missed you. I'm so glad you came today. Don't you look sharp!"

Keefe didn't say anything. But he seemed to straighten just a tiny bit as he glanced down at his outfit.

Rob turned to Wendy, who was sobbing and holding onto Ledder's hand.

"Piggle! Where did you get such a beautiful dress? And those patent leather shoes! You look beautiful, Wendy!"

In mid-sniffle, Wendy looked up and proudly announced, "Mommy bought me this dress!"

Suddenly, Rob felt like a daddy again.

As the three of them slowly became more relaxed, they started to chatter and smile and joke around with each other.

"Do you still have the little red car?" Keefe asked.

"I sure do. Would you like to see it?"

Keefe nodded. Rob picked him up so he could look out the

123

window to see the red Chevette parked on the street. Wendy immediately said that she wanted to see it, too. Rob boosted her to the window as well. Neither child flinched as he held them. Rob knew they wouldn't—and now Ledder knew, too.

Wendy giggled when Rob put her down with the exclamation, "Ooofa-loofa!" Moments later, Wendy looked at Ledder and said, "We don't want to play the game."

"What game is that?" Ledder asked.

"Don't be mean to us," Wendy warned the therapist. "You hurt us and we won't tell you where we live."

Ledder looked at McQueeney, who had sat on the floor between the two children. McQueeney ignored Wendy's remarks and began taking out the pictures and the photo albums. Both children eagerly took the albums. Keefe opened the front cover and printed his name on it. Rob asked if he could put Wendy's name in her album.

"Can you spell 'Wendy?' " he asked.

"W-E-N-D-Y," Keefe promptly answered. He printed Wendy's name on the inside front cover of her album, and proudly tilted the page toward his father. Then Keefe began drawing a man with a bearded, smiling face on the back of his album. "Dats you Daddy," he said as he signed the picture. After complimenting him, Rob asked for a "high-five." Keefe leapt to his feet, brought his arm around in a wide circle and smacked his hand into Rob's—just as he had done during the Super Bowl game seven months before.

As the children were picking out the photographs they wanted to put in their album, Wendy, without looking up, said to Rob, "You hit Keefe in the eye."

Keefe looked at her and sternly said, "Wendy, you're a liar."

Rob asked his three-year-old daughter, "Who told you that?"

"My mommy," she said.

"Liar, liar, pants on fire," Keefe chanted.

Wendy turned to Ledder and Rob, "We don't want to play the game. If you hurt us, we won't tell you where we live."

Five minutes later, Wendy looked at Ledder and said, "You hit Keefe in eye."

When Rob asked who had told her that, Wendy once again said, "My Mommy."

Astonished, Ledder gazed at Rob.

By now, Keefe had chosen the two pictures he wanted: one was of the Labor Day camping trip they had taken the year before and one was a photo of Keefe in the living room of Rob's Bemis Street home. Wendy peeked to see which pictures her brother had chosen, and then chose one of herself taken in Rob's kitchen, and another of herself taken during the camping trip.

As Wendy was struggling to put the photos in the album, she looked at Ledder and said, "You the Bemis Street Man, you bad."

Rob slid into the seat alongside her and asked if she wanted him to help put the pictures in the album.

"Yes, Daddy," she said. Wendy watched as her father placed the photos on the page and folded the plastic covering over them. When he was finished, Wendy looked at Ledder and repeated, "You're the Bemis Street Man, you're bad."

Rob sidled over to Keefe and asked him if he remembered the camping trip.

"Yeah, we had this big, big fire by the tent and we toasted marshmallows and you let me put a stick on the fire and then we put it out. I put some water on it and it went 's-s-s-s-s.' "

"Me put stick on fire, too," Wendy chimed in.

"And 'member your car broke comin' home? It was *really* loud, huh, Wendy?"

Wendy giggled and Rob beamed. He was glad they had remembered the trip, and even that damn muffler falling off.

"What's that other picture you have, Keefe?" Rob asked.

"That's me in the livin' room." he said. "Here's the livin' room, and here's the bafroom and the kitchen and here's my room and Wendy's room." He was waving his hands around to show where each room was located in the house.

Wendy chanted as she crawled over to look at Keefe's album. "If you hurt us, we won't tell where we live. We have a police daddy now." It was unclear to whom she was talking.

Rob slid over to Wendy and asked her if she remembered going to the beach with him.

"No, don't 'member," she said.

"You don't remember when you 'got my nose?' " Rob asked.

Wendy got up, jumped into Rob's lap and, giggling, tweaked his nose.

Keefe then started to talk about Bruce. "Daddy . . . I mean Bruce . . . is gonna take us to the beach next weekend," he said. "We're gonna go in his truck."

"Do you remember when we went to the beach?" Rob asked.

"Yeah, you and me and Wendy was splashin around in the waves."

Rob smiled. "And do you remember when we went toboggaining, and you went down the hill all by yourself?"

"Yeah," Keefe said. "I didn't fall, either."

The hour was over.

"Anybody giving hugs?" he called out as the children and Ledder started for the door.

Wendy, arms outstretched, ran up to hug and kiss her father. "I love you, piglet," Rob said.

"Love you, too," she said.

Keefe had continued walking. A few steps outside the door, he shouted back, "Next week!"

That night, Rob started a journal of the visitations. He was elated, and confident he could quickly rebuild his relationship with the children. He happily concluded his first journal entry: "I am so up for next week!"

The next session was cancelled by Vicki, who said she had to keep both children home because Wendy was sick and she couldn't find a babysitter.

The August 18th session began terribly. The children, who by now had undergone more than two dozen sexual abuse therapy sessions at the Langley Center, were even more reluctant to join their father.

Ledder finally came into the room carrying Wendy, who was again sobbing for her mommy. Keefe had remained with Vicki at the far end of the hall, refusing to go to his father. Ledder put Wendy down and went back to try to convince Keefe to come into the room. Wendy's eyes quickly dried when Rob remarked on her pretty dress and showed her some of the toys that were in the room. Wendy was playing with the toys when Ledder walked in and suggested that Rob try to retrieve Keefe.

Vicki was sitting on a couch with Keefe huddled in her arms.

"Vicki, would you please move away from Keefe?" Rob asked.

Vicki moved a few inches away.

"I don't wanna go in that room," Keefe said, looking down at Rob's shoes. "I don't wanna go wif you."

"Why not, Keefe?" Rob asked. "We had a good time last time, didn't we?"

"I don't know why. I don't wanna go. I don't wanna go."

Vicki, with a snapping look of contempt, said, "He doesn't want to go with you because you hurt him."

Rob ignored her and suggested that the three of them walk to the room. "Wendy's there playing with toys," he said. "Let's all go down and see how she's doing. Rob Ledder said he'd like you to come in, too. Vicki . . . ?"

Vicki slowly got up and the three of them walked down the hall. Keefe held onto Vicki's hand as Rob led the way. Once inside the room, Ledder looked at Vicki, who abruptly turned and walked out. Keefe walked over to a couch, sat down, folded his arms and looked straight ahead.

Rob sat on the floor and began playing with Wendy. Whenever he asked Keefe a question, the little boy would either ignore him or simply nod his head. When it was time for them to choose photographs for their albums, Keefe climbed off the couch and joined them, but refused to participate. After a minute, he went back to the couch.

When Rob produced some paper and crayons, Keefe again joined them. Each child drew a picture and picked out a magnet for Rob to attach the picture to his refrigerator. But, while Wendy was energetic and excited, Keefe remained sullen. As soon as he picked out his magnet, he moped back to the couch.

A few minutes later, Keefe exclaimed, "You're not our daddy. We have a police daddy. We don't love you anymore."

As Wendy was repeating her big brother's words, Rob walked over to the couch and said, "That makes Daddy very sad, Keefe. And it makes me very sad to see you so unhappy."

"I don't wanna play your game," Keefe said. "I hate your game. I hate you. You're bad. You're the Bemis Street Man."

Wendy again repeated Keefe's words. Then, with no pause, she said, "Daddy, I have to go to the bathroom. C'mon."

Rob walked her down the hall and asked Vicki to bring her into the bathroom. Rob stood by the bathroom door as the mother took the little girl inside. A few seconds later, Vicki stepped back into the hall. "You're breaking that little boy's heart," she told Rob. "You should tell him what you did."

She turned to go into the bathroom, and then spun back toward Rob.

"Did your father ever rape you? Do you know how it feels?"

"You're crazy, Vicki. Why are you doing this to me?" Rob cried out as she shut the bathroom door in his face.

When the session finally ended, Keefe walked out.

"See you next week," Rob called to both kids. Wendy gave him a hug and said "Yup!" Keefe didn't look back.

That night, Rob concluded his journal: "And so the resolve to rebuild our lives gets stronger."

The next session was missed when Ledder failed to inform Rob that they would meet in his private office in Hartford instead of in the church.

The next visitation was on September 2nd—Keefe's first day of kindergarten and two days before his fifth birthday. Rob had bought an eighteen-inch-long model airplane for Keefe's present, and had spent hours gluing it together and putting on the decals.

As Ledder escorted the children into the room, Keefe stopped at the doorway and reached for Wendy, who had continued walking. He caught her by the shoulder and began pulling her back into the hallway.

"Hey, stop that," she whined at Keefe.

"Keefe, you should let Wendy do what she wants," Rob said. "If she wants to come into the room, let her come in."

Once inside, Wendy sat on the floor and started to play with some toys. Keefe stood in the corner of the doorway, ignoring his father's entreaties to come into the room.

"Don't you want to see the pictures I brought today?" Rob asked. "Or build something with the Lincoln Logs?"

Keefe remained silent.

"Well, how about coming in and getting your birthday present?"

Still no response.

Ledder suggested that McQueeney go to Keefe and try to gently lead him into the room.

Rob walked out and sat on the floor, facing Keefe. Ledder sat in a chair by the door so he could hear what was happening.

"Keefe, why don't you want to come into the room and visit with Daddy?"

"I'm mad at you," Keefe replied.

"Why are you mad at me?"

"I don't love you anymore," Keefe responded. "You're not my dad. You're the Bemis Street Man. You're bad. You're mean."

"Why am I bad, Keefe? Why don't you love me anymore?" Rob quietly asked.

"Because you hurt me playing the game. You hurt me."

"What was the game, Keefe?" Ledder asked.

"It was Ghostbusters. We were playing Ghostbusters and he did mean things. He hurt me."

"I thought you liked playing Ghostbusters," Rob said. "I thought you liked that movie. That's why I used to play the game with you."

"It scared me," Keefe said, looking distressed. "The Marsh-mallow Man scared me. You scared me. I don't wanna play the game. I don't wanna watch *Ghostbusters* no more."

"Well, can you remember how we played the Ghostbusters game, Keefe?"

"You would chase after me and Wendy and we would scream, but you would keep chasin' us. You were a giant Marsh-mallow Man. You would catch me and squash me. You hurt me."

After about fifteen minutes, Rob was finally able to coax Keefe into the room, where he joined Wendy, who had been quietly playing a few feet inside the doorway.

Without looking up from her toys, Wendy said, "You're going to jail." She looked up at her father, who was sitting on the floor a few feet from her. "You're going to jail," she repeated.

"Yeah, you're going to jail," Keefe echoed.

"Why am I going to jail?" Rob calmly asked.

"Because you're a bad man," Keefe replied.

"But Daddy loves you guys," Rob said.

"We don't love you," Keefe shouted. "We don't love you. You're going to jail."

"That makes Daddy very sad," Rob said. "Daddy loves you, but it makes him very sad when you say you don't love him."

"You're not our daddy," Keefe angrily shouted. "We have a police daddy. You're the Bemis Street Man, you're not our daddy. You're going to jail." Keefe was crying now.

"But I *am* your daddy . . ."

"No, you're *not*," Keefe interrupted, running over to Led-der. Keefe used his hand to shield his mouth as he whispered in Ledder's ear that he wanted to talk to him away from Rob.

Ledder and Keefe walked to a corner of the room, where Keefe told him that he afraid of his father and didn't want to see him anymore.

Ledder reassured Keefe that he wouldn't let anything hap-pen to him, and gently turned him around. They walked closer to Rob.

"You hurt me," Keefe said again. "You hurt me with that game and I don't like you."

"How did your father hurt you when you were playing the game?" Ledder asked him.

"He's a bad man. He hurt me and he's going to jail," Keefe answered.

"Can you tell me how your father hurt you?" Ledder asked.

Rob braced himself for the indictment.

"He pushed on my shoulder real hard," Keefe answered.

Rob sat stunned. Relief flooded over him.

"Can you show me how he did it?" Ledder asked.

Keefe walked over to Ledder and thumped him on his shoulder. Then he walked over to Rob and did the same thing. "You hurt me like that," Keefe said. "You hurt my shoulder."

"What else happened?" Ledder asked. "Was he mean to you in any other way?"

"No. He hurt my shoulder."

"Where else did he hurt you?" Ledder pressed.

"He hurt my shoulder."

"Did he hurt your leg? Your hand? Your back? Your head?" Keefe said "no" to each of the questions.

For the first time, Rob had heard *Keefe's* accusation. The innocence of it angered him. All this was *bullshit*.

Equally dumbfounded, Ledder asked, "When did you play the game?"

"We played after we took a baf," Keefe said. "One time Daddy hid our clothes. Some other times we had our clothes on. He scared me. He hurt my shoulder."

"Was there any other mean thing that he did to any other part of your body?" Ledder asked.

"He hurt my shoulder and he scared me," Keefe said.

"And that's why you're mad at Daddy?" Rob asked.

"Yes."

"And Daddy should go to jail for that?"

"Yes."

Rob let out an agonized sigh and reached for a new set of pictures he had brought. Wendy, who was seated on the couch between Ledder and Rob, immediately started looking at them. Keefe, who was sitting in a chair opposite them, warned his sister, "We're not supposed to look at pictures."

Wendy immediately dropped the pictures, folded her hands in her lap and looked at Keefe.

"We're never coming to your house," Keefe said to his father. "We hate you. You should move away."

"Why should I move away?" Rob asked.

"So you don't hurt the kids next door," Keefe answered. He turned to Ledder for approval.

Rob's heart was breaking. His children had begun to hate him. How had all this happened to him? Why? Did Vicki hate him so much?

"Today was your first day of school, wasn't it, Keefe?"

No answer.

"How do you like kindergarten?"

No answer.

"Do you like your teacher?"

Keefe stared at the floor.

"Do you want to see the present Daddy brought you?"

"I don't want nothin' from you," Keefe said.

Rob got up to get the present from a bag he'd put on a table in the adjoining kitchen. He put it on the couch next to him. With an exaggerated motion, Keefe turned his head away from the couch.

Near the end of the hour-long session, Rob took Ledder just outside the doorway and said he wanted to mention to the kids the last weekend he had spent with them. He wanted to see how they remembered that weekend. Ledder didn't object.

"Do you remember sledding down the hill all by yourself, Keefe?"

Although Keefe had remembered the tobogganing when Rob asked about it during the first visitation, this time he said he didn't remember.

"I 'member!" Wendy exclaimed. "I 'member the sleddin'. Keefe dwove it all alone."

"Do you guys remember what we did when we got home that day?" Rob asked. "Do you remember when I gave you guys a bath?"

Keefe again said he didn't remember. Suddenly, though, he started talking.

132

"I didn't have any clothes on and you was chasin' me," he said. "You chased me."

"When did this happen?" Rob asked as Ledder leaned forward in his chair to listen.

"It was after a baf," Keefe said. "I didn't have any clothes on."

"Do you remember you and Wendy running out of the bathroom sometimes, right after your baths?" Rob asked. "You would run out and I would chase after you so we could start 'PJ time'—and then you'd put your PJs on?"

"Yeah," Keefe said.

"Did that scare you?" Rob asked.

"Yes."

"Was that mean?"

"Yes."

"Should I go to jail for that?"

"Yes. You hid my PJs so's I couldn't find 'em."

Rob couldn't specifically recall doing that on that last weekend, but it was fun to tease them with that prank.

"Well, it's time to go," Ledder said. "We can talk some more next week."

As the two children started to follow Ledder out the door, Rob hurried over to pick up the model airplane he had bought for Keefe's birthday.

"Wait a sec, Keefe. Don't forget your birthday present."

Keefe turned around. Rob was holding the airplane out to him. "Keefe, isn't it neat?"

"I don't want it," Keefe said before turning his back to Rob.

"Bye, guys," Rob mournfully said as they walked down the hall toward their mother. Neither child turned around.

Ledder was angry when he returned to the room. "Obviously, there's been an incredible about-face in the children's behavior and attitude in just three sessions," he said to Rob. "If their mother continues to try to undermine our efforts here, these sessions will become a complete waste of money."

"I want to continue," said Rob determinedly. He was paying for the sessions. "You can't imagine how much this is hurting me," he went on, his voice starting to crack. "I don't think

I'll ever be able to forget the things they've said to me. But, you know, I can deal with that. Somehow, some day, some justice is going to come out of all this. I just hope it's not too late . . . for everybody."

Ledder, though, was concerned about the effect the sessions were having on both McQueeney and his children.

"Well, do you realize that if you didn't do these visitations, it might be better for the kids?" Ledder asked. "This is going to be very hard on them because they're getting conflicting information. You know, here is this guy—you—that has been billed as a terrible person, and the kids come and see that you're not that bad. They get confused."

McQueeney, though, feeling they were his only hope at reestablishing a relationship with his children, insisted on continuing the visitations.

The fourth session was held the following Wednesday, September 9. It was the worst visitation yet. Afterwards, McQueeney began to think for the first time that it wasn't some unknown enemy, but Vicki along with Bruce who were behind his arrest and were now the puppeteers behind his children's increasingly hostile behavior. The thought sickened and, moreover, outraged him.

A few hours after the session ended, McQueeney forced himself to describe it in his journal:

"This was a highly emotional visit," he wrote. "The kids did not want to come in at all and were frightened and spiteful from the start. I could not get near either child; they backed off and huddled near Rob Ledder. The usual proclamations—that I was going to jail, that I was not their daddy and that they hated me—were issued, but today it was with more intensity, more belief and more volume. It was almost non-stop.

"I was equally, if not more, intense. For the first time, Keefe and Wendy saw that Daddy was really mad about this whole affair, not just sad, as before. Keefe often shouted that I was a 'liar.' I would pursue that and we argued a lot. Wendy whimpered or bawled.

"The rejection was paramount, upsetting, depressing. After several references to 'the game,' which Rob Ledder and I again probed Keefe about, Keefe threw us a curve. He said to me, 'You put your penis in my butt.'"

"I was furious! I began to beg Keefe for details, descriptions, proof! Rob Ledder did the same, though in a much more relaxed way. We learned this happened after I put Wendy to bed and jumped on him on the couch, both of us naked. Keefe indicated this happened 'all the time . . . lots of times . . . seven times' and gestured that my penis was approximately twelve inches in length. Keefe's summation was to say that this had 'hurt his feelings.' These were not the voices and faces of my children.

"It is tearing me apart, this growing hatred. These fabricated lies have become nearly factual to Keefe and Wendy. I break down and weep with the realization of losing my own beautiful guys because of this sick plot. A court dismissal is a piece of cake compared to the rebuilding of my fatherhood."

Two days later, on Friday, Ledder went to talk to Hurvitz. He was still upset about Wednesday's visitation.

"When Keefe said to Rob 'you put your penis in my butt,'" it was just the way it came out that was so significant to me," Ledder told the lawyer. "It was just like he said these words and didn't attach any emotion to them. It was extremely matter-of-fact; conversational, I would say.

"And, when the children started talking about how they were worrying that other kids in Rob's neighborhood might be in danger, they were speaking of things that are *eons* out of their range in thought. Their spectrum of experiences are not broad enough to even grasp that stuff," he said, shaking his head.

"During the time that you have seen Rob, has he done anything to encourage such a disintegration in the visitations?" Hurvitz asked.

"I think he has been superhuman not to make it get a lot worse in the face of those kinds of things coming," Ledder replied. "I do believe that, because of the hurtfulness, his intensity has increased, which could have scared the kids somewhat."

"I'm concerned about Rob being hurt more and more," Hurvitz said.

"He has internalized an awful lot of crap the kids have been coming out with," Ledder agreed. "And they can't even understand they are hurting people with the things they say."

The day after the September 9 session, Wendy broke her collarbone in a swing-set accident at her pre-school. Vicki waited for six days before calling Ledder to cancel the September 16 session. She called fifteen minutes before the session was scheduled to begin, telling Ledder that she would be keeping Wendy and Keefe home because she did not have a babysitter to watch Wendy. A few days later, McQueeney's lawyer learned that Wendy hadn't missed one day of pre-school because of the broken collarbone.

The children were supposed to have two sessions the following week—meeting with Rob's mother and father from three-thirty to four-thirty p.m., and then with Rob from four-thirty to five-thirty p.m. Vicki broke in on the session with the grandparents at four-fifteen p.m., saying she had to take the children home because Bruce had to leave for work and she didn't have any other way of getting home. It was the third straight week Rob had been unable to see his children. Angry and frustrated he instructed his lawyer, Henry Hurvitz, to file a motion for contempt of court against Vicki.

The following week, McQueeney was on a business trip to Toronto when his flight home was cancelled. He called at ten-thirty a.m. to tell Ledder that he would be unable to make the session for that day.

On October 7, Rob saw his children for the first time in four weeks. And the downhill slide continued.

For the first time, neither child was crying when they entered the room for their visitation with Daddy. They were sullen and wary, almost as though they were doing an unpleasant, but necessary, chore.

A few moments after the children had entered the room, Keefe looked at his father and said, "Rob, you're goin' to jail for twenty years."

Before Rob could reply, Keefe added, "You're a fuckin' asshole."

"Oh, Keefe, don't say that. You really hurt Daddy when you say things like that," Rob said brokenheartedly, determined not to lose his temper. "You know, that isn't a nice thing to say."

"I don't care," Keefe said. "I don't care about you. I wanna be mean to you 'cause you hurt my feelings."

As Rob was groping for something to say, Keefe burst out, "You're goin' to jail in three days. You're gonna die in jail. You're stupid, you're stupid. You're a jerk. You're an asshole." This time, the five-year-old boy raised his middle finger to accompany his words.

Rob was beginning to feel numb. But he plunged ahead. "Keefe, why are you saying those things? Who told you I was going to jail? Who said I was stupid?"

"My mommy told me. She said you're goin' to jail and that you're stupid, you're a jerk and a fuckin' asshole."

Apparently referring to the contempt-of-court charge McQueeney had filed against Vicki, Keefe shouted, "You're trying to put Mommy in jail, but *you're* gonna go to jail."

Rob couldn't speak. Ledder jumped in. "You know, Keefe, your Daddy and I are friends and it hurts me to hear such words. You see how quiet and gentle your daddy is being. Can you be like that, too?"

"He's a fuckin' asshole," Keefe said, turning from Ledder to give his father the finger. "Rob's a jerk. I hate him. He's not my father. Bruce is my father."

Rob was shrieking now. "I'm your father, you know that. Remember all the things we did together? We fixed up the Christmas tree, visited Santa Claus, went to the beach, went camping. Remember the Super Bowl party? Remember the Flintstones' stories I read to you?"

Keefe took no notice of his father's words. "You're a jerk."
Rob turned to Wendy. "How do you feel about Keefe's language, Wendy? Do you think he should be talking that way to his daddy?"

"I don't have nothin' to say," she said, turning her little face away from Rob.

"This is the last time we're comin' here," Keefe said. "Mommy told us we don't hafta come anymore. Me and Mommy and Daddy and Wendy will come see you after you're in jail to talk about what you did."

At that point, Keefe pointed the squirt gun he had been carrying directly at Rob and shot invisible ink into his father's eye. After he shot the squirt gun, Keefe, with a satisfied look, gave Rob the finger and called him an asshole. Rob turned away from Keefe and reached in his pocket for a handkerchief. Tears ran down his face.

"I seen Nana and Papa and they're fuckin' assholes, too," Keefe continued. "We're not gonna visit them anymore because Daddy said you would steal us. Daddy knows 'cause he's a police daddy."

Just then, Wendy, who was sitting by Ledder, giggled.

"Stop that, Wendy," Keefe said. "You're not s'posed to laugh here, not when Rob is here."

Ledder looked at Rob, who weakly waved his hand in surrender. He couldn't take any more. There were still fifteen minutes to go, but McQueeney had to get out of the room. Ledder found Vicki sitting in the truck, applying nail polish.

The October 14 session was cancelled by Vicki, who told Ledder that she didn't have any transportation to his office.

The following week, on October 20, a court hearing was held to hear arguments on motions for contempt of court that were filed by McQueeney and his parents against Vicki. A counter motion for contempt of court was filed by Vicki against McQueeney—for trying to talk to his children about what had happened during the weekend he was accused of raping Keefe.

Ledder felt compelled to testify during the hearing that the visitations should be suspended between Keefe and Rob.

"At this point, continuing this type of relationship is harmful to—I think—both parties," he said. "Where it's negative for Mr. McQueeney, who appears hurt and disturbed by it. Harmful to the children where they get upset when they come in there, and the relationship appears to be deteriorating from where it initially began."

However, he said there was no reason to halt the visitations with Wendy. Without the influence of her bigger brother, Ledder predicted she could develop a healthy relationship with her father. He also recommended that the grandparents be allowed *unsupervised* visitation with both of their grandchildren.

Barbara Barrett, the Langley Center therapist who reported her view that McQueeney had raped Keefe, told the court that all supervised visitation should be suspended. Neither child should be seeing McQueeney or McQueeney's parents, she said. Four days before the court hearing, Barrett prepared a report that stated her opinion on why the children should not see their father or grandparents.

"Keefe has stated that he does not want to visit his father or grandparents. He has been having a recurring dream in which 'Rob puts his penis in my heinie.' He fears that Rob will 'steal me and Rob Ledder won't be able to stop him.' Keefe does not want to see his grandparents. He feels he was pushed by Mr. Ledder to give his grandparents a hug which he did not want to do. Keefe has been taught in psychotherapy that he has a choice about whom he hugs and who hugs him. Keefe stated, 'I hate my grandparents because they still love Rob even after what he did.' "

Barrett concluded: "Keefe presents as a very sad and angry child who fears for his safety during the visits. He is angry and disappointed that people do not believe what he says his father has done. He is adamant that Rob has played these 'jumping games' and will do it again if given the chance.

"It is my professional opinion that the supervised visitations are not accomplishing the purpose for which they were intended: i.e., a positive rebonding between Rob and the children in a neutral setting. Therefore, I am recommending that, in the best interest of the children, the visitations be terminated immediately. Keefe should continue his individual and group psychotherapy."

She reiterated that opinion to Judge Samuel Freed, telling him that continuing the visitation would harm the children.

Then Hurvitz presented his closing argument to the judge.

"We recognize that there's been problems with Keefe, and we recognize that it has certainly deteriorated," he said. "However, as far as Wendy is concerned, your Honor, I don't think that it has deteriorated. It's granted, as Ms. Barrett says, that she needs the chance to develop, but she also needs a chance to develop with her father.

"Her father has a right to be there; her father wants to be there; and her father should be there. We have one confused child already, and that's sufficient, your Honor."

Richard Dyer had been chosen by agreement of the lawyers for Vicki and Rob to represent the children. McQueeney had only briefly met him. Once again, his future with his children was in the hands of an unknown.

Dyer testified that he agreed with Barrett's recommendation that all visitations be halted. But he summed up his feelings this way: "I also want to make the court aware of my very strong feelings that I think the mother, attitudinally, has not done all that she should to promulgate visitation, particularly with the grandparents. And I think if anything is my feeling here, it's I'm kind of served up with a *fait accompli*, that these children have been horribly splashed with the venom of this divorce. We have some very young children with very old heads on their bodies, and I don't like it one whit."

Before issuing his decision, Judge Freed harshly criticized Vicki for interfering with the children's relationship with their father and grandparents. In fact, he almost found Vicki in contempt of court: "It is obviously a situation where, to me at any rate, Mrs. McQueeney is doing nothing to help it in any way, and that disturbs me very deeply," he said. "I cannot say that I find that the burden of proof has been sustained that she's in contempt of this court, but I believe that she *is*.

"It would certainly be my hope and desire that after, hopefully, a short period of time . . . and getting proper counseling, that the situation can be reversed. But, right now, it seems to be just aggravating it. And I certainly would ask the Langley Center to do whatever it can, particularly Ms. Barrett, to see to it that Mrs. McQueeney does no further damage to the situation, which it is my *absolute* feeling that she had done."

Despite these assessments, Judge Freed halted all visitation, accepting Barrett's recommendation and rejecting the recommendation made by Ledder.

McQueeney concluded his final journal entry with this question: "Can this destruction of two young minds ever be righted?"

■ CHAPTER TWELVE ■

Fear, Love and a Consolation Prize

Not long after the hearing, Rob was scanning the personal columns trying to focus his attention on the fact that there were other people who felt just as isolated and lonely as he did, when a particular ad caught his eye.

> *I know I'm not the ideal woman for everyone and you may not be right for me. But! If you've gotten as discouraged finding a lady like me as I've had finding an unusual guy like you (you may not know how rare you are!), I'm a young-thinking 33, intelligent, inquisitive, enthusiastic, cheerful, active, tempered with understanding, sensitivity and competence. Romantic, responsive, feminine and attractive, but not primped and painted. I just know there's someone out there who's sick of the fluff he meets in bars. I hope he'll meet me instead! No. 3551.*

He responded:

> *Hi 3551!*
> *Lately, I've been extremely discouraged, too. And the rare time I do visit a bar, I don't even seem to meet any fluff! Hence, I appeal to your noted traits of responsiveness and inquisitiveness and ask you to at least take a moment to evaluate this letter-writer. I only offer you a*

brief resume here, hoping to spark your interest for more information.

I am 32, twice-married with two children, professionally active and secure, 5-foot-10-inches and 185 pounds. My many interests include football, hockey, camping, wine, fishing, Studebakers and horror movies. My best friends are my parents and my best girl is my old lab-shepherd.

And I've gone to too many fairs and wine-tastings this year alone.

I have had a great tragedy in my life which has taught me how much every day means and what friendship and devotion really are. I am diligently looking for someone to share life with. I have learned many things from poor marriages: honesty, patience and attentiveness among them.

Through it all, I still believe in romance and commitment and await the wonderful challenge of a new relationship.

The best of luck in your search—stay cheerful and unfluffed. I hope to hear from you.

Rob 584-8389

Please leave a message!!

Happy Halloween

One week after he wrote that letter, on a windy, subfreezing Friday, McQueeney was sitting in his red Chevette in the parking lot outside Chef's, waiting for No. 3551. Her name was Jackie AuCoin—and that's about all McQueeney knew about her.

Rob watched a pair of headlights swing into the dirt parking lot. They belonged to a Mustang, the car he'd been waiting for. It smoothly wheeled into a parking space a dozen yards from McQueeney. In moments, an attractive woman with shoulder-length, curly blonde hair emerged. She wore a white winter coat. As she leaned over to lock the door, a gust of wind blew her hair sideways. McQueeney liked the image.

He got out of his car as she started to walk over.

"Hi, you must be 3551," he said. Then, pretending to consult some notes, he added, "or is it 5331?"

"No," she laughed. "You had it right the first time."

"Oh, good. Well, I'm Rob McQueeney, but I guess you've already figured that out."

"I'm Jackie AuCoin, and yes, I kinda figured you were Rob."

"Hey, if you don't mind, I've *got* to get some gas. It's past empty, and I hate to run out of gas on first dates. It's too conventional, and you'll never believe me when it happens. There's a station down at the corner."

"Oh, no problem," Jackie answered. "Mind if I come along?"

"Not at all."

Jackie watched as McQueeney walked into the gas station to pay the attendant. He was wearing a black, quilted hunter's vest and blue jeans. He had a round, friendly face, framed by a brown, close trimmed beard and glasses. It was too damn dark to see much else.

McQueeney, too, was trying to get a better look at his date. The telephone conversation leading to this meeting had been brief and unrevealing. He slid back behind the wheel, purposely leaving the door open as he stretched his legs to retrieve the keys from his pocket. They both laughed as he noticed the keys already in the ignition. Nevertheless, the dome light had allowed them to surreptitiously eye each other—and pretend that they didn't notice what they were both doing.

When they got back to Chef's, Rob opened the door and let Jackie slide past. He scooted alongside her and immediately gestured to his right.

"Oh, great!" he said. "Nobody's sitting in the table by the fireplace. What luck! C'mon."

Rob took her coat and noticed she was wearing a lavender sweater, which softly outlined her curves. He pulled out her chair and smoothly slid it back under her.

"What would you like to drink?" he asked.

"Oh, I don't know. I don't drink that much. Any suggestions?"

"How about a cranberry juice and vodka? A Cape Codder would go nice on a balmy night like this."

"OK," Jackie answered with a laugh.

"Rob!" exclaimed the waitress who had come over to serve them. "Howya doing, sweetie?" she said, bending over to give him a hug.

"Hi, Joanne. I'm fine, thanks. Joanne, this is Jackie. Jackie . . . Joanne."

"Hi, Jackie. Hold onto this guy. He's a good one."

"Hi," Jackie replied, a little embarrassed.

"I'll have a bourbon and Coke, and Jackie will have a Cape Codder, Joanne."

"Comin' right up!" the waitress replied.

After another drink and a couple more hugs and hellos from other waitresses, Jackie was surprised to find that she felt a little jealous.

But, as the night wore on, it became clear to Jackie that Rob wasn't interested in any of the waitresses. He was interested in her. There were no lags in conversation, even when Rob got up to tend the fire.

"So, whaddya think? A nice birch log, for color, or a nice piece of split oak for warmth? Or, if you'd like, I could run out and see if I could dig up a nice cedar log somewhere, for that perfect bouquet—essence of Chef's. Provided, of course, that I get to it before the dogs do."

Jackie laughed.

"Rob, could you get me a bag of chips, please?" she asked as her third drink arrived just before eleven p.m.

"Are you hungry? Rob asked as he stood up from his chair. "You must be hungry. Let me run out to the kitchen and see if Jimmy can make us some nachos. Do you like nachos?"

She nodded.

"Good, I'll be right back."

Five minutes later, Rob carried a plateful of nachos back to the table.

"Is your dog really your best girl, like you wrote in the letter?" Jackie asked.

"Holly? She sure is," he answered. "I've had her for about twelve years now. She's great."

145

"I used to have a dog, but now all I've got are two cats," Jackie said, almost apologetically. "Oh! Here's something I've always wanted to ask someone about. When I had my dog, he used to clean out the cat box for me. I mean, he actually *ate* the little cat turds. I couldn't believe it. Have you ever heard of that before?"

"Oh yes," Rob answered in his best scholarly tone. "Dogs are known to eat cat turds. Do you know why?"

"No, why?"

"Because they're *sooo* good."

Her mouth was starting to ache from laughing so much. But, God, it felt good. *Sooo* good.

Then they started talking about their parents. When they had exhausted the pet stories and the parents stories, Jackie turned to the subject of children. She told Rob about her son, Paul, who had been born when she was eighteen years old.

When she finished, she asked about his children.

"Well . . . I have a five-year-old son and a three-year-old daughter. Keefe and Wendy. Keefe's just started kindergarten, and Wendy is in pre-school. They're both good kids."

Jackie waited for more. It didn't come.

"When do you get to see them?" she asked.

Rob looked down at the table.

"Would you rather not talk about it," she softly asked.

Rob shifted his eyes from the tabletop to Jackie and nodded.

Jackie changed the subject. She was baffled that Rob, who seemed more open and sensitive than most men, didn't want to talk about his kids. She wondered what had happened to them? Whatever it was, she thought, it was clearly an unapproachable subject.

That was the only awkward moment in a long night filled with conversation and laughter.

While Rob was in the bathroom, Jackie started to mentally chalk up the points he had made. "Everyone seems to like him here, so he can't be too much of a jerk," she thought. "He was worried that I was hungry, and that was nice. He listens well. And he's got a great sense of humor. Hmmm . . . I think I might be interested in this guy."

Rob felt much the same way. "She's laughing at my jokes, and she really seems to appreciate my conversation," he thought. "She seems really genuine, to actually be interested in *me*. This has some real possibilities here."

Jackie, who wasn't used to going to bars, had started to get tired about eleven p.m. But she had hung in, not wanting the night to end. Finally, just before one a.m., her mouth opened in a huge, unstoppable yawn.

"Okay, okay!" Rob said at once. "I took psychology in college. I know what that means. I've become a study in tedium, a wholly tiresome fellow, worse than a rerun of 'The Osmonds.' I'm a sleeping pill."

That kept her there for fifteen more minutes. Finally, though, she told Rob she had to leave, or she would fall asleep at the table.

"Well," he said, "I guess we should go, then. Cinderella had her pumpkin to worry about; McQueeney's got his sleeping pill."

Jackie opened her purse and started to bring out her wallet.

"No, I've got this." Rob said. "I always pay for an appreciative audience. Mostly 'cause they're asleep by the time the bill arrives." He walked over to the register, where he paid the bill.

Both of them were nervous as Rob walked Jackie to her car. It was kiss-or-no-kiss time. Jackie unlocked the door and turned to Rob.

"Jackie, I've never liked it when people play head games. That's one reason why I had such a good time tonight. Everything seemed to be so genuine, so honest. I've always tried to mean what I say and say what I mean. So . . . what I . . . what I want to say is . . . I'd really like to go out with you again. But you don't have to give me an answer right now. There's no pressure at all. Think about it, and then, if you want, we can get in touch next week."

Jackie quickly considered whether she should let him dangle for a little while and decided against it.

"Well . . . yeah, I'd like to go out again," she said earnestly. "Here's my phone number."

Rob suddenly felt shy. He *hated* moments like these, when he didn't know what he was supposed to do.

Jackie wasn't looking for a kiss. But, just before he left, she had an urge to reach over and hug him. Instead, she said goodnight and got into her car.

After several telephone conversations, they decided to go out to see a Newington versus Bristol Eastern high school football game the following Friday night.

Jackie came to Rob's house, where he made a concoction he called "stadium punch." He mixed sloe gin, blackberry brandy and gin, heated it and put it in a thermos.

During the drive to the stadium, Rob asked Jackie where she had grown up.

"Newington."

"So did I," Rob said. "Did you go to Newington High?"

"Yeah," Jackie said, a touch cautiously.

"Wow, me too! I graduated in 1973. How about you?"

"Oh . . . it was one of those years," she said with a nervous laugh.

He glanced at her. "Uh-oh. Do I detect the chagrin of a woman who's been found out? Wait a minute, here. Just how old are you?"

"Well . . ." Jackie reddened.

"Come on, now. Remember—one of the rules is no fluff; not even on your age."

"I'm thirty-six," she confessed.

"Oh, is that all?" Rob said expressionlessly. "That's not *nearly* as bad as I thought."

"Oh, you!" she said, swinging her purse at him.

Just then, they arrived at Muzzy Field in Bristol. It was dark. There were no cars. And no teams.

Rob laughed, "Uh oh, I guess I had the wrong date for the game."

After buying a bottle of Chianti, they picked up Rob's car and went to Jackie's house, where they suddenly decided to get a pizza.

"What do you want on it?" Jackie asked as she was ordering.

"Extra cheese and extra sauce."

Jackie repeated the order into the telephone.

"And extra crust!" she heard Rob yell.

"And extra . . . oh, sorry, never mind," she said, as she heard Rob laughing.

They ate their pizza watching *The World According To Garp.* Then, it was *that* time again.

"Here, before you leave, I saved this New York Giants glass for you," Jackie said. "And don't forget your stadium punch, or whatever it is you call it. And take the rest of your wine home, too."

Rob stood there, his arms filled with stuff. "Anything else? Need your television fixed?"

"No, I think that's about it," she laughed.

They stood, looking at each other for an interminable moment.

"I don't care, I'm going to hug you," Jackie said. "Put that stuff down."

They hugged.

Jackie turned her face up toward his.

Rob lowered his face and fleetingly kissed her on the cheek. A split-second later, he realized that she had closed her eyes and was waiting for a real kiss when he had brought his face close to hers.

Embarrassed, he grabbed his things and called back, " 'Bye."

Rob cursed himself as he was getting into the car. He thought he may have spread a killing frost over their blossoming relationship. Or, at the very least, acted like a dork.

Jackie stood in the doorway, watching his car recede.

"Damn," she thought. "When is this man going to wake up?"

The following Friday night, they returned to Muzzy Field. This time, the two teams were there as well. Rob and Jackie's alma mater, Newington High, won the game. Afterwards, they met Jackie's sister and brother-in-law at a local bar. But only Jackie was invited back to Rob's house.

And, later that evening, they kissed. It was a real kiss, warm and lingering.

Afterward, Jackie said, "You know, Rob, it's strange. I've only known you for two weeks, but I already feel closer to you than I've ever felt to anyone else. You're so easy to talk to, and so nice just to be around."

Rob smiled. And kissed her again.

After their third or fourth kiss, Jackie opened her eyes and was startled to see a look of absolute misery on Rob's face.

"What's the matter?" she asked.

Rob didn't answer.

"Rob, you look like you're in pain. What's wrong?"

Again, there was no response. Rob felt a dreadful weight pressing on his chest.

Confused by Rob's silence, Jackie asked, "Are you upset about something?"

"No," he answered, looking off into the distance. "I'm afraid?"

"Afraid?"

"Jackie, there's something that I have to tell you. But I can't tell you right now. I'm sorry. I just can't."

Suddenly, Jackie was frightened. What could he be afraid of? What is going on?

"Well, I'm not going to push you," she said after a few moments. "When you're ready to talk, I'll be ready to listen."

She gently backed away. "It's about time for me to get going home anyway." She was silently thankful that she had driven to Rob's house before they went to the game.

"Bye, Rob. You take care. Give me a call over the weekend." She gave him a peck on the cheek and left.

Neither of them slept that night.

Rob had never been able to keep things inside. He *had* to tell her. But he felt that when he did, it would be the last he would see of Jackie.

When they had been kissing, Rob suddenly realized just how much he stood to lose. As hard as he tried to convince himself otherwise, he knew that he was no longer an ordinary guy entering a relationship. *Nobody* was going to commit to a relationship with someone who was accused of raping his own son. Jesus, what was going to happen if it went to trial? Never mind the publicity of a trial . . . he could actually end up in jail. And that, he knew, would ruin his life forever.

What hurt the most, though, was that he knew he couldn't blame Jackie for leaving. As he pulled the bed covers more tightly around him, he wondered how he would find the courage to tell the woman he wanted to love a story that would surely drive her away.

In another bed, seven miles away, a thousand questions were buzzing around Jackie's mind. Was he still married to someone? Was he in some sort of trouble? What was it that she didn't know about him? Jesus, you finally meet someone you really like, someone you could have a future with, and then you find out something's going to wreck it. Could he be sick, she wondered? He had said he was "afraid." What could make him afraid?

Rob went over to Jackie's house the following Friday night. She had to work Saturday morning, so they decided to stay in. Jackie sensed that Rob was going to tell her something; Rob wasn't sure he could.

They were on the living room couch in the downstairs den of Jackie's split-level home on Rossi Drive in Bristol. They had been chatting about inconsequential things for about an hour. It was now close to ten p.m. They were sitting close to each other, talking in subdued voices.

"So, tell me more about your children," Jackie carefully said. "Do you see them very often?"

Rob began to pour out his story. He told her how he had dreamed of having a son since he'd been in high school. Before he was old enough to drive a car, he had settled on a name for the boy he knew would one day be his—Keefe Michael McQueeney.

"When it happened, it was the most incredible thing," he told her. "I didn't think it was possible to be so happy. He looked just like I pictured he would. Even as he grew older, he always looked like that picture I had in my mind so many years before."

Rob talked about Wendy, as well, describing her as "a little bubble" who was so tiny, she didn't even make the pediatrician's growth charts.

"She was like a little wisp," he said with a sad smile. "You wouldn't want to take her outside on a windy day. And she just adored Keefe."

He paused and sadness crept into his voice.

"I really loved that little girl, but I'm not sure she knew it," he said. "When Vicki left me, I thought I would miss Keefe the most. I missed him a lot, Jackie. But I missed Wendy even more. I don't think I was a very good father to her. I didn't spend as much time with her as I did with Keefe. Even now, when I talk about her, I get that dull aching feeling in my stomach, you know? It's that feeling you get when you've lost something precious, and you know you won't get a second chance at it. Sort of an empty feeling, I guess."

Jackie was silent for a few moments. She wondered whether his children had died, but dared not ask. Then, she said, "Does this have something to do with whatever it is you're afraid of?"

Rob sat up and looked at the blank television opposite the couch. He remained silent for a minute or two. Finally, he turned and looked at Jackie. Their eyes met briefly before he looked away. The pain and the sadness Jackie saw were so potent that she became frightened.

Rob took a deep breath.

"The children had never been tobogganing before . . ."

Rob talked for more than five hours. He tried, with mixed results, to keep his emotions under control. He doggedly plodded through each disjointed part of the story. He jumped from the tobogganing weekend to the day Vicki left him. He talked about his parents and their relationship with the children. He told her about the night that Keefe asked him if he had lost the moon. It was a long time before he got to his arrest and the charges he faced.

For the first hour or so, Jackie had no idea where the story was leading. Still, her heart was pounding, as she tried to imagine how the story would end. Rob tried to tell the story impersonally. But he couldn't stop himself from reliving the events. He broke down several times, crying for his children and crying for himself. It was eerie the way his tears would suddenly splash over his mechanical words. Jackie became more afraid each time it happened.

It wasn't until Rob told her about the first phone call from the police, and his meeting with Hurvitz, that she found out what had happened.

Pain washed over Jackie. For much of the story, she had kept her face buried in his shoulder. For long stretches, she hugged him as she listened. It was like watching someone be tortured, she thought. As Rob neared the end of the story, he felt weirdly numb. He was hoping they could part with dignity, but he was so emotionally drained, he almost didn't care. He had always known that it would be unfair to drag her into his problems; or to even ask for her support. He was relieved that he was finally telling her, and he hoped she would believe him. He couldn't ask for more than that. A single thought had kept emerging while he was talking: when the story was over, the relationship would end.

Rob was too frightened by what he might see in Jackie's eyes, so he avoided them. It was nearly four a.m. when he finished talking. Jackie leaned her head on his shoulder.

"I've never heard anything like this," Jackie finally said. "I'm so sorry for what you've gone through."

She paused and wiped away a tear before continuing. "You know, when we first met, you told me that you always try to mean what you say and say what you mean. Well, that's what I feel right now. And, for whatever it's worth, Rob, I believe you. And I respect you for telling me. I mean it."

Rob stared at the wall for a few seconds before he spoke. "If you recall, there was something else I said during that first date, too," he said. "I told you that you didn't have to decide right away whether you wanted to see me again. Well, I think that applies even more in this situation. I've dumped an enormous, heavy load on you, and you've got a lot of things to think about. I would be a liar if I said that I expect you to accept all this and continue the relationship. I honestly don't know what I would do in your place. But I do know that this has got to be your decision, Jackie, and *only* your decision. And, please believe this, whatever you do, I won't hold it against you."

Before she could reply, Rob lifted himself off the couch. "I'm utterly, utterly exhausted," he said. "And you have to leave for work in about three hours. I've gotta get going."

Jackie got up and touched Rob on the arm. He looked at her for a moment before he turned away. She watched him slowly climb the steps and make his way to the door. She heard the door quietly close behind him.

After Rob left, Jackie remained on the couch until she had to get ready for work. She was exhausted, but sleep was impossible.

Jackie had no doubt about Rob's innocence. His story, she had seen, had come from his heart. He was more hurt than angry, and Jackie felt that if someone was trying to hide something, it would be easier to hide it behind anger than it would be to feign hurt.

During the next several days, she forced herself to consider ending the relationship. Although she believed with her whole heart that Rob was telling her the truth, she thought it would be foolish not to at least examine whether the alternative was possible.

In some ways, Jackie was more of a rational person than Rob. She did not allow her heart to rule her mind. She often thought she was *too* rational, and sometimes criticized herself for not being more spontaneous and intuitive.

She searched for inconsistencies or cracks in his story and found none. She searched for clues that might hint at the slightest possibility that Rob's personality or behavior was dysfunctional. She found none. She was more troubled by one seemingly unanswerable question: Why would Vicki do this to Rob?

On Monday, Jackie told her best friend at work what had happened. It helped to talk about it.

"You know, I detected a lot of pain, loss, hurt, fear . . . but not much anger, even against his ex-wife," she said. "You could tell it was wrenching his heart out, just to say those words. There was more confusion than anger; like how you would feel if a stranger walked up to you and punched you in the face. You'd be stunned before you became angry. That's how he seemed. Stunned. And confused.

"There was no false table-pounding rage. Nothing like

'How could they do this to me' or 'I'm innocent' or 'They can't prove it.' In fact, there was never a specific denial. He didn't jump up and shout 'I didn't do this, I swear I didn't.' I think I might have worried a little more if there had been. But there was nothing. No denial . . . other than the story itself.''

While Jackie talked to her friend and wrestled with her decision on their future, Rob's despair deepened. In relating the story to Jackie, Rob felt as though he was being squeezed from both sides. There was the savage pain of the story itself; and the bitter certainty that it would end the first real relationship he had had since Vicki left.

Rob spent a lot of time that weekend grieving for what he was about to lose. For more than a year, he had sorely missed the one-on-one sharing of thoughts that he so loved when he was close to someone. He had also missed the physical closeness that a relationship brings. Most of all, though, he had been lonely. For three buoyant weeks, Jackie had allowed him to escape that loneliness. Now, he was terrified he would lose her.

Rob was sure Jackie would decide to end the relationship. Even worse, as he continued thinking about it, he began to wonder whether Jackie had truly believed him. He had loved and trusted Vicki completely. Her leaving had left a gaping wound. He wasn't sure if he could ever again fully believe in a woman.

Rob and Jackie spent hours on the telephone that week, talking about what had happened. To save money, Rob had again turned down the heat in his house. He would lie under several blankets, with only his head and the telephone showing. On Wednesday, he was elated when Jackie invited him to her house the following Friday night, although he wondered if the invitation was extended so she could say good-bye to him in person.

When he arrived, they continued talking, much as they had on the telephone. They talked about life, about themselves and about what Rob was facing. He never asked her if the relationship was going to continue. And Jackie never said she was going to stand by him.

But, later that night, she did something better; she began to make love to him. When it was over, Rob turned away and sobbed uncontrollably into his pillow. For him, the lovemaking had cemented a silent understanding that she would stay with him. It was a crossing of the line; something she had done with complete knowledge of what Rob had gone through and what he might be facing in the future.

When his crying subsided, Rob finally spoke.

"I just didn't believe it was possible for somebody to believe in me so much," he managed. "I just didn't believe it was possible."

Jackie pulled him tight and wrapped her arms around his heaving chest. They cried together for awhile, and then Rob fell asleep. As she listened to his even breathing, Jackie whispered, "You're not alone anymore, Rob. You're not alone." Rob stirred slightly when she kissed him lightly on the lips. But he didn't awaken. In a few minutes, Jackie, too, was asleep.

■ CHAPTER THIRTEEN ■

Truth and the Therapist

Barbara Barrett's qualifications looked good on paper. The fifty-one-year-old social worker had a Bachelor of Arts degree in social work from prestigious Wheymore College in New York, and a Master of Arts degree in child welfare from St. Marion's College in Connecticut. She used three initials after her name— M.C.W. And she had an important job in one of the state's most highly regarded mental health institutions, the Langley Center.

However, as Schoenhorn, Rob's lawyer, began to research these qualifications, other—less impressive—facts surfaced.

Barrett received her degree from Wheymore in 1976 without ever taking a class there. She had enrolled in a "University Without Rooms" program, which gave her college credits for her work at the Langley Center and for her "life experience," which included a brief stint at a clothing store.

While pursuing her master's degree, which she received in 1985, she did not take any courses in child psychology or child sexual abuse. Her experience with those subjects was limited to on-the-job training.

It seemed, too, that, while a Master's degree in Child Welfare is technically offered at St. Marion's, it is rarely, if ever, used by other professionals—most of whom have Master's degrees in Social Work and call themselves M.S.W.s—not M.C.W.s.

The deposition of Barbara Barrett took about four and one half hours over a period of two days. On October 29, 1987, and again on November 12, 1987, Hurvitz and Schoenhorn questioned Barrett as John P. Clifford, Jr., Vicki's lawyer, quietly observed. When the questioning was over, McQueeney's two lawyers had compiled a remarkable record on Barrett—and Schoenhorn had started to methodically build his criminal defense.

Barrett told the lawyers, under oath, that she concluded Keefe had been sexually abused when she first met him—on February 5.

During that first session at Langley Center, she said, Keefe told her what he had already told Vicki—that his father had put his penis in his heinie.

Hurvitz was surprised. "On the date of the intake he reported that to you?" he asked.

"Yes."

"What else did he report at the first session?" Hurvitz continued.

"He described the jumping game, which was his lying on the couch and his father jumping up and down on his heinie," said Barrett. "The marshmallow game was described in two ways. One that his father wet on his tummy and his shoulder. Another version was connected to Ghostbusters, which is one of the children's games."

Hurvitz questioned her about each of the sessions she had with Keefe before she made her videotape and sent it to the police. He asked about her use of anatomical dolls, about her contacts with Vicki.

Then he asked her about her work in general over the past three years.

"My case load is sexually abused children," said Barrett.

"All the children that you see are sexually abused?"

"Are alleged to be sexually abused, yes," she said.

Hurvitz asked her to estimate how many children she had seen since she began evaluating sexual abuse. She estimated between fifty and one hundred children.

"Okay," said Hurvitz. "How many cases of alleged sexual abuse have you determined to be unfounded?"

"None."

"Oookay," Hurvitz gulped. "Thank you . . . And also, of

the allegations of sexual abuse, how many of these cases have been in the midst of a dissolution action or a custody fight or question of visitation?"

"That's relatively small," said Barrett. "I would say not more than a half dozen."

"And have you found there to be sexual abuse in all of these cases?" asked Hurvitz.

"Yes," said Barrett firmly. "I believe the child."

Schoenhorn handled much of the questioning at the second deposition session. He and Hurvitz had subpoened Barrett's files on Keefe, and Schoenhorn directed Barrett's attention to a three-page evaluation-treatment summary that she had prepared in August.

"Now," he said, "what did you do with the notes that you used to write this report?"

"I always grind up my notes," Barrett calmly answered.

"You do *what*?" Schoenhorn exploded.

"Grind them up."

"Is that like shredding?"

"Shredding, right."

"Do you have a shredder in the Langley Clinic?"

"Yes, we do."

Schoenhorn paused, a growing look of disbelief spreading across his face.

"I'm going to ask you to go back to the subpoena from our office," he said. "And I ask you to read number three under what you're asked to bring. Read it out loud."

"All notes, records, memorandum, reports," read Barrett dutifully. "All letters sent and received and all other material concerning medical and/or mental examinations and/or accounts of Keefe, Wendy and/or Vicki McQueeney."

"Well, you know that a subpoena is a legal document, don't you?"

"Yes, sir."

"And it's basically an order from a court to produce certain materials?"

"Yes, sir."

"Do you ever disregard subpoenas without at least having an attorney maybe move to dismiss a subpoena or quash it?"

"No, I don't."

"You don't. Yet you knew we were requesting all the notes and records that you had pertaining to Keefe, Wendy or Vicki McQueeney."

"I wrote my report, and I shredded my handwritten notes, which is my normal procedure," she said.

"Now I take it you understand and realize that the allegation that is made is a serious one. Is that right?"

"That's right."

"And I'm going to ask you, then, to be very careful with your answers concerning when certain things occurred, and with that in mind—"

"I believe I've tried," Barrett interrupted.

"I'm going to ask you to say again . . . you indicated that the allegations by Keefe concerning the jumping game and sexual abuse were told to you on February 5, 1987. Is that correct? At the very first session?"

"I believe I said that."

"Would you show me one place in all of these notes anywhere that indicates that that was told to you on February 5?"

The lawyers called a recess to allow Barrett time to review her case management notes, which she had not shredded.

Schoenhorn resumed the questioning.

"You agree with me that any kind of specific statements by Keefe would be significant information that you'd want to record," he said. "Is that correct?"

"Any statements by Keefe? Yeah." Barrett was fidgeting with her hands in her lap. One of her feet was rapidly tapping the floor.

"A statement that would relate to alleged abuse is something you'd want to record, is that right?"

"Yes . . . yes."

"And isn't it a fact that in none of these documents is there any mention of such statements being made on February 5, and in fact the first time any such statements are made in any of them . . . according to your materials here . . . is February 19?"

"Right."

"Do you wish to explain that omission?"

"I can't explain it."

"Isn't it a fact that February 19 is the first time that Keefe made any such statements about a jumping game or bumping heinies or anything else?"

"Those are the . . . that's the first date that I refer to, yes," said a stuttering Barrett.

"And isn't it a fact it was the mother who made the allegations on February 5?"

"The mother had made statements, yes."

"And that Keefe said nothing about the allegations on February 5?"

"My recollection is that he . . . I don't know that I state that he didn't," Barrett was floundering. "So I would have to believe that he also stated those to me on that date."

"How is that again, please?" an incredulous Schoenhorn asked.

"I do not specifically say . . . and I'm looking just to make sure . . . that I do not specifically say that he *didn't* tell me anything on those dates."

"So you're sitting here and under oath stating to us that because you didn't say that he didn't say anything, we can assume he did make specific allegations of sexual abuse by his father. Is that what you're saying to us?"

"I am saying to you that I believe that I had gotten the information in the first session," said Barrett, her voice trembling. "That is what I am saying to you."

"You're willing to swear under oath that Keefe McQueeney, on February 5, 1987, made the specific comments about jumping games and all of the specific allegations that are referred to in this report as having occured on February 19?"

"Those are on February 19. I'm telling you if that's what I have stated in my letter and in my evaluation, I will say that it . . . those were stated to me on February 19, yes."

Schoenhorn rocked back in his chair, took a deep breath and looked toward Hurvitz. Then he leaned forward again, his eyes intense, focusing on the social worker.

"Do you recall stating today, approximately fifteen minutes into the interview, that during the intake session Keefe described the abuse and the jumping game? Do you remember saying that today?"

"Yes, I do."

"And do you wish to correct that testimony?"

"I address it specifically to February 19 because I don't have it in my records as being specific to February 5." She said it slowly, cautiously. She looked beaten, her eyes down.

Schoenhorn abruptly changed the subject, asking her about the games that Keefe described. One of them was what the social worker referred to as the second marshmallow game.

Barrett described that game as the one "where he said the father put something white on him, on his shoulder and on his stomach."

Schoenhorn asked Barrett to re-read her February 19 report. After she had done so, he asked, "What did you say on February 19, 1987?"

"That he wets on him."

"Wets on his tummy," Schoenhorn prompted.

"Uh-huh." Barrett was fidgeting with her hands again.

"So where do you get white stuff, or did you imagine that?"

"I don't believe I imagined it."

"Where is it in any materials?"

"It's not in any of my material," she admitted, "and I will take it back if you like . . . and say 'wets' which is what I have put in my report. I am not imagining things, sir."

"Mrs. Barrett, my concern here is that we're taking a deposition under oath."

"I am trying to answer to the best of my recollection and ability."

"And this isn't a matter of saying something under oath and then saying, 'gee, I'll take that back.'"

A few minutes later, a beleagured Barrett excused herself to get a drink.

Later, Schoenhorn turned his attention back to Barrett's written materials from the Langley Center files.

"These case management notes from October for Keefe, is this all your handwriting?" he asked.

"Yes, it is."

"Was this all filled out on one date, or on each of the dates?"

"No, it's filled out on one day."

"The whole thing is filled out on one day?"

"Yes, it is."

"You don't take any notes after each of the group sessions or interviews with the child?"

"I don't usually, no."

"Are you familiar with the term 'confabulation?'" Schoenhorn asked.

"I'm not sure that I know the exact meaning of it."

"Do you have a general understanding of what it means?"

"That somebody is helping someone to fabricate a story."

"No," said Schoenhorn. "It's where you start off with some basic facts, but you twist it around to either exaggerate or fabricate so that it's a combination of truth and fantasy."

He paused, then pressed on: "Would you find it significant that the father reported that Keefe had a rash on his anus, and he had applied a [powder] to the child, and the child had gotten upset because he had placed his finger on the child's anus?"

"Would I find that significant?" asked Barrett, surprised. "I was not aware of any of that that you've just mentioned."

"Would you find that of significance?"

"I think that would have been important information, yes," Barrett answered.

Schoenhorn then asked Barrett several times whether her opinion that Keefe had been sexually abused by McQueeney might have changed if she had been aware of the additional information. She refused to acknowledge that her opinion would have changed.

Schoenhorn did not give up. He knew it was important to show *why* Keefe had suddenly accused his father of putting his penis, instead of his finger, in the child's rear end. Schoenhorn could explain why his client had put his finger in Keefe's rear end; but McQueeney's penis in Keefe's rear end was unexplainable—and punishable by a long prison term.

"Were you aware that Keefe told his mother that his father put his finger in his heinie and it hurt?" Schoenhorn asked.

"No," she answered. "I don't know that I remember that. Did I . . . is that something I have put down?"

"No," said Schoenhorn. "If I told you this is in the affidavit that Vicki McQueeney gave to the police and that's what Keefe told her and that's what she swore to, would you find that significant?"

"Yes, that would be important information."

He asked her about Pandit's examination, and she said she was not aware of the results.

He continued to press, until Barrett acknowledged that if she had been aware of the additional information Schoenhorn supplied, she would have postponed any finding of molestation until after she had pursued questions raised by the information.

Schoenhorn then returned to the Ghostbusters images Keefe had relayed to her. Barrett had not seen the movie.

"If you were also aware in the movie that there are ghosts without arms or legs that fly around buildings, and there is also a giant marshmallow man that jumps on top of people and crushes then and chases them, would you find that significant in your evaluation?"

"I would feel that it was an important piece of information, yes," Barrett replied.

"And finally," said Schoenhorn, "if you were aware of all these other facts, you would have dealt with Keefe in a different manner. Is that right? You would have treated him differently, you would have questioned him differently. Is that right?"

"I would have asked him additional questions, yes."

"And you would have done that before you reached your conclusion, is that right?"

"Yes, I would have."

"No further questions."

■CHAPTER FOURTEEN■

Searching For Experts

After hearing Barrett's unconvincing and disturbing testimony, Jon Schoenhorn, who had taken Rob's case only because Rob was a client of his firm, was deeply troubled. He decided to hire an expert in child sexual abuse to review Barrett's methods and her deposition. Schoenhorn, who had started to educate himself by reading literature on child sexual abuse, thought Barrett's methods were, at best, questionable if not incompetent.

Schoenhorn's research made him increasingly nervous. He found the percentage of guilty verdicts in child sex cases was extraordinarily high. Selecting an unbiased jury would be practically impossible. In the courtroom, it seemed, judges were willing to allow prosecutors to do virtually anything for the sake of a child. He found that appellate courts almost never overturned child molestation convictions.

He figured an appeals court would not want to put a child through a second trial, no matter how many mistakes the judge might have made or how weak the evidence was.

Schoenhorn hoped the McQueeney case wouldn't get that far. His aim was to stop the prosecution before it got to trial. But he knew the odds were against him.

He didn't tell Rob everything he had found out. The guy had enough problems already.

The next morning returning to his Oak Street office, Schoenhorn lugged his dark brown trial briefcase up the stairs. The third floor pretty much belonged to him. Though his office was isolated from the rest, it had one advantage. It was next to his firm's law library, where he did most of his research. He also had a kitchen and bathroom on the third floor.

In the five years that Schoenhorn had been practicing, he had developed a growing reputation as an aggressive, somewhat flamboyant defense lawyer who threw himself into his cases.

Most of Schoenhorn's work on the McQueeney case was stuffed in files two stories below, intermingled with the divorce case, in bulky accordion folders on the floor by the front windows in Hurvitz's office.

Schoenhorn took off his suit jacket, flopped into the chair behind his desk and picked up the telephone. He dialed the number of Nancy Eiswirth, a clinical psychologist in Hartford who had agreed to testify as an expert witness in the McQueeney case. Her job would be straightforward—to demolish Barbara Barrett's testimony, showing it to be unreliable, if the case ever got to court.

As he waited for Eiswirth to answer the phone he thought back to his first meeting with her.

Schoenhorn had met Eiswirth at a party about a year earlier. She had talked to him earnestly about her and other professional psychologists' and psychiatrists' growing distress that false claims of child abuse were being increasingly used to gain leverage during divorce cases. What immediately struck him about the McQueeney case was that the timing of Vicki's rape allegation was classic, coming days before a custody hearing.

The day McQueeney was arrested, the CBS Evening News had aired a report on "the newest weapon in the custody war." The broadcast said sixty percent of 1.5 million child abuse cases reported in 1986 were either determined to be unfounded or dropped for lack of evidence. Schoenhorn had heard about the broadcast and ordered a transcript.

When his law firm was formed in 1985, he and his partners agreed they would shun sex cases. They did not want any involvement in them.

Finally, she got on the line. Schoenhorn was indignant. "Nancy, we had Barrett's deposition yesterday. This social worker is outrageous, incompetent, and totally unsure of herself," he told her. "This is a snow job. She just made stuff up. She's a danger."

He wanted Eiswirth to write a critical report on Barrett's evaluation and treatment of Keefe. He told her he would send her copies of Keefe's Langley Center records that he had obtained. He also wanted her to read a transcript of Barrett's deposition before writing her report.

Eiswirth promised to get back to him as soon as she had the necessary information. When she did, Eiswirth told him that there were thirteen general categories that should be included— at a minimum—in any assessment of a preschool child suspected of being a victim of sexual abuse.

Barrett, she said, had failed to meet even minimal standards in twelve of the thirteen categories.

"Keefe has undergone a number of major life stresses and these are given no credit to his psychological functioning at the time of the [three-page evaluation/treatment summary] report," Eiswirth wrote. "Not only has Keefe experienced the separation of his parents, and their impending divorce, he has also undergone a move to a new house, removal from his nursery school, loss of friends, a new man living with his mother and the complete loss of his father following the allegations.

"Such a number of stresses cannot be ignored in the functioning of a four-year-old child, and included in evaluating a child for possible sexual abuse."

Eiswirth found other problems as well.

"In general, the clinical records kept in this case inadequately document Keefe's psychological functioning, his familial role and the allegations of sexual abuse.

"Part of the documentation in all treatment cases, including abuse cases, should include session-by-session notes. The progress notes in both Keefe's and Wendy's clinical records are outstandingly minimal, and are only written once a month, as stated in Mrs. Barrett's deposition.

"A final point in this review involves the lack of information about the children gathered from other sources. The information included in both Keefe's and Wendy's records was obtained solely from Mrs. McQueeney and from the children's play sessions. Reports from Keefe's pre-school teachers would have been valuable in establishing a baseline for his prior functioning. The reporting source in this case is solely the mother, who is also seeking sole custody of the children. This is a rather narrow source of information."

The first significant hole had been found in the armor of the allegations. Now, all McQueeney had to do was to wait. And watch. And try to get on with his life as best he could—while the weight of over forty years in prison hung over his head.

■CHAPTER FIFTEEN■

Past Issues

On a dark afternoon in early December 1987, when Schoenhorn got back to the Oak Street office, Henry Hurvitz was watching for him. As Schoenhorn quickly parked his oversized boxy briefcase along one wall in the lobby and began thumbing through his phone messages, Hurvitz approached.

"Jon, I need to talk with you about the McQueeney case," he said, stroking his goatee. "I don't think we can stall the divorce any longer . . . and Rob wants to settle."

Schoenhorn looked up. His drooping mustache accented a frown. "Let me take this call first," he said. "I'll just be a minute."

For months Judge Herbert Barall had pushed Hurvitz to find a way to end the divorce litigation, now almost a year and half old.

One of Barall's toughest jobs as presiding judge in charge of family matters in Hartford Superior Court was to chip away at the huge backlog of divorce cases. The judge knew that Hurvitz and Schoenhorn had been using the divorce during the past nine months to question potential prosecution witnesses for McQueeney's criminal case, even though the lawyers claimed the depositions were for the divorce.

The judge also understood that the criminal case put Hurvitz in a bind. Hurvitz could not put Rob on the witness stand in the divorce case while sodomy charges were hanging over his head. Because of the case, custody was out of the question, but Rob needed to testify to have any chance of winning the right to visit his children. Barall urged Hurvitz to settle the divorce while leaving the visitation issue open.

When Hurvitz told Rob he thought the idea had merit, Rob thought about his new relationship with Jackie. Keeping the divorce open wasn't fair to her. His only real worry was money. A settlement meant he would have to sell the house on Bemis Street. He had asked Hurvitz how much Vicki could get out of the house. The answer was half.

Rob gave Hurvitz the go-ahead to settle the divorce.

Now Hurvitz needed Schoenhorn's nod.

Schoenhorn didn't do divorce cases. He didn't like dealing with emotions. The way he looked at it, he wasn't a social worker, paid to soothe somebody's hurt feelings.

His job was to give his clients the best criminal defense their money could buy, pretty much regardless of the personal consequences. And in the McQueeney case that included keeping the divorce open. It was a tremendous advantage.

Defense lawyers in Connecticut were limited in what information they could get to prepare for trial when it came to prosecution witnesses. Schoenhorn had used the divorce to depose Vicki, Pandit and Barrett. Without the divorce, he wouldn't have been able to subpoena the Langley Center records on Keefe.

He wanted to keep the divorce open in case any new, unexpected witnesses emerged. And if the criminal charges ever got to trial, an open divorce case would continue to provide Vicki with a motive he could attack. He would have to convince a jury that she was so obsessed with getting sole custody of the children that she would do almost anything to Rob.

Schoenhorn put down the phone. "So Rob wants to settle," he sighed, rubbing the cold out of his hands.

"I don't think we have a choice," said Hurvitz. "Barall is all over me on this. But he'll let us leave the visitation open."

"I'd like to have the whole thing left open," Schoenhorn said. "But you're probably right . . . I can't think of anything else we need the divorce for right now. And we don't know how long the state is going to let my case sit. I suppose it's time for him to get on with his life."

"Okay then," Hurvitz said quickly. "I'm going to go ahead

and settle." He spun around and headed back toward his office in the front of the building.

Schoenhorn figured his biggest obstacle in the criminal case was Jack Bailey, the Hartford County State's attorney, son of the strongest political boss in the history of Connecticut. Bailey's father ran the Democratic party in Connecticut from 1946 until his death in 1977, helped get John Kennedy elected president and was the Democratic National Chairman from 1960 to 1968.

And now Jack Bailey, the son, was in charge of a powerful office. A prosecutor for seven years before he was appointed State's attorney in 1979, he had not tried a case since assuming the position. He had thirty-five prosecutors working for him and viewed his job as administrative.

McQueeney knew Jack Bailey from watching television, where he was frequently seen on the evening news, making tough statements from crime scenes or from the courthouse steps after one of his prosecutors won a conviction.

The Bailey Rob knew from television reminded him of a powerful prohibition-era prosecutor, with his slicked-back, dark receding hair and steely eyes behind wire-rimmed spectacles.

Bailey was well-known for his love of publicity and his sensitivity to politics and public opinion. And that was what worried Schoenhorn. Risking public outrage by dropping charges against an accused child molester was not something that he could reasonably expect Bailey to do.

If the charges were going to be dropped, Schoenhorn figured, it would have to be with the permission of the victim's family. And it didn't look like Vicki was going to do that.

The McQueeney case had been assigned to Herbert Carlson, Bailey's chief assistant State's attorney, who tried many of the most serious cases in the district. More than half his cases were murders. Carlson had been a prosecutor for over fifteen years. He had started in private practice, and had even worked part-time as a public defender for a year before joining the State's attorney's office.

Schoenhorn regarded Carlson as the most ethical of Bailey's prosecutors, and for that reason he was willing to share information with him. His strategy was to raise enough suspicion about Vicki and Bruce that the state would drop the charges.

Schoenhorn had talked to Carlson about the case every time he saw him in the courthouse around the corner from his office.

"This isn't an abuse case," Schoenhorn would tell him. "This is the classic divorce-custody situation."

Carlson, a tall, trim man with brown receding hair, wire-rimmed glasses, a deep voice and a subdued manner, had shared some information himself, but not his feelings about the evidence. He grumbled that Vicki was constantly calling him, insistent on pursuing the charges and keeping Rob away from the children.

Vicki's deposition had made Schoenhorn increasingly wary about her ability to act independently. He had begun to look more closely at Barbara Barrett and the State Department of Children and Youth Services and the part they had played in Vicki's charges.

The arrest warrant had been based almost solely on Barrett's testimony that Rob had molested Keefe. And Vicki had testified during her deposition that a DCYS worker threatened her with arrest if she did not file charges against her estranged husband. The DCYS staff had certain police powers, but they weren't trained to be police officers. In Schoenhorn's experience, they operated like storm troopers.

In addition to Schoenhorn's questions about Barrett's role, he had also been hearing stories about Bruce Johnson from Rob and others. Johnson began to look more and more like he was playing a Machiavellian role.

The more Schoenhorn learned, the weaker the State's case looked. Keefe's pre-school teacher gave Rob a strong endorsement and offered to help in any way she could. Pandit, the pediatrician, had said he found no physical evidence of abuse.

During the summer, Schoenhorn had stepped up his pressure on Carlson. He started feeling more confident the case wouldn't get to trial.

"You have to meet the boyfriend," he told the prosecutor. "Get him and Vicki into your office. Talk to them. This just is not an abuse case."

Carlson seemed receptive. The McQueeney case was taken off the trial list, and a series of pre-trial meetings were scheduled in August so that the prosecutor could talk with Vicki and Bruce. But they never got together. On August 31, the case was returned to the trial list.

Despite this, Schoenhorn kept pushing. Every time he saw Carlson throughout the fall, he tried to convince him that McQueeney was innocent and the State had no case against him. During one of those brief conversations, Carlson joked that if Schoenhorn didn't stop hounding him, he might turn the case over to another prosecutor, known as a conservative fanatic willing to do almost anything to get a conviction.

Schoenhorn eased off the pressure. He knew Carlson as a decent, moral man. He wanted him to stay in charge of the prosecution. Since Rob wasn't in jail, the charges could linger a little longer.

Schoenhorn had become more convinced of the absurdity of the allegations against McQueeney when he had deposed Barrett.

In the meantime, he had asked Eiswirth to put together a package of articles on false allegations of child sexual abuse for him.

Schoenhorn wanted at least one more expert witness, preferably someone with a national reputation. He was anxious to get his hands on the articles, which might lead him to another expert.

Eiswirth was supposed to get the information to him before Christmas, which was less than two weeks away.

On the morning of December 18, a Monday, Rob McQueeney and Henry Hurvitz slowly climbed the worn stone staircase to the third floor of the Superior Court on Washington Street in Hartford.

Rob was weary of these stairs and this place.

The third floor of the civil court was where people yelled at each other, where they went to get divorced and to fight for custody of children and visitation rights. Rob had been coming to the third floor for sixteen months, nearly once a month for the past year.

Today, if everything went as expected, Rob would get divorced. Because of the criminal charges, Judge Barall had suggested waiting to settle visitation matters. And custody . . . Rob couldn't even think about it.

The murmur of conversation grew louder as they reached the third floor by Courtroom 300.

Back in March, Rob had put on quite a third-floor spectacle himself. He did it on a balcony that rimmed the center of the old courthouse. It was the first time he had to go to court for the divorce. After Vicki had him arrested.

She had drawn up a list of possessions she wanted from the Bemis Street house. When the list was passed from lawyer to lawyer to Rob, he snapped. She wanted . . . the corn pot, the can opener . . . *the can opener.*

All the anger that had been building up inside him was unleashed in a forty-five second, machine-gun-like outburst.

"What do you think this is, a fucking tag sale?" he exploded. "You run out on me. You steal my kids and have me arrested. You're nothing but a tramp . . ."

Hurvitz put his hand lightly on Rob's shoulder as he ran out of breath, his chest heaving.

Vicki was sobbing. "He's on drugs," she screamed to anyone who could hear. "He's on drugs."

Later that spring day, as McQueeney and Hurvitz walked back to the lawyer's office, Rob stopped him. "Hank," he said, "I have to ask you a question. Why didn't you stop me in there?"

"I figured it was good for you," Hurvitz said. "But that's your one chance to vent your hostility. It's the only one you get. You had your say and now you keep your mouth shut."

"Well," Rob grinned, "I appreciate it."

In the months since the outburst, Rob's anger and despair had been replaced by a stubborn, desperate belief that the criminal case would eventually be dropped.

He was trying to look forward to life after Vicki. He was trying to focus on the fact that it would just be a matter of time.

Hurvitz spotted Clifford across the crowded lobby outside Courtroom 300.

Vicki was with Clifford. And Bruce Johnson was with her. The sheriff, riding shotgun. Rob and Vicki exchanged glances, but no words this time.

The two lawyers moved off to a conference room to do their work while Rob waited, passing time by wandering the familiar routes through the courthouse that he had traveled so many times before. But he didn't walk far.

Several times the lawyers emerged from their conference room, huddled with their clients and returned to the negotiating table to settle the terms of the divorce. Hours passed slowly.

Hurvitz began writing the terms on a blank form titled, "Agreement."

Because of Vicki's accusation against Rob, the first item was no longer in dispute. Custody went to the plaintiff and the visitation rights of the defendant were suspended pending further review. Then came insurance. Rob would maintain medical and dental coverage for the children and all unreimbursed expenses would be equally split. Then child support. They had finally settled at $70 per week for each child. Then the house. Vicki would sign away her right to the property in exchange for a promissory note of $24,500 that earned eight percent interest and was payable July 1, 1988. Then taxes. Vicki got to claim Keefe as a dependent. Hurvitz made sure Rob got Wendy, which would give him a dependent for a few extra years.

Hurvitz's handwriting got progressively smaller as he worked his way down the form. By the time he got to "personal property," his writing was so squeezed for space it was barely readable.

The negotiations were completed in early afternoon. Rob signed the handwritten form, and then Vicki. Hurvitz quickly lined up a judge to make the settlement official.

While they were waiting, Hurvitz took Rob aside. "I've got a surprise for you," he said. He opened his briefcase, reached inside and handed Rob a check.

McQueeney looked at it, confused. A check from an insurance company for more than $600.

"What's this?" he asked.

"Do you remember Vicki's car accident?" Hurvitz asked back.

175

Rob started to laugh.

Vicki had cracked up the car he had bought her five days before she left him. Since the insurance was in Rob's name, the company sent the check to him, and he had turned it over to Hurvitz. The lawyer had kept the check for more than a year.

"They never asked for it," Hurvitz smiled. "It's in your name. It's your check. It's your money."

Rob was elated. After all Vicki had done to him, he finally had gotten retribution, small but meaningful.

Clifford signaled that the judge was ready. Hurvitz ushered his client into Courtroom 300.

Vicki was asked to take the witness stand, and Clifford led her through the process.

"Mrs. McQueeney, you're the plaintiff in this marriage are you not?"

"Yes I am."

"You married Robert McQueeney in Bristol, Connecticut on April 17, 1982. Is that correct?"

"Yes."

"You have two children issued of this marriage, is that correct?"

"Yes."

"Now, you've claimed for dissolution of marriage, is that correct?"

"Yes."

"And you've claimed that your marriage has broken down irretrievably?"

"Yes."

"Is there any chance for reconciliation?"

"No."

"Now, you and Mr. McQueeney have come to an agreement this day, is that correct?"

"Yes."

"And it provides for custody of the children and visitation as set out in the agreement. It also provides for child support in the amount of $70 per week. Do you understand that?"

"Yes."

"Do you believe this is a fair and equitable agreement?"

"Yes, I do."

"And you'd like the court to enter this as its order?"
"Yes."
Clifford looked to the judge, who turned toward Rob.
"Mr. McQueeney," the judge said, "you heard your wife testify?"
"Yes."
"Is this a fair and equitable agreement under the circumstances?"
"Yes."
"Dissolution granted. Agreement approved."

Later that afternoon, when Jon Schoenhorn got back to his office, the package he had been expecting from Nancy Eiswirth, was waiting for him. She had sent a pile of new information.

One piece that quickly caught Schoenhorn's eye was a paper written by two psychiatrists, one of them a woman named Diane Schetky who had a private practice in Rockport, Maine and a national reputation.

The paper, which had been presented at a professional conference, focused on faulty assessment of child abuse. The two psychiatrists had served as consultants to defense lawyers, and they had used some of the cases as examples.

"Increased awareness of child sexual abuse has caused the pendulum to swing the other way to the point where unsubstantiated reported cases may now outnumber documented ones," Schetky and her co-author wrote. "In some areas overzealous reporting and investigation of child sexual abuse has contributed to an atmosphere of hysteria reminiscent of the Salem Witch Trials."

Schoenhorn reached Schetky a few days later. She was willing to work with him.

Experts were absolutely necessary in child sexual abuse cases. That point was made in nearly all the articles Schoenhorn had read on the subject. But experts were expensive.

Two days before Christmas, Schoenhorn sent a short letter to his client:

"Dear Rob,

"We have hired one of the foremost experts on the proper (vs. improper) method of interviewing children where child abuse is alleged in a divorce case. She has written books on it. Her role will be to attack Barbara Barrett's work as incompetent.

"You must immediately send $1,000 as a retainer to hire her. The sooner we get her involved the better. Please send the money to us before the first of the year."

Below his signature, Schoenhorn added:

"P.S. I think having her together with Nancy Eiswirth is the best shot at getting the prosecution dropped."

CHAPTER SIXTEEN

Marriage, Memories And Future Fears

Just before Christmas, Rob moved into Jackie's home on Rossi Drive in Bristol.

No longer would he spend nights alone, haunted by the relics of a lost life in the cold ranch house in the woods off Bemis Street. A "For Sale" sign would soon be planted in the yard.

But the change of scene did little to soften the sorrow that accompanied the holidays. Memories of the kids were everywhere, in the decorations, the lights, the cookies, the music.

Right after Christmas they started to clean out Rob's house. The hardest part was dismantling the bedrooms where Keefe and Wendy once lived; rooms that had been virtually untouched, their doors closed, since their mother had taken them away a year earlier.

They went through Wendy's room first. Almost every item required consideration before a decision could be made. Rob wanted to keep it all. Jackie had to remind him they didn't have the space.

When they got to Keefe's room, they were weary, and it was getting late.

Rob opened the closet. Inside were all the superhero and monster toys he and Keefe used to play with as they waged epic battles of good and evil.

He stood motionless, staring into the closet for a long time, memories swirling through his mind, the squeals of the kids ringing in his ears.

Jackie saw him from across the room. The back of his neck looked very red. Then his shoulders started to heave. She heard the sobs as he sank to the floor.

With the spring sale of the Bemis Street house, the outlook for 1988 brightened briefly.

Rob paid Vicki her $24,500. He gave his parents $5,000 to repay the money they had put up for Schoenhorn's retainer. He paid Hurvitz's bill of $4,000. After covering the mortgage and the real estate commission, he had about $30,000 left. Of that, $20,000 went into a certificate of deposit.

The sale pulled McQueeney out of a financial hole, but soon afterward the torment of the past year that had touched every corner of his life caught up to him.

Sharp pains began shooting through his chest, making it feel at times like it was about to cave in. He had headaches so strong that he could hardly stand up. His doctor prescribed pills for hypertension.

In May, McQueeney quit his job.

He felt burned out, not only in his private life but at the office. Tension surrounded him.

The tiny company for which he worked had not achieved the promise he envisioned when he joined it three years earlier to design custom gauges for measuring anything from telephone components to surgical scissors.

McQueeney was grateful to the owners, Tom and Dan, for the support they had given him after the arrest. But since the beginning of 1988, he had hardly seen them in the office. They had drifted apart, each concentrating on other ventures.

McQueeney had effectively become the company's general manager, supervising himself, doing almost everything.

Finally, Rob told Dan he couldn't work at the company

any longer. They agreed it was time to go their separate ways.

Through the hot summer, Rob was unemployed.

He read the help-wanted ads each day, but found no engineering jobs that suited his qualifications. He figured he had the experience to expect a management position.

On weekends, Rob and Jackie traveled to flea markets, looking for parts for his Studebaker. They made one overnight trip to Carlisle, Pennsylvania, site of one of the largest car-part flea markets in the country.

As summer worn on, Jackie grew frustrated with the lack of any information on the criminal case.

When she had invited Rob to live with her, she told him the arrangement would either lead to marriage or the end of their relationship. She had never lived with anyone before.

She wanted the criminal charges out of the way before they talked seriously about marriage. So she asked Rob to call Schoenhorn.

"I just can't tell you what's going to happen," the lawyer said.

But Schoenhorn had an idea. He encouraged Rob to file a lawsuit against Barrett and the Langley Center.

Eiswirth and Schetky had produced reports ripping Barrett apart. Schetky had told Schoenhorn that, in her opinion, the materials she had reviewed constituted a clear case of malpractice.

Schoenhorn thought it would be a conflict to handle the civil lawsuit and the criminal case, but John Andreini, the big, bearded lawyer who had helped Ray and Ruth last fall, was interested.

Rob and his parents decided to sue. The claim would be that they, as well as the kids, had been injured by Barrett's flawed findings. She had destroyed the children's relationship with their father, and with their grandparents as well—two people who wanted nothing but a chance to continue loving their grandchildren.

181

Andreini advised the McQueeneys not to file the lawsuit until after the criminal case was resolved. He did not want Rob to be deposed by lawyers for Langley Center as long as the sodomy charges were hanging over his head.

While McQueeney waited, he bought another Studebaker.

The house on Rossi Drive began to look like a used car lot. Jackie and Rob had had a two-car garage built earlier in the summer but in addition to his two Studebakers, Rob had a Buick Riviera he bought with money from the sale of the Bemis Street house. He had sold his little red Chevette. Jackie had a Ford Mustang and a Honda Prelude. And her son Paul had a Sapporo. Luckily, a 1968 Chevy panel truck that Rob also owned was at the body shop.

McQueeney now had three cars, a truck and no job. But he was no longer bothered by chest pains, headaches and dizziness.

In late July he and Jackie drove to South Bend, Indiana for the annual gathering of Studebaker fanatics from across the continent. The event was extra-special because South Bend was the home of Studebaker's factory before the car went out of production in the United States in 1964.

On the second day of the convention, Rob challenged Jackie to a game of miniature golf at the Holiday Inn where they were staying. It was a close game, but he won.

"There is a consolation prize, though," he said.

"Really" she asked warily. "What?"

"Come here." Rob walked her to their room, where he began rummaging in a knapsack that was filled with used car parts. He pulled out a small box that had a novelty button attached to the top.

"Will you marry me?" asked the button. "I'm aging visibly."

Inside the box was a diamond ring.

Jackie was both tearful and joyful as Rob put it on her finger.

McQueeney missed his old friends, particularly a small group of boyhood pals who had stayed close through the years —that is, until the arrest. He hadn't seen his closest friend in the group, Brian Samsel, in almost two years.

In October Rob called Brian to see if it was possible to renew their friendship.

A few days after they talked on the phone, they had a heart-felt get-together over a pitcher of beer at Roma's, a pizza restaurant in New Britain where they used to hang out.

The conversation was awkward at first. Brian had heard about the arrest soon after it happened. His mother was a good friend of Ruth McQueeney. Rob told his story, and Brian apologized for not staying in touch and offering support. He said he was disappointed in himself, but hadn't known what to say or how to say it. As they rekindled their friendship, Rob asked Brian to be his best man.

Rob and Jackie were married on Saturday, November 5, 1988 at Avon Old Farms Inn, a quaint country restaurant—three hundred and sixty-five days after they had first met.

Rob wrote the ceremony.

"On this day of their marriage, Jackie and Rob stand somewhat apart from all other human beings, within the charmed circle of their love," read a justice of the peace. "Ideally, love knows no limit to its endurance, no end to its trust, no dashing of its hope. It can outlast anything. It is, in fact, the one thing that still stands when all else has fallen.

"The essence of this commitment is the taking of another person in his or her entirety, as lover, companion and friend. It is a decision to be undertaken with great consideration and respect for both the other person and oneself. We must give ourselves in love, but we must not give ourselves away.

"Will you, then, Rob, take Jackie to be your wife, pledging to share your life openly with her, to speak the truth to her, to honor and tenderly care for her, to cherish and encourage her fulfillment through all the changes of your lives?"

"I will."

"Place the ring on her finger and repeat, 'This is my beloved and my friend.'

"And will you, then, Jackie, take Rob to be your husband,

pledging to share your life openly with him, to speak the truth to him, to honor and tenderly care for him, to cherish and encourage his fulfillment through all the changes of your lives?"

"I will."

"Place the ring on his finger and repeat, 'This is my beloved and my friend.'

"Paul, will you, their son, grant them your blessings and pledge them your love and acceptance?"

"I will."

"Since Jackie and Rob have vowed to be loyal and loving toward each other, formalizing in our presence the existence of the bond between them, it is my pleasure, ladies and gentlemen, to present to you, Mr. and Mrs. Robert McQueeney."

As they turned and walked back down the aisle, Ruth McQueeney couldn't stop staring at the simple pink and blue ribbons that Rob and Jackie wore. The pink ribbon was for Wendy; the blue one for Keefe.

Everybody thought Ruth was crying with happiness for Rob.

They were mistaken.

McQueeney had started a new job two weeks before the wedding.

The job was one that wouldn't have interested him during the summer—before he grew desperate. The advertisement was for a "quality technologist" and the company, MRC Bearings, was in Winsted, a thirty-five to forty minute commute from Bristol.

As it turned out, McQueeney was offered a supervisory position running the quality assurance operation with a staff of seven, making sure the ball bearing components that rolled off the assembly line were within critical tolerances, measuring them to within millionths of an inch.

Throughout the job application process, the criminal case lurked in the background like a dark shadow.

Rob kept his secret to himself. Since he was sure the

charges would eventually be dropped, he figured there was no reason to worry anyone at the company.

The approach of the holidays heralded the promise of a new life together for the newlyweds. But, once again, Christmas was a chilling reminder of how much had been lost. It had been more than a year since Rob had seen his "little man" and "piglet."

Jackie had begun to think about a different child—the one she and Rob wanted to have together.

At her age, she knew she couldn't wait very long. She couldn't understand why, after almost two years, nothing was happening in the criminal case. And worse, nobody seemed to care.

For the first time, Jackie began thinking that her husband could conceivably be convicted—and sent to prison—if the charges ever did get to a trial.

She had raised one child alone, and didn't want to do it again.

Gently at first, then more insistently, she urged Rob to get in touch with Schoenhorn. Rob, not wanting to stir up anything, hadn't talked with his lawyer for months.

On Saturday afternoon two weeks before Christmas, she and Rob drove to his parents home in Newington. A dusting of snow was swirling across the pavement ahead of them.

"Have you talked to Schoenhorn yet?" Jackie asked quietly.

"Haven't had the chance." Rob's eyes remained riveted on the road.

"I know this is hard on you," she went on. "I wouldn't keep bringing it up if it wasn't important. But I need to have more information if we're going to have a baby."

"Schoenhorn doesn't know," Rob barked. "It's always the same answer every time I talk to him. Lawyers don't give any guarantees."

"I know there aren't any guarantees," she said, trying to soothe him. "But you haven't talked to him in a long time, and I just need to know what he thinks."

"What difference does it make?" Rob asked. "He can't predict what's going to happen."

"It would just make me feel better if we knew something," she said softly. "Chances are this is going to be my last pregnancy. I want it to be a happy one. If we only have to wait a few months, then I want to wait."

Rob knew how painful the memories of her first pregnancy were. Paul had been conceived out of wedlock when Jackie was eighteen, and her family had been very upset.

"You know who's fault this is?" Rob finally blurted. His voice was trembling. "It's Vicki again . . . She's already taken away two of my kids. Now she's taking away a baby that we don't even have yet . . . She's going to ruin that for me, too."

Jackie looked down at her hands folded in her lap. For several minutes, the only sound in the car was the steady click-click-click of the windshield wipers.

"Look." Rob broke the silence. "I'll call Schoenhorn. But you've got to understand, there aren't going to be any guarantees."

"I know that," said Jackie. "I'd just like to know whether he thinks there's going to be a trial. I want some odds."

The following Monday, McQueeney called Schoenhorn from work. His lawyer surprised him.

"Don't bet the house on it," Schoenhorn said, "but I don't think there's going to be a trial."

For Jackie that was good enough—more than she had hoped for.

In late January, Jackie happily told Rob she was pregnant. They pinpointed New Year's Eve as the beginning of their child's life. In September they would have a baby. Maybe 1989 would be a better year.

A week later they got a telephone call from Andreini. He needed their go-ahead to file the malpractice lawsuit against Barrett and the Langley Center. A two-year statute of limitations was about to expire. Andreini was confident he could stall any attempt to depose Rob before the criminal case was resolved.

The legal complaint was filed in Hartford Superior Court

February 15, in the names of McQueeney, his parents, and Keefe and Wendy. It was almost two years to the day since Barrett had sent her statement to the police, concluding that Rob had sexually molested his four-year old son.

The lawsuit listed twenty-nine reasons why Barrett was negligent in her evaluation and diagnosis of the children.

"As a result of the defendant Barbara Barrett's negligence and carelessness," said the eighteen-page complaint, "the plaintiff Robert McQueeney was caused to suffer grievous mental suffering, shame and embarrassment, medical and legal expenses and permanent and irreparable damage to his professional and personal reputation."

Further, it said, "Robert McQueeney, who was entitled to the companionship, love and affection of his children, lost such companionship, support, love and affection and the paternal relationship between himself and his children."

Ray and Ruth McQueeney had suffered the same losses, the lawsuit declared, and the children had been deprived of the companionship and guidance of their father and grandparents.

In March, a few weeks after the malpractice action was filed, Schoenhorn got a call from Herb Carlson.

The prosecutor asked for a copy of Vicki's deposition. It was the first real interest Carlson had shown in the case in two years.

Schoenhorn agreed to give him the deposition. He expected Carlson would conclude that the state did not have enough of a case to go to trial. He alerted Carlson to some of the points he wanted him to notice in the deposition.

Schoenhorn figured he had nothing to lose and a lot to gain.

In early May, McQueeney knew something was terribly wrong when he got home from work one day. His dog Holly hadn't greeted him at the door. Holly had been Rob's companion through so much—three wives, two divorces, the loss of his children, the arrest—and had never showed anything but love and support.

He found her on the kitchen floor, so weak that she could hardly lift her head. He carried her to his car, put her on a sheet in the back seat and scratched her head as they drove to the veterinarian.

The next day the vet determined that the 14-year-old lab-shepherd had massive internal bleeding, caused by a ruptured tumor. There was nothing that could be done.

Rob held his "best girl" as she was given a fatal injection.

■ CHAPTER SEVENTEEN ■

New Riddles

When Rob got home from work the evening of June 7, Jackie told him he had a letter from Schoenhorn's office. "Probably wants money," Rob grumbled as he opened it. He hadn't talked with his lawyer since the winter.

Schoenhorn didn't want more money—at least not yet. The letter said a meeting had been scheduled on the criminal case in court on June 27. Schoenhorn called it a "status conference." He wanted McQueeney to call his office so they could discuss it.

Rob tried to remember the last time he had to go to court on his criminal case. It had been more than two years. He didn't know what Schoenhorn meant by a status conference.

A little nervous, Rob telephoned his lawyer from work the next day.

"A status conference means the judge is saying, 'what's going on with this case, guys,'" explained Schoenhorn. "It means that Judge Arena, who's the presiding judge in Hartford, sees nothing happening, and he's saying to the State, 'either you move this case or you drop it.' He doesn't want it on his trial list any more."

"What you're saying is this could be it?" Rob asked.

"It looks that way," Schoenhorn said. "I met with Carlson last week, and he was talking like he wasn't interested in pursuing the case. But he said he had to talk to Vicki."

"So what do I have to do?" asked Rob.

"Well, I want you to be at the court just in case you're

needed," he said. "You should probably bring your wife, too. Carlson and I will talk to Arena. We'll tell him what the case is all about and see what happens. Arena's job is to get these cases moving. Your case has got to be one of the oldest."

"You sound really optimistic," said Rob.

"It looks good," said Schoenhorn.

From all that he had been through the past three years, Rob had a grasp of the basic rules of court. He thought about Henry Hurvitz's lecture on tiebars as he, Jackie and his mother walked with Schoenhorn the block and a half from his office to Hartford Superior Court.

Rob always wore a tiebar. He had a good assortment of them. Many were replicas of handguns, gifts from his father who was an accomplished target shooter.

One day, when Rob had a court appearance in the early stages of the divorce case, he had met Hurvitz in his office. The lawyer took one look at Rob's gun tiebar, threw up his hands and ordered him to "lose it." Rob was puzzled. "You are not to wear anything like that, anytime, whether you're going to court or not," Hurvitz said flatly.

Rob had followed his advice. Today, his tiebar was an innocuous gold clip.

All of them were dressed well, thinking they would have reason to celebrate. Jackie wore a new outfit—black pants and a tailored white top—that she had bought for this occasion. She anticipated the case would be dropped, after which she and Rob would go out for dinner to toast the occasion.

They waited for more than an hour on a hardwood bench while Schoenhorn conferred with Carlson and Judge Arena.

When Schoenhorn finally emerged, they jumped up eagerly.

"How'd it go?" Rob asked.

"We'll know in two weeks," Schoenhorn said. "That's how much time the judge gave Carlson to decide what he's going to do."

"Did the Judge say anything about the case?" asked Rob.

"Not really," said Schoenhorn. "I don't think he was too impressed with it, but Carlson is the one who has the final say about whether it goes to trial."

Rob wanted to know more. He pressed his lawyer for details of the conference, which had been held in the judge's chambers.

Schoenhorn said he had been the one who did most of the talking. He had laid out his reasons why he thought Carlson didn't have a case—the allegations made by Vicki and Bruce in the midst of the custody dispute, Barrett's incompetence, Pandit's examination and the lack of any physical evidence.

"When the judge asked Carlson about it," Schoenhorn said, "Carlson told him he hadn't had a chance to really look at the file."

"What does he mean, he hasn't had a chance to look at the file?" bellowed Rob. "Jesus Christ. What's he been doing all this time? We've been here on pins and needles for twenty-seven months, or however long it is, and he hasn't even looked at the file?"

Again Schoenhorn said he got the impression Carlson would not take the case to trial. He said Carlson was going to meet with Vicki and Bruce to try to get them to drop the case.

But Schoenhorn also reminded them of the Bailey factor—that the State's attorney probably wouldn't risk a public outcry.

"We'll know in two weeks," he said again.

Despite his impression that the case was going to be dropped, the next day Schoenhorn had his secretary send identical letters to Nancy Eiswirth and Diana Schetky.

"This is to inform you," read the letters, "that the trial of the above-captioned matter might begin as early as the first week of July. It is possible that the charges against my client will be dismissed, but I still need to know your availability for the month of July and the beginning of August in the event that the trial will proceed.

"Please contact me at your earliest opportunity."

As Schoenhorn's letters went into the mail, Rob was preparing to tell John Agnew, his boss, about his dark secret—just in case.

Agnew was going to go on vacation at the end of the week while the MRC plant was on its annual two-week shutdown. Most Connecticut manufacturers that supplied parts for the aircraft industry were idle during those weeks.

McQueeney and Agnew had a good relationship. He had never felt uncomfortable about not telling him of the criminal case when he applied for the job. It just hadn't seemed necessary. He was sure Agnew would understand.

Now, Rob wanted to be the one to tell him. He didn't want his boss coming back from vacation and finding out that the engineer who ran his quality control operation wasn't around because he was on trial for raping his four-year-old son.

On Wednesday Rob asked Agnew if he had a minute to talk. "Just in case," he began, "there's something I've got to tell you. . . ."

The conversation lasted an hour. It was quite a shock for Agnew, but he was sympathetic, and caring. He said he personally felt that Rob's job should be secure. "In this country," he said, "you're innocent until proven guilty."

Agnew agreed to talk to the plant manager and corporate executives to prepare them for the worst.

The MRC plant was abandoned, as expected, on Monday, July 3rd. McQueeney was among a handful of staff who worked during the first shutdown week so they could take a week of vacation later in the year.

He planned to take Tuesday off to observe July 4th, but otherwise was going to work ten-hour days through the week.

Jackie was in the kitchen making dinner when he got home from work Monday at five p.m.

He went down the short stairway to their unfinished basement office and switched on his answering machine, as he usually did, to check for messages. He and Jackie had two separate phone lines in the house. The one connected to the answering machine was mostly for business purposes.

From the kitchen, Jackie heard Rob close the office door after checking for messages. But he didn't come back up to the kitchen. She went to the edge of the stairs to see what he was doing.

She was terrified at what she saw.

Rob was standing at the bottom of the stairs with a tortured look of horror.

"What's wrong?" Jackie's voice trembled.

Rob struggled to speak.

"We're going to trial," he answered in a flat voice. "Keefe is going to testify."

Jackie's heart began to beat rapidly, but she kept her voice calm.

"When?" she heard herself asking.

"In two days."

They stood motionless, staring at each other from opposite ends of the stairs.

"Was that Schoenhorn?"

"No." Rob started slowly up the stairs, gripping the handrail. "It was on the machine. I don't know who it was . . . a secretary or an answering service. I don't know. It wasn't him."

He snatched the telephone in the kitchen and dialed Schoenhorn's office. He was getting angry. He got an answering service.

"I'm sorry, the office is closed," he was told. "Would you like to leave a message?"

Rob knew Schoenhorn and John Andreini were good friends, and Andreini frequently worked late. It was five-twenty p.m. He decided to call Andreini.

Rob's hand shook as he dialed and the lawyer answered. Rob practically shouted.

"John, I just got this message that the case is going to trial. Keefe is going to testify. I can't get a hold of Schoenhorn. Do you know what the hell is going on?"

"I'm afraid it's true," Andreini said softly. "They're going to put Keefe on the stand. I heard the news late in the afternoon."

"I have to talk with Jon," said Rob. *"Now."*

"Let me see what I can do," offered Andreini. "Stay on the line. I'm going to put you on hold."

Rob waited.

Andreini came back on the phone after a minute, saying he was connecting Schoenhorn to the same line.

"It's true," said Schoenhorn flatly. "We're going to trial. I got word from a clerk this afternoon."

Rob stammered. "I can't believe it. How could this happen? I mean, a week ago, Carlson hadn't even looked at the file, and the judge didn't think he had a case. How can they do this? I just can't believe it."

Schoenhorn muttered that, for whatever reason, Carlson had suddenly decided to take the case to trial. Schoenhorn reminded Rob that he had always told him there was that chance.

"We're prepared," the lawyer reassured him. "I'll see you Thursday. Meet me at my office."

Schoenhorn's voice betrayed no emotion; he acted like this happened all the time.

■CHAPTER EIGHTEEN■

Voir Dire

By virtue of his position as Jack Bailey's chief assistant, Herb Carlson's office on the first floor of Hartford Superior Court was larger than those of the other prosecutors.

His massive oak desk was centered at one end of the office, and prominently displayed next to it was a bright-colored, framed embroidered message:

"If you can't do the time, don't do the crime."

At the other end of the office, near the door, was a small round conference table where Carlson and Schoenhorn now sat opposite each other.

Schoenhorn flipped through the pages of the state's attorney's file on Robert McQueeney. There were a couple of minor documents that he hadn't seen, but no real surprises.

Carlson was one of the few prosecutors Schoenhorn knew who allowed a defense lawyer to look at the state's file before trial.

He closed the folder, slid it across the table and leaned back in his chair.

"You know," Schoenhorn said, "you look at everything in that file and you combine it with everything I've given you, and what have you got?"

He grimaced, "Do you really think this case should be tried?"

Carlson stared for a moment at the file on the table in front of him and folded his arms across his chest before meeting Schoenhorn's eyes.

"I've read all the information," he said carefully, "and I can't personally say that a crime was necessarily committed. I've got the child's story, and I've got an angry mother . . ." he stopped in mid thought, reached for the file and picked it up.

"Maybe he did it, maybe he didn't do it," Carlson went on. "But I can't make that judgment. We've got to do what we have to do."

Schoenhorn got out of his chair and picked up his boxy briefcase.

"Thanks for letting me look at the file," he said, his voice flat, his face flushed, turning toward the door. "I'll see you tomorrow at voir dire."

McQueeney was alone when he drove into the small parking area behind the offices of Hurvitz, Hershinson & Schoenhorn Thursday morning.

He had told Jackie she should go to work. They would need every paycheck they could get. She, like Rob, would have to take an unpaid leave of absence from her job once the trial started. Schoenhorn's trial fee had been $400 per day when Rob signed the contract more than two years ago.

Rob parked next to Schoenhorn's car. It had two bumper stickers on the back.

"Question authority," implored one.

"Liberty's last champion," proclaimed the other. "Your criminal defense lawyer."

Still numb from the message on his answering machine three days before, Rob slowly made his way into the lobby.

A secretary buzzed Schoenhorn in his office. "You can go right up to the third floor," she said.

Rob listened to his creaking footsteps as he climbed the old oak staircase. A pad of paper was tucked under his arm. Though he felt like he was forgetting something, he didn't know what else to bring.

Turning the corner, he climbed the next flight to the third floor. Never had he felt so helpless.

"Hi Rob."

Schoenhorn was at his desk in a blue short-sleeved shirt. "Take off your coat . . . Can I get you a cup of coffee?"

McQueeney was bothered that his lawyer was greeting him like this was just another day. Depressed, he sank into a chair next to Schoenhorn's desk.

"I can't believe I'm here," said Rob, his voice anguished, "I can't get over that message on my answering machine. I wish it had been you and not some stranger."

"The most important thing was to let you know as soon as possible," Schoenhorn said. "I was in court when I found out. I called back here for messages, and they told me the judge's clerk had phoned, saying we were going to trial. I told my secretary to get a hold of you right away."

"It's just that I can't believe this is going to trial." Rob went on. "How could it happen? For two and a half years the state did nothing."

"Rob," said Schoenhorn. "We've known all along this could go to trial. I told you how Bailey's office handles these kinds of cases."

Schoenhorn related his conversation with Carlson the previous afternoon.

"Carlson's one of the good guys," he said. "What is important at the moment," Schoenhorn said, "is the trial."

Rob had to force himself to concentrate on what lay ahead. He couldn't let the past matter anymore.

Schoenhorn said he was already working on a series of standard motions that he filed before trials. One was a motion for sequestration of witnesses—meaning they would not be able to listen to each other's testimony or talk about it. His motions were designed to pave the way for possible appeals as much as they were to influence the course of the trial.

Schoenhorn's first step in preparing Rob for the trial was an explanation of the jury selection process, known as voir dire, a French term meaning "to speak the truth."

"We're going to go over to court this afternoon and look over some jurors," he said.

Connecticut was one of the few states that allowed the prosecutor and the defense attorney to question individual jurors outside the presence of other jurors. Schoenhorn considered voir dire one of the most important parts of the trial process, because it was the only opportunity the jurors had to get to know him and his client as people—not the scum they expected to see.

Schoenhorn's approach was to try to draw out prospective jurors by involving them in conversations instead of simply asking questions which required yes or no answers.

During the last two and a half years, the basic rules of courtroom behavior had been pounded into Rob: dress nicely, keep quiet, don't laugh, don't mutter, don't wear tie clasps with guns, if the judge speaks to you, stand up.

Schoenhorn had some special instructions for voir dire: don't shy away from looking over the jurors; make eye contact with each of them; pay attention; watch their body language.

Schoenhorn said, "I'll use voir dire to sensitize the jurors to what the case is all about. The rules prevent me from asking them directly about the particulars of the charges. But I'll probe them about their attitudes toward children, divorce and custody."

He told Rob he was looking for jurors who had been through a nasty divorce or had a relative who had been through one. Or people who didn't necessarily believe everything a child said was true.

"Beyond that, he said, "I want people who are fairly intelligent or well-read. I think men will probably be better able to understand your situation." If there were any engineers on the panel, he said, they might identify with Rob.

One device Schoenhorn had found effective was asking jurors who they thought the defendant was when they first saw them sitting at the defense desk—him or Rob?

"I'll be doing some things like that," he said. "I want to convey that often the first impressions that people get about these cases are completely skewed. I'll do it if I think someone may have trouble grasping the notion of presumption of innocence.

"Carlson and I will each have eight peremptory challenges; the chance to dismiss jurors without having to give a reason."

Schoenhorn looked at his watch. "It's time to head over," he said. Motioning to Rob, Schoenhorn began gathering his trial materials and stuffing them into his briefcase.

As they were walking around the corner to the courthouse, Schoenhorn kept talking.

Rob would be asked to stand in front of the jury panel that afternoon while the charges against him were read. Schoenhorn said he would introduce Rob a second time, physically touching him to show the jurors that he wasn't some monster.

He went through his introduction: "I'll say, 'This is Mr. McQueeney, he's an engineer, he works at' . . . where *do* you work?"

"MRC Bearings in Winsted," Rob responded mechanically.

"I'll say he's an engineer, he works at MRC Bearings in Winsted . . . He lives in Bristol with his present wife Jackie, who's here in the courtroom today."

"You wanted Jackie today?" asked Rob, surprised.

Schoenhorn nodded. It's important that she be with you on the first introduction to the whole jury panel, so they can see that you have the support of your family."

Jackie didn't have to be at voir dire every day. But first impressions were important.

"Could she get down here this afternoon?" Schoenhorn asked.

"I'll see what I can do," said Rob. "She's at work."

"You can use a phone in the courthouse."

Rob called Jackie shortly before noon. She said she'd leave right away. She had already told her boss she would be taking off soon for an indefinite period of time. Her boss said she understood because her husband had once been involved in a lawsuit.

The new Hartford Superior Court building was just three years old. It was built because the old pillared stone courthouse across the street was not big enough to handle the volume of civil and criminal cases. Now all criminal justice was dispensed at the new courthouse.

Courtroom 3A, while air-conditioned, was small, cramped and windowless. It had hard red brick walls, and microphones protruded from every piece of wood furniture in the front section.

Just three benches were provided for spectators in the rear of the chamber—two benches behind the defense desk on the right and one bench on the prosecution side.

The long jury box was on the left, extending from the prosecutor's desk to the witness stand, adjacent to the judge's bench. Between the jury box and the witness stand was a door where jurors were escorted in and out of the courtroom.

The McQueeney case would be heard by a jury of six, although eight would be chosen. Two of them would be alternates who could step in if one of the regular jurors was unable to complete the trial.

The judge presiding over voir dire, fifty-six-year-old John F. Mulcahy Jr., would also run the trial. He had been a federal prosecutor during the 1960s, then a state prosecutor in the 1970s before being appointed judge in 1979. He was a small man with graying brown hair. He had a patient, thoughtful manner and a soothing voice.

The judge's bench was flanked by an American flag on one side and a Connecticut flag on the other.

Rob scrutinized the scene carefully, worriedly. He imagined he would be a spectator at his own trial, watching helplessly as a group of strangers debated whether he would spend the rest of his life in prison.

He was surprised later that afternoon when Schoenhorn, while questioning one of the prospective jurors, leaned over to him and asked, "What do you think?"

Schoenhorn actually wanted his opinion. Rob felt better. He would be involved in the case. He would have some control —quality control at least over the composition of the jury.

He turned around. Jackie and his mother, who had met them at the courthouse, were in the spectator section four feet behind him. He gave them a weak smile of reassurance.

Awkwardly, they smiled back. It was difficult to be cheerful in this place, Rob thought squirming.

The spectator benches were hard and the seats sloped sharply from front to rear. When they to tried shift positions by edging forward, they would slide back. The benches bordered on torture for a pregnant woman.

When Mulcahy adjourned court late Thursday afternoon one juror had been selected—Rose Emma Aceto, a fifty-eight year old keypunch operator and porcelain artist who lived in Manchester, a suburb a few miles east of Hartford.

She was questioned for more than two hours before she was accepted. Much of the questioning centered on her opinions about divorce and its effect on children.

She had grown up in a Rhode Island orphanage with a twin sister whose first name was also Rose. Now she and her sister lived two miles away from each other and each had three children—two girls and a boy. Emma had six grandchildren.

She seemed tense while answering questions from the witness stand. What Schoenhorn and Rob didn't know was why she was nervous.

Emma Aceto was fighting herself. She knew McQueeney was supposed to be presumed innocent, but she couldn't help feeling that he was guilty the minute she heard the clerk read those horrible charges. "He's going to have to prove something to me," she thought to herself as she left the court.

Rob began taking notes on each juror the first day. That weekend he bought a law dictionary so he could understand the language that was routinely used in the courtroom. He also bought loose-leaf binders and put copies of all the depositions in them. He had seen Schoenhorn using yellow Post-it stickers to mark passages in his copies of the depositions. Rob did the same.

During the second week of voir dire, Rob began carrying a briefcase. He spent time at the public library studying literature on sexual abuse. Diane Schetky had written some of it.

He telephoned his boss, John Agnew, to tell him the worst had happened. Agnew said he had talked with the plant manager and higher-ups. Rob could have an unpaid leave of absence, and his job would be waiting for him when it was over.

Jury selection was ponderous, but it had a few memorable moments. Rob was stunned when Schoenhorn asked matter-of-factly what one prospective juror thought of anal penetration. Schoenhorn whispered to Rob he wanted to find out how squeamish the person was.

Schoenhorn asked five prospective jurors who they thought the defendant was when they first saw him and Rob sitting at the defense desk. The competition ended in a tie. Schoenhorn got two votes. Rob got two, and the fifth person thought it could be either of them.

When he was not in the courtroom questioning members of the jury panel, Schoenhorn was researching court decisions, working on motions, lining up his witnesses and preparing notes for direct examination of his witnesses and cross-examination of the state's witnesses.

His days started at six-thirty a.m.—with a brisk run through the neighborhood where he lived in West Hartford—and usually didn't end until midnight. The pace was exhausting, but also exhilarating.

Trial work was why Schoenhorn became a lawyer. His role as "liberty's last champion" was one he relished.

A trial for Schoenhorn was like a movie. He got to write the script, act, direct the production and watch it—all at the same time.

One of his most important scenes in the McQueeney trial would come during cross-examination of Keefe. It would require careful, sensitive preparation. Schoenhorn wasn't married, and his contacts with children were limited to seeing cousins every once in a while.

While jury selection progressed, Schoenhorn met with Eiswirth and talked with Schetky about how to prepare for questioning the little boy.

They told him that children can remember a lot more than most people think, but they warned him to watch out for memorization. They advised him to have a normal conversation, not to talk down to the boy. To get Keefe to open up, they suggested doing something that would make him laugh.

Schoenhorn figured a toy should do the trick. He dug into a collection of wind-up toys he kept at home. Some had been given to him as gag gifts and others came from the lobby of the law office, where they had been broken and left behind.

One of his favorites was a set of walking teeth that chattered. He considered an ice-cream cone that shot a sponge ball out the top, but dismissed it as too dangerous. He settled on a gorilla that did flips. The chattering teeth would be his backup.

He called John Andreini and arranged to borrow his son for an hour one day to practice.

He wanted one other prop for Keefe's cross-examination, something that could get the boy talking about *Ghostbusters*. A law student working at Schoenhorn's office tried to find a coloring book with a picture of the Marshmallow Man. But he came back with something better—a six-inch Marshmallow Man doll.

As jury selection neared an end, Schoenhorn grew more and more agitated at Carlson, who had used his peremptory challenges to excuse a number of jurors that Schoenhorn wanted. Four of them were men who had gone through divorces.

Schoenhorn argued to Judge Mulcahy that if it was unconstitutional to exclude jurors on the basis of race, as the Supreme Court had recently decided, then it should also be unconstitutional to exclude on the basis of gender.

Mulcahy overruled him.

As voir dire neared an end, Schoenhorn drew up a motion calling for dismissal of the jury because the state had used five of its peremptory challenges to dismiss men.

The motion was filed the morning of July 18, immediately after the acceptance of the final alternate juror—Richard Allison, a vice-president with Aetna Life & Casualty, the same company Jackie had worked for since 1972.

Schoenhorn's motion was quickly argued and denied by Judge Mulcahy, who set the beginning of the trial for later in the afternoon.

While Carlson, Schoenhorn and Mulcahy worked out last-minute details before the trial, Rob sat at the defense desk going over his notes, petrified at what was to come.

The atmosphere of the brick courtroom, where blue-uniformed sheriffs followed his every move, seemed hostile.

He angrily thought about Barbara Barrett, how she had appointed herself his sole judge and juror twenty-eight months before. She had never asked for his story. This time it would be different. This jury would hear both sides of the case.

It had taken two weeks to pick the jurors, four men and four women. Two of them were engineers, and a third had a brother who was an engineer. Four were grandparents. The average age was fifty-one.

McQueeney had taken detailed notes on the jurors and knew their faces. He would be able to connect names to each of them when they took their places in the jury box in a couple of hours.

He carefully reread his notes from voir dire:

• *Emma Aceto*, the white-haired grandmother from Manchester and the first juror selected, a porcelain artist and part-time keypunch operator. A little stern, but "auntly."

• *Lois J. Goodin*, a forty-four year old legal secretary from Glastonbury, married, with two sons in their twenties. Short dark hair swept back and streaked with grey, big blue eyes, a long face. Articulate and sure of herself.

• *Robert Luff*, a fifty-nine year old engineer from Simsbury, married, with two children in their twenties. Slight build, grey thinning hair, sharp facial features, glasses. He had served on a civil jury before and said he would have a hard time believing a six-year-old child. His answers had been short, to the point. Introspective.

• *Paula R. Gorobzov*, a petite sixty-one-year-old red haired grandmother from Windsor. Worked as a sales clerk in the lingerie department of a clothing store. One of the few college graduates on the jury—from Brown University. Had also once served on a civil jury. She liked the Matlock television detective show. A quick mind, but seemed a little flighty.

• *Maurice Back*, a sixty-four year old retired engineer with a Master's degree, also from Windsor, a grandfather with curly silver hair and an uncompromising way. His answers during voir dire had been forceful. He was a naturalized citizen who had been born in the Netherlands and had a strong Dutch accent. Had been a juror in a murder trial in Florida in 1970. He was a Bible school teacher at his church. Serious, stoic.

• *Hillary Jefferson*, the youngest juror at twenty-three. Attractive, with big eyes. Lived in Hartford, where she was born and raised, and worked as a supervisor at Sears. She had been raised by her grandparents and had one brother, who was an engineer. Described herself as a religious person who believed anyone who swore to tell the truth would tell the truth. Quiet, serious.

The two alternate jurors were both professional men.

• *James G. Stewart*, fifty-one years old, of Wethersfield, married, but with no children. He had twenty years experience in television production and now worked as a supervisor in the Corporate Communications department of CIGNA, one of the major insurance companies headquartered in the Hartford area. He worked nights directing the ten p.m. news at a local independent television station. Distinguished looking with silvery-white hair and glasses. Thoughtful, articulate.

• *Richard W. Allison*, a slender, handsome forty-nine-year-old vice president with Aetna Life & Casualty, had a Master's degree in marketing, had been through a divorce and had managed to retain custody of his children. He knew Jack Bailey through a fund-raising drive for a private school. He had spent two hours on the witness stand during voir dire, much of it answering questions about his ability to presume innocence and be impartial in light of one statement he made. "If the state didn't have a strong case," Allison had said, "we wouldn't be here."

These were the people on whom Rob's fate depended.

■CHAPTER NINETEEN■

The State vs. Robert McQueeney

The oak door to the right of Judge John F. Mulcahy, Jr. swung open at three twenty-seven p.m., and a sheriff led the eight jurors into the courtroom.

They filed solemnly past the witness stand and up one step into the jury box.

"Good afternoon ladies and gentlemen," Mulcahy's imposing voice greeted them. "Now we're going to proceed with the case of State vs. McQueeney. We'll begin by having the clerk take the required and necessary roll call."

Each juror stood, expressionless, as his or her name was read.

"Thank you, ladies and gentlemen," said the judge. "You may be seated."

The clerk, a young brown-haired man seated to the left of the judge, stood and turned toward McQueeney. "Will the defendant please stand," he asked.

Rob took a deep breath, eased back his chair and rose slowly, trembling, and tugging at his suit coat to straighten out the creases.

"Ladies and gentlemen of the jury," the clerk went on, "the accused has been charged in the following substituted information.

"In the Superior Court for the Hartford/New Britain Judicial District at Hartford, July 17, 1989, in Docket Number 53031, State of Connecticut vs. Robert McQueeney, in the first count John M. Bailey, State's attorney for the Judicial District of Hartford/New Britain, accuses Robert McQueeney of Bristol, Connecticut, of the crime of sexual assault in the first degree and alleges that on or about January 30th to February 1st, 1987, at or near 44 Bemis Street, Terryville, Connecticut, the said Robert McQueeney compelled another person, namely "K," to engage in sexual intercourse, the insertion of the penis into the anus, by the use of force against such person, or by the threat of the use of force against such person, which reasonably caused such person to fear physical injury to such person, in violation of Section 53a-70(a) of the Connecticut General Statutes."

Everyone was looking at the bearded man with his hands braced on the defense desk to steady himself. Rob's eyes never left the jurors. Their faces showed no emotion.

"In the second count," the clerk continued, "the State's attorney further accuses the said Robert McQueeney of the crime of sexual assault in the second degree, and alleges that on or about January 30th to February 1st, 1987, at or near 44 Bemis Street, Terryville, Connecticut, the said Robert Mc-Queeney engaged in sexual intercourse, the insertion of the penis into the anus, with another person, namely "K," and said other person was under the age of sixteen years, in violation of . . ."

McQueeney tensed, getting ready for the next wave.

"In the third count," the clerk droned on, "the said State's attorney further accuses the said Robert McQueeney of the crime of injury or risk of injury, and alleges that on or about January 30th to February 1st, 1987, at or near 44 Bemis Street, Terryville, Connecticut, the said Robert McQueeney did an act likely to impair the health or morals of the child, "K," namely the touching of the anus of the child with his penis, in a sexual and indecent manner . . ."

Rob lowered his eyes, humiliated and embarrassed.

Behind him his family could only imagine how he felt and what his face looked like to the jurors, a group of strangers who probably believed what they were hearing.

Ray had his arm around Ruth. There were tears in her eyes.

Jackie felt dizzy.

Her mother and son, Paul, had come. They had finally been initiated into the small circle of people who knew Rob's awful secret. Jackie's sister, Aimee, was in the spectator section also. They all wanted to show their support, though they wouldn't be able to come every day.

The clerk droned on: "To this information ladies and gentlemen of the jury, the accused has pled not guilty. It is your duty, therefore, to inquire whether he is guilty or not guilty. And if you find him guilty or not guilty, you will say so by your foreperson, and say no more. Kindly attend to the evidence.

"The defendant may be seated."

McQueeney groped behind him to find the arms of his chair and dropped into it. He exhaled and looked over at Schoenhorn, who gave him a reassuring nod.

Well, Rob shuddered to himself, here we go.

Mulcahy was explaining to the jurors in his patient, soothing voice that the substituted information was the document filed by the State in order to initiate prosecution.

"The document is simply accusatory in nature," he said. "It is certainly no evidence of guilt. And certainly no inference of guilt should be drawn or can be drawn from the fact that the State has filed this document."

Mulcahy went over the format of the trial, told the jurors that the burden of proof was on the prosecution, which would present its case first. Then the defense could also present evidence if it chose to do so.

"But please bear in mind always," the judge nodded to the jury, "that the State has the burden of proof in a criminal prosecution and that burden of proof is to prove all of the elements of each offense charged beyond a reasonable doubt."

He explained that the lawyers might object to the admission of certain evidence and that he might excuse the jury while the objection was debated.

"The province of the jury is to determine the facts of the case—what the facts are—from the evidence presented, and only from the evidence presented here in court during the orderly course of the trial," Mulcahy said. "You should thus, as the factfinding body in this proceeding, listen very carefully and attentively to all of the testimony of all of the witnesses and examine all of the exhibits very carefully and very thoroughly.

"All right, with those preliminary remarks, ladies and gentlemen, we will proceed with the evidence."

Carlson, dressed in a dark blue suit, got up from his desk and walked out the back door of the courtroom.

The McQueeneys watched Carlson as he returned with Vicki. She was dressed in a pink shirtwaist, cinched with a wide matching belt. Her young face was flushed, and she smiled to the jurors as she walked to the witness stand, giving them a glimpse of her dimples and her wide blue eyes.

She stepped up into the witness box, swore to tell the truth, gave her new name, Vicki Johnson, and her address. Feeling his anger rise, Rob leaned forward to catch the last words. He hadn't known where she and the children were living.

The clerk asked Vicki to spell the name of the street where she lived:

"I'll try," she giggled, flashing another smile.

Before Carlson began, he asked for permission to approach the bench. Schoenhorn joined him in a whispered huddle with Mulcahy.

The two lawyers presented quite a contrast.

Carlson was tall and stiff. He wore dark suits and kept his suit coat buttoned. When he wasn't adjusting his glasses, he would plunge his hands into pants pockets or fold his arms across his chest. He had a curious way of tucking his chin into his neck without bending his head while getting ready to say something.

Schoenhorn was slightly shorter, and looser. He wore light-colored suits and never buttoned his coat. His body was athletic, expressive. He always seemed to be moving, and as he walked and talked he waved his hands, making his coat flap.

The two men went back to their desks.

Carlson turned toward Mulcahy with a serious look. "I would ask that the jury be excused for a moment, your Honor."

Mulcahy turned toward the jury box. "Ladies and gentlemen, if you'd be kind enough please, to return to the jury deliberation room."

Carlson waited for the door to close behind them.

"The reason that I asked for that," he said, "is that just as I was going out to ask Mrs. Johnson to come in, she was in the process of being served with a motion for modification, signed by Mr. Hurvitz. And all I wanted to do was to find out from her whether or not she needs in any way to," he paused, "needs a few minutes before she starts her testimony. That's really all I wanted to inquire about."

Mulcahy gave him permission to question Vicki.

"Do you need time to read this or do you want to proceed with your testimony," Carlson asked.

"Can you explain it to me some?" she asked in the shy school-girlish voice which Rob had once totally believed.

"No," he said, "I really can't. That's not my job. I think you have a lawyer in this case, is that correct?"

"Yes," she said. "Yes, I do. He's not here at the moment though."

Schoenhorn offered an explanation.

"There was an understanding or suggestion that the witness was going to be moving out of state to Florida," he said. "And since her address was unavailable . . . all I know is that the only opportunity that Mr. Hurvitz had, to make sure she received notice concerning that would be in court."

Further, Schoenhorn said, he understood she was going to be served with the legal papers after she testified.

"When she comes in to testify in a criminal case, which I'm sure is traumatic for her, as it would be for any witness, to suddenly have a sheriff meet her out in the hall and serve her with a piece of paper that deals with the custody of a child . . ." The judge paused in mid-sentence and turned his attention to Vicki. "Do you have custody of the child now?"

"Yes I do."

Mulcahy asked Carlson for the state's position.

"Well," he responded, "it depends on the witness's state of mind now. That's all I'm interested in, your honor, is as to whether or not the witness was in any way upset by this."

"I can't understand why that would be done," said Mulcahy, shaking his head. "Well, what do you wish, ma'am?"

"I'm upset by it," said Vicki softly.

Mulcahy called a recess, so Carlson could have a few minutes with his witness. Schoenhorn had suffered his first setback less than half an hour into the trial.

When they returned to the courtroom at four-fifteen p.m., the judge decided to suspend Vicki's testimony and excuse the jury until the following morning. He asked a sheriff to bring the jurors back.

"Thank you ladies and gentlemen," he began. "You will recall that a few moments ago in my preliminary instruction to you, I did indicate that there may be occasions when we have to take up some matters outside of your presence, and it turns out that that instruction became quite accurate very quickly."

He excused the jurors until the next morning at eleven a.m.

"I want to caution you not to discuss this case with anyone, not to listen to any comments whatsoever by anyone concerning this case, and not to seek any information regarding the case at all from any source whatsoever," he said. "Now, if there are any media reports—I don't expect there will be any—but if there are any, you should not read any newspaper accounts of this case. You should not listen to or watch any television or radio accounts, if there are any regarding the case. And if anything along that line should come to your attention through inadvertence, you should immediately put that aside and direct your attention elsewhere."

He wished them a very pleasant evening.

All the McQueeneys were petrified that the press might hunt them down. Every time a strange face appeared at the rear door of their homes they looked for a reporter's notebook. It was reassuring to hear Mulcahy say he didn't expect any media reports.

After the jurors left, Mulcahy asked Schoenhorn to elaborate on what had happened.

"It was my understanding, your Honor," he said, "that information came to our office this morning from a relative of the witness—a close relative—that it was his understanding that she was either already in the process of transferring her residency to Florida or was about to do so. I shared that information with my partner, Attorney Hurvitz, who represents Mr. McQueeney in the domestic matter and in the custody matter and had represented him in the divorce matter."

Schoenhorn said Carlson told him earlier in the afternoon that he had been aware of the planned Florida move, but that Vicki and her husband didn't go because a job fell through. Instead they had moved to Glastonbury, near Hartford.

Of concern to Hurvitz, Schoenhorn said, were the issues of custody and visitation.

"It's been almost two years, your Honor, since my client has seen his children," he continued. "There was a belief that the witness intended, right after her son's testimony tomorrow, to possibly relocate out of state, and therefore, be outside the jurisdiction of the court. My partner, with at least reason, put together a motion for a hearing on that issue."

Carlson pointed out that Vicki still had a job in Connecticut.

"I've made my feelings known," the judge said. "I certainly don't think that it's appropriate to serve a witness in a criminal case with a motion to modify custody."

Mulcahy turned his attention to the matter that would be taken up the following morning.

"As I understand it," he said, "what the defense intends to put on is the evidence of an expert or experts concerning anatomical dolls. Is that correct?"

"That's correct," said Schoenhorn. "It'll just be one, I believe."

The judge brought up another issue before adjourning for the day. He noted that the trial was being tape-recorded by a court monitor.

"Counsel have brought to my attention that they believe other recordation equipment is present in the courtroom," Mulcahy said. "Is that correct, gentlemen?"

"Well," Carlson growled, "I didn't bring it to your attention."

"I understand there may be a microcassette recorder in the courtroom, your Honor," said Schoenhorn.

He had learned about the tape recorder through a note passed to him by Ray McQueeney. Jackie's mother had spotted it first, lying on the bench next to a young woman. Schoenhorn knew the firm of Gould, Killian and Wynne represented Barbara Barrett and Langley Center in the malpractice lawsuit.

212

"Specifically," said the judge, "I take it, it's a young lady on the left side of the courtroom?"

He turned toward the spectator benches.

"Ma'am, I don't know if you have any connection with this case or not . . . Would you care to identify yourself?"

The young woman stood nervously twisting a lock of her hair. She appeared to be about twenty years old. "My name is Nancy Gould," she said. "And I'm with the law firm of Gould, Killian and Wynne."

"I see," said Mulcahy. "Now are you an attorney, ma'am?"

"No, I'm not."

"Are you a paralegal?"

"I'm in law school and . . ."

"Oh, I see," said the judge. "Whereabouts do you go to law school?"

"Boston University."

"Oh," he said. "I would suggest that before anything is recorded in court, that an attorney with your firm be here and request permission to do so." Mulcahy asked whether Carlson or Schoenhorn had anything to say.

"Yes, your Honor," said Schoenhorn. "I believe that her firm represents one of the State's witnesses."

Schoenhorn told Mulcahy he was concerned about the recorder for two reasons.

"If it picks up conversations of people that do not consent to that conversation, it's a federal crime, number one, aside from the whole issue of recording things that go on in a courtroom," he said. "There's also an issue of a sequestration order."

"That's primarily what I was concerned with," the judge said. "The person who's represented by that firm will be a witness in this case? Is that correct? Mr. Carlson, do you have any thoughts on it?"

"Well, probably," responded Carlson, "but none that I'd like to put on the record right now."

Gould was asked whether she had recorded anything.

"No," she said, "it hasn't been turned on."

Mulcahy advised her to inform the lawyers at her firm of what happened in court.

"Anything further at this point?" the judge asked.

"Sounds like enough for one day to me," said Carlson.
"All right," said Mulcahy. "We'll adjourn."

The next morning Schoenhorn presented his first witness
in the case, but the jury wasn't allowed to hear the testimony.

Dr. Kenneth Robson was called to testify before the judge
in support of a motion Schoenhorn filed to present evidence
opposing the validity of Barbara Barrett's testimony. The motion asked Mulcahy to bar the State from presenting any evidence or testimony based on the use of anatomically-correct
dolls.

Robson was a child and adolescent psychiatrist associated
with Yale University, the University of Connecticut, and the Institute of Living, a prestigious psychiatric hospital in Hartford.
He was an expert in the use of dolls and had worked extensively
with three- to five-year-old children.

Robson, a short balding man with white bushy eyebrows,
strode to the witness stand.

Schoenhorn moved toward the empty jury box, clasped his
hands together at belt level, and began by leading his witness
through his qualifications. After fifteen minutes, Mulcahy declared Robson fit to testify as an expert in child psychiatry.

"Incidentally, Doctor," Schoenhorn went on, "are you familiar with the professional title of MCW?" (Referring to the
initials Barbara Barrett used after her name.)

"No, I'm not, Mr. Schoenhorn."

"Or the title, Masters in Child Welfare?"

"No, I'm not, Mr. Schoenhorn," Robson frowned.

"Are you familiar with the use among child mental health
professionals of so-called anatomically-correct dolls?"

"Yes, I am."

"Would you please indicate what your familiarity is with
that subject?"

Robson said he did not use anatomical dolls, but had
worked with professionals who did and had kept current with
literature on the subject. "So I'm familiar with their use and

familiar with the controversies surrounding their use and the hazards as well as the benefits of their use," he said.

"Using dolls to explore allegations of sexual abuse can lead to unreliable conclusions," he said definitively. "One of the major problems is that children three to five years old are preoccupied with anatomy in general, and are particularly curious about genital anatomy.

"It is difficult to separate the normal developmental interest of such children in those areas from what appears to be sexual abuse," he said. "Children of that age have seen genitals while bathing with parents or bathing with siblings. They've frequently made contact with genitals, playfully, as children that age do.

"It's easy to confuse that kind of developmental play with sexual abuse. And the hazards are so serious and the consequences so grave that I have felt that that is a significant hazard in their use."

Robson spoke masterfully and methodically, choosing his words carefully. He leaned forward in his chair when making a point, and demonstrated with his hands.

Schoenhorn said he had no further questions, and Carlson got out of his chair to begin his cross-examination. He stood at the corner of his desk, arms folded across his chest, and asked Robson to describe anatomical dolls.

"Dolls in which the genitalia are explicitly designed and incorporated into the dolls so that there is no mistaking male from female," he explained, continuing that the male doll had both a penis and anal opening.

"You have already told us some of the hazards, I guess," Carlson said. "Could you tell us some of the benefits, please?"

"Children of that age," said Robson, "often have a hard time remembering events clearly. They tend to do so more readily when they see a familiar stimulus that helps them recognize. And in recognizing, they remember more readily and, allegedly, more accurately. That's one of the potential benefits."

Carlson asked him about his opinion that anatomical dolls, when used in isolation, could lead to unreliable conclusions. "What other types of information would you suggest be sought after?" the prosecutor asked.

"One would want a careful developmental history of the child," Robson said patiently, "and that would require a good deal of time. It would include such things as toilet training, sleep habits and the family ecology in terms of who sleeps where, and whether bathroom doors are open or shut, what bathing practices and toileting practices are—extremely important information."

Other information, he said, should include a school history; the relationship between the child and each of the parents; the relationship of the parents to each other; the clinical status of the parents; the early lives of the parents and their sexual habits; whether a divorce is contemplated or in process; the details of the divorce; custodial wishes of the parents; what custodial arrangement would be in the best interests of the child; and a medical history of the child, including a thorough physical examination.

"You certainly covered many factors there," Mulcahy interrupted. "One that I just didn't quite understand. You said the clinical status of either or both parents?"

"Yes," answered Robson.

"What did you mean by that, sir?"

"Well," said Robson, leaning forward, "particularly in situations where abuse has been, sexual abuse has been alleged, and if a divorce is being contemplated or is in process, generally for most adults, that is a time of increased psychological vulnerability and stress.

"And if they're a parent, frequently they are desperate in terms of feeling that perhaps the only thing they can keep is a child. All of us know about those situations in one way or another, unfortunately. And the clinical status of a parent—for example if they're sufficiently troubled or disturbed—is likely to contribute to the distortion of information that they might share."

"By clinical status, you mean the psychological stress level or status of the parents?" the judge asked.

"Yes."

Carlson asked Robson to explain why he would be interested in the custody wishes of the parents.

"There are few situations where human desperation

reaches the points it does in the dissolution of families," Robson answered shaking his head slowly. "Information from parents in such situations is highly suspect. And it's very difficult to determine the accuracy of it."

Mulcahy broke in with a question. He asked whether the scientific community shared Robson's view that dolls, used in isolation, are not reliable.

"I would say among fully-trained mental health professionals, it is very much the prevailing view," he answered. "There are varieties of professionals or semi-professionals or non-professionals conducting such allegations around the country with increasing frequency, and this isn't the setting in which to discuss that. But there is no quality control for unlicensed professionals."

Rob swung his swivel chair toward his family behind him and grinned. Robson was really doing well.

The judge, fascinated by Robson's testimony, questioned him extensively.

Mulcahy asked why people resort to using such things as dolls, drawings and coloring books while investigating allegations of sexual abuse.

"They resort to them generally because particularly in the three-to-five year old age group, verbal communication and memory are poor substitutes for play," Robson said. "In general the three-to-five year old's language is play, rather than words for the most part."

Mulcahy pressed Robson, trying to get him to admit dolls and drawings could be legitimate ways of communicating with a child. The doctor didn't agree.

"Actually, it's for the benefit of the child, is it not, in terms of assisting the child in communicating?" asked Mulcahy.

"That's the design, Your Honor. Though it is at the same time the hazard."

It was almost noon.

The judge excused Robson and called a recess, saying he would not rule on Schoenhorn's doll motion until it was time for Barrett to take the witness stand.

■CHAPTER TWENTY■

For The Prosecution

The next morning the prosecution recalled Vicki to the stand. The clerk reminded her she had already been sworn.

After he asked some preliminary questions, Carlson said, "I think you are going to have to keep your voice up."

"Perhaps if you could just talk closer to the microphone," suggested Mulcahy.

Vicki smiled at the jurors, who were back in their seats. She smiled again while Rob's heart thudded. He knew just how charming that smile could be, and how deceptive. She shifted her chair forward and nodded to the prosecutor, who continued his questions.

When Carlson asked Vicki if she was presently married she replied, "Yes, I am."

"Alright, and to whom are you married?"

"Bruce Johnson."

"And for how long have you been married to Bruce Johnson?"

"A little over a year."

"Alright, do you have children?"

"Yes, I do."

"I'm going to show you a document marked court's exhibit A." Carlson walked to the witness box with a piece of paper. "And there's a name on there, correct?"

"Yes."

"Alright. And whether or not the person whose name appears under the 'name of witness' in court's exhibit A is your son?"

"Yes, it is."

"What we'd like to have you do from now on, then, is refer to that individual as 'my son,' rather than by either his Christian name or his surname."

She kept glancing toward the back of the courtroom during pauses between some of Carlson's questions. Rob, watching the jurors intently, noticed they, too, were watching her.

"Now were you at some point in time married to an individual named Robert McQueeney?"

"Yes, I was."

"Alright. And is Robert McQueeney here in the courtroom today?"

"Yes, he is."

"Point him out please."

"Right over there," she pointed. Rob's glaring eyes locked briefly with hers. Then she quickly lowered hers and answered a few more specific questions about Rob's attire.

"All right," Mulcahy said. "The record may reflect that the witness has identified the defendant."

Rob's stomach churned, his anger rose once again. How could she have done this to him? He stared at Vicki with as much disgust as he could reflect in his eyes. Behind him, his mother and Jackie were doing the same, hoping that their reflected feelings would rattle her, make her finally admit Rob's innocence. They hadn't taken their eyes off Vicki since the moment she walked into the courtroom.

Rob had warned his mother before court not to say anything out loud or make any sounds. "You don't want to get thrown out," he had said.

Carlson continued his preliminary questioning—the date of Vicki's marriage to Rob, the date when she had left him and filed for divorce and the places she had lived after leaving him.

At one o'clock p.m., Mulcahy adjourned for the luncheon recess.

When court reconvened, the clerk announced that one of the jurors, Paula Gorobzov, the red-haired grandmother, was having trouble hearing Vicki's testimony.

The court monitor was asked to replay the audio tape of the final questions and answers before lunch. "Certainly, if there's any problem with hearing," the judge told the jurors, "please bring that to our attention right away by raising your hand, just so that we know about it."

Carlson resumed this examination, taking up his post at the corner of his desk next to the jury box. There were long pauses between questions as he meticulously studied his notes on the desk. He had a military way of phrasing each question.

He asked Vicki "whether or not during the upbringing of your son and before the last weekend in January of 1987, you had taught your son about body parts?"

"Yes, I had."

"Alright, can you tell us how it is that you did that, or what you did?"

"Just explained it to him. Like if he was going to the bathroom, I'd say that's his penis, or . . ."

"Alright. And as it relates, for example, to the word penis, what word—I mean, excuse me—to the body part known as the penis, what would you use?"

"He would say penis."

Carlson worked his way to the weekend of January 30, through February 1, 1987, and what Vicki saw the night Rob returned the children to her after tobogganing.

"Now, as to whether or not there was any conversation or interaction between your son and Mr. McQueeney?"

"Yes, there was."

"And could you tell us what that was, please?"

"Rob had bent down to say good-bye to the kids and Keefe screamed out, 'You hurt me. You hurt me,' screaming at the top of his lungs. Rob grabbed my son, held him tight and said, 'It's okay, it's okay.' And after a minute or two he calmed down."

Rob was on the edge of his chair, scribbling hard on his note pad. That's a lie, he screamed to himself. Can't they all see she's lying?

"Who was it who calmed down?"

"My son."

"And then whether or not there was any further conversation about this between or among you, your son and Rob?"

"No, we didn't discuss it."

Vicki motioned to the judge for a drink of water. She sipped slowly as if she were faint, then nodded to Carlson that she was ready to continue.

"Now whether or not there was any conversation between Mr. McQueeney about any physical condition as it relates to your son?"

"He told me that he had given Keefe a bath, and when he was washing him, Keefe complained that his bottom was hurting, his anus."

"Alright. And whether or not that Mr. McQueeney indicated to you that he had done anything in relationship to your son because of that complaint?"

"He said he had put some powder on it."

The judge interrupted. "Now I know it's difficult to keep it in mind, but I have stressed to counsel, and I would just stress that in compliance with the necessary directive under the rules, if possible, we should try to refer to your son as simply your son."

"I'm sorry," Vicki murmured.

"No," said Mulcahy, "I understand."

Carlson continued, "Would you indicate to us please, what it is that you did to check your son, physically?"

"Well, he was laying in the bed, and I pulled his buttocks apart and checked his anus. And it was red, inflamed, and swollen. There was a big circle. I put some vaseline on it, and I believe cornstarch powder."

"Had you ever seen a mark like that on him before?"

"No, I hadn't."

"What is it that your son told you on the evening of Sunday, February 1, 1987, as it relates to how it is that he came to be in that physical condition?"

"He talked about playing a game, Ghostbusters, and the Marshmallow Man jumped on little kids, and he kind of said 'smothered them.' And if they didn't lay still, they had to stay in their room the next day. And he kept repeating that story. He was upset toward it."

"Okay. And was there anything further that your son said

other than what you've just testified to . . . on that evening, I mean?"

"I believe that evening, I'm almost positive it was the same evening, he said that his father had stuck his hand in his anus so far until it hurt." Vicki pointed to her elbow.

The judge interrupted.

"Ladies and gentlemen," he turned toward the jurors. "That testimony by this witness, as you're aware, is a statement made by the witness concerning the out-of-court statement of the complainant, the witness's son. And I want to caution you that ordinarily out-of-court statements by an individual are not admissible in evidence.

"However, our law does have an exception to that rule, and that is the exception referred to as constancy of accusation. And that evidence is presented solely for the purpose of undertaking to demonstrate that the complainant child was constant in the accusation. It is not offered as direct proof that a particular incident took place."

Mulcahy motioned to Carlson to continue.

Carlson questioned Vicki about Keefe's first visit to Langley Center and then asked whether she talked with her son before she took him the second time.

"Yes."

"Alright. And would you tell us what that conversation was?"

"He talked more about Marshmallow Man, and he said that it was his father that had put his finger in his rectum." Her voice was fading. "He told me he didn't want to tell me a lot about it because I wouldn't like it." She looked toward the jury box, tears in her eyes.

"Alright. Whether or not your son told you where it was that this game was taking place?"

"At his father's house."

"Whether or not your son indicated to you what happened after this game was over, or at the time the game was ending?"

"He said that his father used to wash him up," she whispered.

Mulcahy leaned over the edge of his desk next to the witness box. "Try to keep your voice up, ma'am, please," he said.

Vicki nodded meekly.

Carlson asked whether her son had told her anything else. "It had to be after the second visit." She seemed to be struggling to talk. "It was really close together that he had said his father had put his penis in his heinie. I'm not sure what visit it is though."

"And did your son describe to you any more particularly exactly how that was done?"

"He was on the couch, and I guess he was having him sleep there with him. Keefe said that it was really cold in the house."

Vicki slumped in the witness chair, weeping.

Rob groaned to himself. She could be so damned appealing if you didn't know her.

"Alright," said the judge. "We'll just take a moment, and again, remember you have to keep your voice up, ma'am. We'll take a moment."

Schoenhorn and McQueeney intently watched the jurors, trying to gauge the effect of the breakdown. It was the kind of scene Schoenhorn had worried about since the deposition.

Vicki brushed the tears away, took a deep breath and nodded toward Mulcahy.

"All right. Perhaps we could proceed now. Mr. Carlson?"

"Can you tell us where it was that you were when you had this conversation between your son and you?"

"I believe in the living room, on the couch."

"And whether or not any other person or persons were present at that time, if you remember?"

"I believe Bruce was."

Rob put down his pen and frowned as Carlson completed his direct examination. The judge excused the jury and called the afternoon recess. Ruth and Jackie followed Vicki with their beam of hate as she walked past them out of the courtroom.

When the trial reconvened, Schoenhorn began his cross-examination.

He had been preparing for two weeks. Schoenhorn looked over at Rob, then got out of his chair, nodding a little to indicate to his client that he was ready. He slowly walked to within a foot of the witness stand. He stared directly into Vicki's eyes for a long moment and then swung around toward the jury box.

"I guess we're all interested in the answer to this question." He was talking to Vicki, but looking at the jury. "When you had your son at Dr. Pandit's, and he was examining your son, what did you see at that point?"

"I just saw him examining him."

"Well," Schoenhorn paused and spread his arms. "Did you see anything wrong with your son at that point?"

"I had been . . ." she hesitated.

"I'm asking at Dr. Pandit's office."

"I didn't look at his rectum at that point."

Schoenhorn hesitated, his face thoughtful and questioning, "You didn't look?" Schoenhorn let the words hang in the air.

Moments passed before Vicki's quiet answer.

"No."

Schoenhorn picked up the pace.

"In any event, without saying what anyone told you after you had been to the doctor's office, you were aware of the fact that there were no medical findings, correct?"

"Yes," Vicki answered meekly.

He began asking questions about Vicki's marriage to Rob.

Then he turned to the subject of the divorce, "You left Rob in 1986, correct?"

"I believe so."

"In fact, you left without him knowing where you were going, correct?"

"Yes."

"And that was before he got served with the papers, correct?"

"Yes."

"In other words," Schoenhorn turned toward the jury box, a momentary annoyance creeping into his voice, "one day you were just gone with the children, and then a few days later, he found out by getting the divorce papers, correct?"

"No, he was supposed to be served that day, when he came home from work."

"But you didn't mention to him you were going to serve him with divorce papers, did you?"

"No."

"Just one day you were gone, right?"

224

"Yes."

"Was he at work when you packed?"

"Yes."

Schoenhorn turned his attention to Bruce. "At some point you moved in with Bruce Johnson, correct?"

"Yes."

"And in fact, you met Bruce Johnson prior to the time that you left Rob, correct?"

"Yes," Vicki looked distinctly uncomfortable now.

"And in fact, on at least one occasion, you had been out socially with Bruce Johnson prior to the time you left Rob, yes?"

"Not only with him."

"Well, did you or did you not on at least one occasion go out socially with Bruce Johnson prior to the time that you left Rob. Yes or no?"

"Depends how you're referring to 'with Bruce Johnson.' Not alone with him, no."

"Well . . ."

"In a crowd, yes."

Rob felt she seemed to be avoiding Schoenhorn's questions.

Schoenhorn turned to Mulcahy. "Excuse me, your Honor. I think maybe the witness needs to be directed to answer the specific questions."

"Well, yes," the judge said. "The answer should be as direct as possible, and it cannot be answered with a question back to counsel."

"I'm not sure exactly how he's saying it," said Vicki, turning meek again.

"All right," said Mulcahy. "But do your best."

Schoenhorn tried again, enunciating his words as though he was talking to a third-grader: "This is a yes or no question, alright? At any time, did you go someplace with Bruce Johnson prior to the time that you left Rob?"

"Yes, I did."

As the questioning continued, Vicki's shy demeanor visibly changed, she grew increasingly combative. She refused to admit that she didn't want Rob to see the children after she left him, and that she wouldn't tell him where she was living.

Schoenhorn went back to the defense desk and got a copy of the deposition to remind Vicki what she had said more than two years earlier.

Jackie and Rob's mother were convinced at this point that Vicki was rattled. She kept glancing back toward them between questions, as if checking to see if they were still glaring at her.

"Now your divorce lawyer, I think you already indicated, was John Clifford, correct?"

"Yes, he was."

"And how did you end up with Attorney John Clifford? Who recommended him."

"I called their office."

"Isn't it a fact," Schoenhorn looked toward the jury box, "that Bruce recommended him?"

"Not him, per se, no."

"Isn't it a fact," he was still looking at the jurors, "that he recommended his law firm?"

"Yes, he recommended the law firm."

Schoenhorn said he also understood that Bruce recommended she take the children to the Langley Center.

"Yes, he did."

"In fact, he called for you, didn't he?"

"Yes, he did."

"And he had a friend who was either the director or the assistant director of the Langley Center, correct?"

"I'm not sure who his friend was, but he had a friend that . . ."

"Somebody in some position of authority at Langley Center?"

"I don't know what position he held."

"OK. Do you remember testifying at the deposition that you believed it was the director or assistant director? This was back in March of 1987."

"I don't remember."

"Would you like to have your memory refreshed, perhaps?"

"Sure." Vicki said it as though she were humoring him.

Schoenhorn frowned, turned away from the witness stand

and walked slowly to the defense desk. He slapped his hand down onto a copy of the deposition. The sound shot through the courtroom. He returned to the witness box and handed the transcript to Vicki.

"Starting here," he pointed, "and just read down to there. See if it refreshes your memory."

He looked at the jurors, shaking his head slightly, as she read.

"Yes," she said finally.

"Now, didn't you testify that Bruce knew the director there? Isn't that what you said?"

"I said it, but to this day, I don't remember if he was a director."

Schoenhorn asked her whether the children had a rough time with the divorce. Once again, she said she couldn't remember, and he handed her the deposition. She studied it and admitted they did have a rough time.

"Isn't it true that some months before the weekend in question that we're talking about, Keefe started having problems wiping himself after going to the bathroom?"

"For a period of time—I'm not sure exactly how long—yes."

"And you never mentioned to Rob about that at all, did you? That he should watch out for that or be careful because Keefe . . . sorry, K is not wiping himself. Anything like that?"

"I believe I did, but I can't remember if I did or didn't."

"This is a true or false question. You believe that Rob didn't really know much about raising kids. Isn't that right?"

"True."

"And that's why you wanted sole custody of the children, with just visitation rights with Rob, correct?"

"No."

"Well, isn't it true you wanted sole custody of those children?"

"Because of the fact that I think he wasn't really interested in them that much."

McQueeney clenched his teeth.

Schoenhorn began questioning Vicki about *the* weekend,

227

when Rob returned the kids to the Goshen house where Vicki was living with Bruce.

"Now, let's talk about the specific words that Rob said to you concerning Keefe's bottom, okay? What specifically did Rob say to you about your son's bottom?"

"He said that he was giving him a bath. He was washing him, and I believe he said the Keefe was crying that his bottom hurt, and he put some powder on it."

"He didn't mention that he saw it looked red?"

"I don't remember."

"You don't remember?" Schoenhorn looked toward the jury, incredulous.

"No."

"Well again," he sighed, "let me show you your deposition. Again, I'm doing this just to refresh your memory."

"Sure."

"And again, during the whole deposition back in March of 1987, you were under oath, correct?"

"Yes."

"And I take it also your memory was a lot better in March of 1987 as to what happened one month before than it is now, two and a half years later? Is that a fair statement?"

"I would say so."

He asked her to read a portion of the deposition.

"Now specifically, did Rob tell you that your son's bottom was red?"

"Today, I don't remember. But back then I said it, yes."

"All right. And as far as you're concerned, you were telling the truth back in 1987. Is that correct?"

"Yes."

Schoenhorn asked her to turn her attention to her sworn statement she gave to police on February 10, 1987.

"If I remember correctly, I cried through that statement."

McQueeney swiveled toward his family with a look of disgust. They knew how Vicki could turn on the tears.

"In fact," Schoenhorn went on, "in the statement of February 10th, there was not yet any allegation proven, or even shown, regarding sexual abuse. Isn't that true? On February

10th, that was before there were even any statements from your son that would suggest there was something sexual?"

"He said that he had put his fingers in his rectum."

"Fingers or finger?"

"I don't remember the exact words," she said hesitating again.

"Well, you were trying to be fairly accurate when you gave the statement, weren't you?"

"Yes."

Schoenhorn handed her a copy of the statement she gave to the police. "Didn't you say that Keefe said his father put his finger in his heinie? Isn't that what he said?"

"That's what it says there."

Schoenhorn frowned. He asked Vicki how she applied the vaseline to Keefe's bottom when she saw the redness.

"My finger," she answered.

Schoenhorn paused, then looked at her with a stern expression.

"This is a serious proceeding that we're involved in here, correct?"

"Yes."

"So you want to be as accurate as possible, is that right?" Schoenhorn said speaking slowly.

"Yes."

"You don't want anyone to say you're making things up, right?"

"Of course not."

He handed her the statement again. His voice was stronger now. "Isn't it correct that in your statement, the only thing you said was, in that regard, Keefe said his father put his finger in his heinie real far and it hurt. Do you remember writing that, or signing that?"

"I read it and signed it, yes."

"Just so we're clear on that, whatever . . . whether he said it was hand or finger, he never said penis at that point, correct?"

"Not that I remember, no."

"And, if he had, I assume you would have put that down, right . . . Yes?"

Vicki nodded.

"You have to answer out loud," Schoenhorn reminded her. "Yes."

He asked whether she took her son to see Keefe's pediatrician immediately after seeing his red bottom.

"No, I didn't."

He paused and shook his head.

"It was not of concern enough for you at that point to go take your son to a medical doctor, correct?"

"It wasn't that it wasn't of concern. I figured it was him not wiping his bottom."

Schoenhorn reminded her that she had taken her son to Dr. Pandit at the request of Langley Center. He asked whether she ever told anyone at the center that examination was negative.

"I don't remember."

"Do you recall telling Mrs. Barrett that your son had said his father put his finger up his heinie, and it hurt, or up his bottom, and it hurt?"

"No, I don't remember."

With surprise, Schoenhorn turned toward the jury, "You don't remember?" he said again letting Vicki's words hang into the air.

"I don't think I did, no."

"Did you tell Mrs. Barrett about the custody dispute, that you wanted sole custody and Rob wanted joint custody?"

"Not that I remember, no." Vicki colored slightly.

"Nobody ever asked you about that?"

"Not that I remember."

"And correct me if I'm wrong, you yourself, as an adolescent, were—there was an attempt to sexually molest you, correct, by a neighbor, right?"

Carlson, who had been watching with his arms folded across his chest, jumped out of his chair.

"Well, I'm going to object to this," he said, "on the grounds of relevance and materiality, plus privacy. But that's less important at the moment."

The judge excused the jury before hearing more.

Schoenhorn asked that the judge also excuse Vicki. "I'm

going to suggest to the court things that I intend to prove and offer," he said, "and I don't think it's appropriate for the witness to hear about other evidence."

Carlson said he had no objection to sending Vicki from the courtroom, and the judge excused her.

After Vicki left, Mulcahy let Schoenhorn speak first.

"The defense in this case is based on fabrication, not just by the child, but by the mother and the mother's then-boyfriend," said Schoenhorn forcefully. Carlson's voice had a deep methodical tone. Schoenhorn had a broader range. His voice ranged from a resonant whisper to a roar. "The fact that she, herself, had been molested as a child and had had some dealing in how these things are treated and what to do about them is certainly relevant to the defense."

The judge questioned the connection between a prior sexual assault and fabrication. "Simply because she has been the victim," he asked, "how does that indicate that she would be inclined to fabricate?"

"We are talking," said Schoenhorn, "about the heart of the defense, that it was fabricated for purposes of denying him visitation, taking an incident, using that as the basis for getting not only sole custody, but no visitation by him. Under those circumstances, her own involvement, she'd know what to do."

Mulcahy overruled his point.

"The objection is sustained."

But the point had been made to the jury.

It was nearly five o'clock p.m. The judge called Vicki back into the courtroom and reminded her of the sequestration order.

"I want to instruct you that as part of that order, that you're not to discuss your testimony at all, your testimony today, or what you will be testifying to with anyone since you will be resuming the stand tomorrow," he said. "And of course, that's true after your testimony is completed. It should not be discussed with anyone at all. Do you understand that?"

"Yes, your Honor," she smiled.

"You may step down," he said. "All right, Sheriff, you can adjourn court please."

Vicki had to walk through the McQueeney stares as she left the courtroom to go home to Glastonbury—and Bruce.

Schoenhorn began his questioning Thursday morning with a copy of Vicki's deposition in his hand.

The defense attorney told her he wanted to talk about the night Rob returned the children to the house. He reminded her what she had said on the witness stand Wednesday while Carlson was questioning her.

"When your son said, 'You hurt me, you hurt me,' you said that Rob grabbed him. Is that right?"

"Right."

"He hugged him," Schoenhorn said flatly. "Isn't that what you mean?"

She paused. "That's what I said in the deposition, didn't I?"

"Right . . . Well, that's the truth, right? He hugged him. Correct? And then after a couple of minutes, your son stopped crying, correct?"

"Ummm hmm . . . Yes." Schoenhorn's eyes searched her face.

"And then I believe you said that your son was fine. Correct?"

"Yes, he was."

Through the next hour and a half, Schoenhorn continued to hammer at her story, using the deposition to expose what he considered the many inconsistencies and contradictions.

He centered on one crucial point. The date when Vicki remembered Keefe saying that his father had put his penis in his anus—the day that a seemingly innocent finger applying powder to a sore spot became a penis—and a rape.

"So let's talk now about the specific allegation, which you know, you have to say, that's a very serious allegation. Isn't that? Don't you agree?"

"Yes, it is."

Schoenhorn reminded her that she testified Keefe told her

his father put his penis in his bottom. "You don't remember exactly when that occurred, correct?"

"I believe it was . . ."

"I'm not asking what you believe," he said exasperated. "Whether you know, right now, what day that was?"

"It was after I made the police report."

"In other words at least through the date of February 10th, correct, he hadn't said it?"

"Right."

McQueeney nodded almost imperceptibly to himself as he took notes, mentally cheering on his lawyer.

Trying a different tact, Schoenhorn asked whether Vicki remembered getting a copy of Barbara Barrett's February 19th, report that was given to the police.

"I couldn't tell you," she said softly. "I got a lot of papers from Langley Center."

"Isn't this something that Bruce went and picked up and gave you a copy of?"

"I don't know. I couldn't tell you."

The judge interrupted. "I'm sorry, ma'am. I can't hear. Keep your . . ."

"I don't know. I couldn't tell you." It was almost a yell. Vicki's composure was disintegrating.

"Isn't it a fact," Schoenhorn asked, "that as far as anything that your son told you about penis and Rob, it was after you received a report from Langley Center? The first of whatever number of reports you received?"

Her voice shook as she answered. "I couldn't tell you. I don't know. I can't remember the date of the first time he told me that."

Schoenhorn went back to the deposition, once again playing to the jury, trying to expose the truth.

"Isn't it true that nowhere during the deposition did you ever say that your son—and again the deposition was in March, right?"

"Yes, it was."

"Nowhere during the entire time of that deposition did you ever say that your son told you that Rob put his penis in your son's bottom?"

233

"I don't recall." She was avoiding Schoenhorn's eyes.

He continued to press the point, but Vicki refused to admit it.

Schoenhorn turned his attention to the Marshmallow Man game. He asked Vicki if she had seen the movie *Ghostbusters*.

"Yes, I did."

He asked how many times Keefe had seen the movie. Vicki couldn't remember, but said it was one of the boy's favorite movies.

"And isn't there a Marshmallow Man in that movie?"

"Yes, there is."

"If I could just have a moment, your Honor?" Schoenhorn walked to the defense desk and picked up a photograph. He showed it to Vicki.

"Who's this?" he asked, looking at the jurors.

"Marshmallow Man," she said softly.

"You'll have to speak up so the jury can hear you."

"Marshmallow Man." Her voice sounded hollow.

Schoenhorn had the picture marked as an exhibit. It was handed first to the judge and then passed through the jury.

Carlson suggested two of his exhibits, photographs of Keefe and the Bemis Street house, be shown to the jurors as well because they had not seen them.

As the photographs were circulated, Paula Gorobzov raised her hand. "I just had a question about the pictures," she called to the judge.

"I'm sorry, jurors can't ask questions," Mulcahy said kindly. "These are exhibits and at this point, the members of the jury should look at and view those exhibits carefully."

Schoenhorn resumed his cross-examination by asking Vicki about the role of Marshmallow Man in the *Ghostbusters* movie.

"If I remember correctly, he walked through the town at the end."

"It looks like he's fairly large, isn't that right?"

"Right."

"Much bigger than the cars, correct?"

"Correct."

"And, in fact, doesn't he crush cars?"

"Yes, he does."

"In other words, he's this giant monster, isn't he?"

He asked her what words Keefe used to describe the Marshmallow Man game. She said she couldn't remember.

He showed her the statement she gave to the police, and read one sentence of it into the trial record: "K said Marshmallow Man jumps on little kids, covers their mouth. He squashes them."

Schoenhorn completed his questioning shortly before noon. Carlson's redirect examination was brief. One of the issues he addressed was the description of the Marshmallow Man game Vicki gave in her police statement.

"Mr. Schoenhorn asked you about a certain sentence that you gave in there," Carlson said. "Is that correct?"

"I believe so, yes."

"And whether or not there was a complete recitation of what you said at that time about the Marshmallow Man?"

"No, it wasn't complete . . . what he said."

"All right. If you could just read the next sentence after the sentence that Mr. Schoenhorn either read to you or had you read, which included the word, 'squash'." Carlson left his post by the corner of the prosecution desk to hand her a copy of the statement.

"My son said Marshmallow Man jumps on little kids, covers their mouth. He squashes them. They have to stay very still. If they move or talk, they have to stay in the house the whole next day."

"All right. And whether or not there is other information about the Marshmallow Man in there?"

"Yes."

"All right. Would you read that information, please?"

Vicki's face looked composed again.

"When they play Marshmallow Man, they go to sleep on the couch. He said his father don't have any clothes on, and he has to lie still and be quiet. His father rubs him and tells him how much he loves him. K said his father puts his finger in his heinie real far and it hurts."

"All right. Did he say what else?"

"K said after they are done playing Marshmallow Man, it's

very messy. K said his father covers him up with a sheet, brings him in the bathroom, cleans him up very well. K said it's sandy, and then puts his PJs on, and he goes back on the couch."

Carlson completed his questioning, and Schoenhorn followed up on the issue of the police report.

"Did you also say in your statement on February 10, 1987: 'I have asked Keefe to play Marshmallow Man with me. Keefe said you wouldn't like that, and that it took a long time and you're very very tired afterwards?' "

"Correct."

Minutes later Vicki was excused from the witness stand. She had testified for almost six hours over two days.

Ruth focused her exhausted eyes, burning with contempt, on Vicki as she walked by for the last time.

CHAPTER TWENTY-ONE

A Small Boy

After arriving at court Friday morning, the jurors were escorted to the deliberation room while the lawyers and the judge attended to matters the jurors were not allowed to hear.

They pulled out chairs around a large conference table. The women sat at one end of the table near the door. The men sat by the window.

The jurors talked about the steamy July weather, their families, their jobs, their hobbies, the vacations some of them were worried about missing if the trial went on too long.

They talked about anything that came to mind except the one topic they wanted to, the one subject the judge had warned them to avoid—the evidence they had heard during the first three days of the trial.

Some jurors were also trying to avoid Paula Gorobzov, the sixty-one year old redhead who had asked the judge to replay some testimony and identify some exhibits that were passed to the jury.

Paula had had trouble hearing Vicki and remembering all the dates that had been mentioned while she was on the witness stand.

She asked the other jurors for help, but was told firmly that they could not talk about it.

"We don't want to get into trouble," said Emma Aceto, the porcelain artist who, like Paula, was a grandmother, "or have a mistrial."

"I have to ask," Paula pleaded.

"You'll get your chance to ask at the end of the trial," Emma said gently. Then she confided in a whisper, "I'm taking notes."

Paula wanted desperately to see the notes, but Emma refused.

"Not until later," she said.

The judge had told the jurors they could not take notes during the trial. But Emma had been working on them at home from memory.

Each night, she waited for her husband to go to bed after the eleven p.m. news, wrote for an hour or so and then hid the notes in a drawer. She hadn't talked about the case with her husband and didn't want him to know about the notes. She was saving them for the deliberations. She was sure they would be useful.

Finally, at eleven a.m. a sheriff summoned the eight jurors to the courtroom. As they passed solemnly, single-file through the door to the brick-walled chamber, they were staggered by what they saw.

Perched on the edge of the witness chair, which sat in an oak box adjacent to the judge's bench, was a small boy, his short blond hair neatly brushed back. He was dressed in a blue suit, as though he was going to church. The jurors could see his little feet, dangling above the floor. He looked tiny and vulnerable.

The jurors had not known that a child—*the child*—was going to testify. They filed slowly toward their seats in the jury box.

Staring heartbrokenly at his son, Rob wasn't thinking about the jurors. He was trying to deal with his own feelings. He had been agonizing over this moment more than any other in the trial. His dream was that Keefe would tell the judge it was all a lie, jump off the witness stand and run into his arms. Rob waited numbly for reality to blot out his dream.

The preparations for Keefe's testimony had taken up part of the previous afternoon and the first hour of Friday morning. Barbara Rhue, a zealous Hartford lawyer known as a

238

crusader for children's rights, had been appointed Keefe's guardian while he was a witness.

Rhue had filed a motion to institute special procedures for Keefe's testimony. She had asked that Keefe be seated in the courtroom before the jury was let in. She did not want anyone to enter or leave the courtroom while he was testifying, and she asked the judge to order the sheriffs to guard against any unnecessary noise.

She had made arrangements for the boy to go to the bathroom without coming in contact with the jury, should he need to go. She asked that the spectator section be closed on the side of the courtroom where the jury was seated. She wanted to sit next to the boy to make him feel more comfortable, but promised she would not talk to him while he was being questioned.

Rhue had asked that Schoenhorn and Carlson remain seated if they felt the need to raise any legal objections during Keefe's testimony. Both lawyers agreed and arrangements were made to have a baby-sitter available to be with Keefe while Rhue was in the courtroom. That job was given to Noreen Wilcox, a victim advocate who worked for the State.

Schoenhorn and Rhue had sparred on several points that afternoon. Schoenhorn had no problems with most of the special procedures, but he did not like Rhue. She acted like a prosecutor.

The jurors—unsettled by the sight of the cute little boy in the big witness chair playing such a crucial role in a drama that could send his father to prison for a long time—dropped into their chairs.

Those sitting closest to the witness stand were less than four feet from the boy. Before they heard him say anything, several were thinking ahead—past the trial—trying to figure out how the ordeal would affect the child as he grew older and who should be blamed for putting him in that position.

"Ladies and gentlemen," the judge addressed them. "The person on the witness stand at this point is the child witness who was identified in the court's exhibit A, which was previously circulated among you.

"I want to advise you that before we begin with the testimony, the court did place the witness under oath, outside of your presence . . . I think at this point, we're ready to proceed. Mr. Carlson?"

Carlson stood up at the corner of his desk, as he had while questioning Keefe's mother.

"Good morning."

"Morning," answered Keefe.

"Can you tell us how old you are?"

"Six."

"Can you tell us whether or not you go to school?"

"Not yet."

"Did you go to school this past year?"

"Yeah."

"What grade were you in?"

"First."

Carlson was unnatural. His voice was louder than it had been, and he spoke very slowly, enunciating each syllable, pausing after each word, as though he was talking to someone who didn't speak English.

"Would you tell us who you live with now?"

"Bruce."

"Anyone else?"

"My mom." Keefe squinted.

Rob adored that expression. He was trying to take notes, but he didn't want to take his eyes off his son.

Carlson asked about Bruce: "Do you call him Dad now?"

"Yeah."

"Do you know whether your mother works?"

"Where my mom works?"

"Yes."

"Mmm . . . New Britain."

"Can you tell us where in New Britain she works? I mean what place?"

"No, I don't know."

"Have you ever been there?"

"Yeah."

"And do you know where Bruce worked?"

"The same," answered Keefe, "but no more."

"And what did Bruce do there?"

"He was a sheriff," the boy said with pride.

Carlson adjusted his glasses, folded his arms and tucked in his chin.

"Do you know what the difference is between what's true and what's not true?"

Keefe thought for a few seconds. "Like say I told my sister we're going to Florida. And she asked mom and dad. And she said yes. That would be the truth."

"Okay. If I told you I had a green necktie, would that be true?"

"No."

"Do you know what happens when you tell something that's not true?"

"Get in trouble."

"And who do you get in trouble with?"

"Your family."

"You know where you are right now?"

"Yes."

"Can you tell us where it is you are right now?"

"I'm in the court."

"And if you told something that wasn't true, could something happen to you?"

"Yes."

"Alright. What do you think could happen to you?"

"Like, I'd go to jail."

"Have you ever seen a jail?"

"Yes."

"Do you think that's a place you'd like to be?"

"No."

"Will you tell the truth in here?"

"Yes."

Carlson walked to the witness stand and showed Keefe a picture of the Bemis Street house and asked him what it was.

"Rob's house."

"Did you ever live there?"

"Yes."

241

He had Keefe describe the layout of the house as he moved back to the prosecution desk.

"The person that you call Rob, is he here today?"

"Yes."

"In the courtroom? Could you tell us where in the courtroom?"

He pointed to his father: "Over there."

Rob and Keefe's eyes met for the first time since the fall of 1987.

"Can you tell us what he's wearing?"

"Peach suit."

"Does he have glasses or not?"

"Yes."

"Beard or not?"

"Yes."

Carlson noted the identification.

Rob was struck by the clarity of his son's speech. No more cute mispronunciations. He had grown up so much. And the "peach suit" description. Wrong color, but very poetic.

"Now," Carlson asked, "before you called him Rob, was there something else that you called him?"

"My dad."

Rob swallowed hard at the sound of the word. He wanted to savor it, but Carlson was pushing on.

"The last time you visited Rob at his house, did something happen to you?" the prosecutor asked.

"Yes."

"Okay. When this happened to you, where were you?"

"In the living room."

"And can you tell us what, if anything, you were wearing?"

"Nothing."

"And can you tell us what it is that happened to you?"

"I got hurt."

"Can you tell us how it is that you got hurt?"

"How it happened?" Keefe asked.

"Yes."

"Or do you want me to tell you the story?"

Carlson gulped. "I'm sorry?"

"Do you want me to tell you what he did to me?"

"Yes, I do."

"All right." Keefe sighed, and then he began a non-stop recitation:

"Well, on a day that Mom dropped me off, it was Christmas. It was Christmas that day, or starting Christmas. And after we had . . . we didn't have dinner that night. And then after we went to bed. Then the next day we took a bath, and we got out. Then I was in my room. He started chasing. After a while, Wendy . . . he started chasing Wendy around the house. And then after he found . . . got her, he pushed her into her room and locked her. And then after a while . . . still running around . . . then he got me. Then he was hitting me on the back. And then after, he put his front into the back of me. And then he hit me with the belt. We didn't have dinner that night. He hit me with his belt to my ear, to my eye. And then he pushed me into my room. The next day, he brought us to Litchfield. Then we got there at night. And then when Mom and Bruce found out I had the sting, I told them . . . my scratch . . . I told them why it . . . what had happened, how he did it. And then that was the day when Mom and Dad almost got married . . . Mom and Bruce."

"All right." Carlson paused.

Keefe told his story with no emotion.

Rob couldn't believe his ears. Where had the belt come from?

Who had been telling Keefe these things?

Carlson was leaning over his desk, studying his notes. Finally, he straightened.

"When you say about Rob's front, what do you mean by that?"

"His penis," Keefe answered promptly.

"And can you tell us what a penis is?"

"Something you go to the bathroom in."

"And can you tell us what it is again that Rob did with his penis?"

"He stuck it into my behind." Still no emotion.

"Now, when this happened, exactly where were you within the house?"

"In the living room."

"And whether or not you," Carlson caught himself. He started again, pronouncing each word slowly.

"Did you have any clothes on?"

"No."

"When Rob was chasing, did he have any clothes on?"

"Only his shirt."

"When Rob put his penis into your bottom, as you've said, how did it feel?"

"Rough."

"After he put his penis into your bottom, what did he do next?"

"He took his belt and he hit me in the eye—to my ear."

McQueeney swiveled toward his family with an agonized look on his face. Ruth was crying quietly. Ray had his arm around her.

"Did you get dressed?" asked Carlson.

"No, he just pushed me into my room. Next day we got dressed. Then he dropped us off at Litchfield. We didn't get there 'till night. And then when they . . . at dinnertime . . . they found out I had the big scratch. And then I told them why. And then . . . now is the night with it was Christmas. So that's after, when we opened our presents."

Carlson paused and turned his attention to Keefe's sessions at the Langley Center with Barbara Barrett.

"Can you tell us what Barbara looks like?" he asked.

"Well, she has blond hair. It's curly. She's short, and she's pretty fat . . . And that's about all I could say."

"And when you went to see Barbara, what did you do there?"

"Well, we would talk about what Rob did to me. And then after a while, we would play with the clay she had."

Carlson completed his questioning and sat down.

"All right, thank you," said the judge. "Mr. Schoenhorn?"

Schoenhorn grinned toward the boy on the witness stand. Playfully he pushed himself out from behind the defense desk, still in his chair. He rolled across the courtroom floor toward Keefe, paddling with his feet.

"Hi." Schoenhorn's voice was cheerful.

"Hi," Keefe answered a little surprised.

"My name is Jon. Do you know who some of the other people are in the courtroom here?"

"No, not really."

He pointed to Carlson.

"Do you know this man's name?"

"No."

"Have you seen him before now?"

"Yeah."

"Where? Downstairs?"

"Yeah."

"Did anybody ask you some of these questions downstairs?"

"Yes."

"Was it this man?" He pointed again to Carlson.

"Yes."

For this cross-examination, Schoenhorn did not play to the jury. He kept his eyes on the youngster and spoke naturally.

"I'm going to ask you a question," he said. "Do you believe that I have a gorilla in my jacket?"

"Noooo." Keefe was skeptical.

"I do." Schoenhorn gave him a mischievous smile. "Want to see him? Want to see him do a trick?"

Keefe nodded shyly.

"I'll have him do a trick right here."

Schoenhorn reached into the pocket of his suit coat and pulled out a toy gorilla holding a yellow banana. He wound it up with a little key on its back and put the gorilla on top of the wooden rail in front of the witness stand. It whirred and flipped over backwards, landing on its feet.

"He jumped over, didn't he?" Schoenhorn held out the toy to Keefe. "Do you want to see him."

Keefe started giggling, softly at first, and then the giggles grew into a hearty laugh.

"Do you believe he could do that?"

"No."

"Do you want to see him do it again?"

Keefe nodded, and Schoenhorn had the gorilla do another flip. "Do you like playing games with toys?" he asked.

"Yes."

"And what toys do you have now?"

"Well, not really any yet, because we just moved in."

"You just moved to a new house?"

"Yes."

Schoenhorn eased Keefe into talking about the places that he had lived. When Keefe was asked where he lived before Goshen, the boy sighed heavily.

"A red house," he answered. "Rob's house."

Schoenhorn asked whether Keefe remembered his grandparents, Rob's parents.

"Yes."

"When's the last time you saw Grandma and Grandpa?"

"After . . . no . . . before Rob hurt me."

"Before Rob hurt you?"

"Yes."

"You haven't seen them since?"

"No."

"Do you want to see them?"

"No."

"Can you tell me why?"

"Well . . . another thing . . . it's not really." Keefe was struggling. "It's hard to say," he said finally. "But I'll think about it."

Schoenhorn asked if it was hard for him to think of a reason.

"Yes."

"Okay. So I'll ask you something else."

"Right."

"Right. Don't want to ask you hard questions."

"Right." Keefe looked relieved.

Ray and Ruth McQueeney were aching. Ruth was crying quietly again. Ray put his arm around her.

"Do you want to play with the gorilla while I'm talking to you?"

"Mmmm," Keefe grinned. "Sure."

Schoenhorn passed the gorilla to him.

Keefe started giggling again. He played with the toy while Schoenhorn continued his questioning.

"Let me ask you this." He motioned toward Carlson. "Do

you remember a few minutes ago that this man here asked you about, you, the difference between lies and truth?"

"Yes."

"What's the difference . . . Do you know the difference between a dream and true?"

"Yeah."

"What's a dream?"

"Some dreams are like . . . Some nights my sister has really, really bad dreams when she watches movies that . . . like *Ghostbusters*."

"Oh yeah?"

"When she watches those, she gets the ghost in her head. Then she has the dream like that."

"Now, have you ever had a dream about *Ghostbusters*?"

"No, not really."

"You've seen the movie, haven't you?"

"Yeah."

"You saw it more than once, didn't you?"

"Yeah," Keefe giggled. "A lot more."

Schoenhorn rolled his chair toward the clerk's desk and asked for defendant's exhibit, a picture. He showed the picture to Keefe and asked if he knew who it was.

"Marshmallow Man," he exclaimed.

"What did Marshmallow Man do in the movie?"

"He was scaring other people away."

"Was he crushing other people?"

"Yeah, crushing other people . . . cars."

"He was real big, wasn't he?"

"Yeah, real big."

"And he'd chase people, right?"

"Yes."

"I want to show you something else," Schoenhorn said, rolling his chair toward the defense desk. He reached inside his boxy briefcase and pulled out a six-inch puffy white doll with a blue cap and sailor collar.

"Do you know who this is?" he asked.

"Marshmallow Man!" Keefe's eyes widened.

Schoenhorn had the doll be marked as an exhibit, then asked Keefe whether he wanted to hold it.

The boy giggled again as he pointed to the wooden rail and said, "You can put him right here."

The judge interrupted. "I suppose I should hold Marshmallow Man myself," he said in a childlike way.

Schoenhorn handed the doll to Mulcahy, who turned it in his hands before giving it back.

When Keefe got the doll, Schoenhorn asked what the Ghostbusters did to Marshmallow Man.

"Make him get burnt."

"They blow him up, right?"

"Yep."

"With their special guns?"

"Yes."

"Do you ever watch the Ghostbusters television show too? Cartoons?"

"Yeah."

"And isn't there another ghost in it that's friendly?"

"Yeah, Slimer."

"Why do they call him Slimer?"

"Because he slimes."

"He gets everything wet, right?"

"Yeah—with slime."

Schoenhorn asked Keefe whether anything in the *Ghostbusters* movie was true.

"No."

"It's just a movie, huh?"

"Yes."

"Okay. And I was going to ask you—before you came here today, did anyone tell you that you'd be telling a story here today?"

"Yeah."

"And who told you?"

"My mom," Keefe answered. "She told us we had court today."

"And what did she tell you about court?"

"Well," Keefe paused. "She told me 'don't lie.' That's one."

"Umm hmm," said Schoenhorn.

"And 'always tell the truth.' "

"Okay."

"And that's about it."

"Okay. Did you tell her the story that you were going to tell today?"

"Yes."

"Did she ask you to?"

"Yeah."

"Now, do you know why you don't live anymore with Rob and your mom?"

"Yes."

"Why?"

"Because Rob hurt me . . . us."

"Hurt us, meaning who?"

"Me and Wendy."

"And that's why you don't live together any more?"

"Yes."

"Okay." Schoenhorn thought for a moment.

"And you said that the last time you were over at Rob's house, that he hit you with a belt?"

"Yes."

"And was it like real hard?"

"Yeah."

"And you said from the eye all the way over to the ear?" Schoenhorn drew an imaginary line across the side of his face with his finger.

"Yeah."

"And did you have like a bruise there?"

"It was a *real big* cut."

Schoenhorn asked Keefe if he wanted Rob to go to jail.

"Yes."

"You do? And who first told you about jail?"

"Well, where Mom works, she showed me all the jails and what they looked like. And you can see all the bad people in them."

"And Bruce, your present dad, also worked in the jail, didn't he?"

"Yes."

"At the same place where your mom works, right?"

"Now he's working for a jail."

"He was working for a jail, right?"

"No. He was a sheriff before. But now he's working for a jail, and he's going to be a sheriff . . . He owns a jail," Keefe said proudly.

Schoenhorn was nearing the end of his examination. He started bouncing from one point to another.

"Now do you think Rob would do this bad thing to other kids, too?"

"I don't know."

Schoenhorn was surprised. "I'm sorry?"

"I don't know."

"Did you ever say that you think he'd do it to other kids?"

"No."

"Did your mom ever say to you that she thought he might do it to other kids?"

"Maybe. She said it once."

"She said that to you once?" he turned toward the jurors for the first time.

"Yeah."

He swung back toward Keefe, asking whether he had been able to think of any reasons why he didn't want to see his grandparents.

"I can't think," the boy said.

Schoenhorn went back to Rob. "You think that Rob's a bad man, right?" he asked.

"Yes."

"Who else thinks he's a bad man?"

"My mom and my dad . . . and my sister . . . and my grandma."

"Your sister and your grandma?"

"Yeah."

"Now, this is not *this* grandma here, right," Schoenhorn pointed toward Ruth McQueeney, who was seated directly behind Rob.

"No," answered Keefe.

Ruth's tear-filled eyes locked with Keefe's for a moment. She wanted to run up to the front of the courtroom, hug him and take him in her arms away from Vicki and all that she had done.

"Do you think your mom would be worried if you were friends again with Rob?" Schoenhorn asked.

"Yes."

"Why?"

"Well," Keefe stopped to think. "I won't even think Mom . . . Mom doesn't even like Rob any more. I think she would be really mad if I was."

Schoenhorn asked if Keefe remembered telling his mother that Rob had put his finger on his bottom.

"No," Keefe said firmly. "I never said that."

"Never said that?" Schoenhorn played to the jury once again.

"No," said Keefe, confused. "He never even wanted . . . to them . . . tell them . . . because I told them that—what he did to me and Wendy."

"And you never said anything to your mom about him putting his finger real hard in your heinie?"

"He never did that."

"Did you ever say that?"

"No."

Schoenhorn asked Keefe whether he remembered playing Marshmallow Man with Rob chasing him around the house.

"Yes."

"Did that scare you a little bit?"

"Yeah, I was scared a little bit."

"You're not scared of the movie anymore, are you?"

"No."

"But you're older now, right?"

"Yes."

"Didn't it scare you a little bit back then?"

"Yeah."

"And you were only four years old then, weren't you?"

"Yeah."

"And a lot more scared you, huh?"

"Yeah."

"And now you know it's just a movie, right?"

"Yeah."

"Know what?" Schoenhorn leaned back in his chair and

extended his arms. "I don't have any more questions. Thank you. You've been a good boy."

Judge Mulcahy called a recess, sending the jury out of the courtroom before excusing Keefe from the witness stand.

The McQueeneys were numb.

During the recess, Keefe was entrusted to the care of Noreen Wilcox who took him to a small hearing room near the courtroom.

Wilcox, a plump, attractive woman with brown hair and glasses had worked for the State as a victim witness advocate, attending to the needs of crime victims for the last year and one half. Before that she was a police officer. But today she was just babysitting. It was the first time she had met Keefe.

The first thing the cute blond boy had asked her was how long he was going to be there.

Wilcox told him she didn't know how long the two of them would be in the room. A recess, she said, could be short, or it could be long.

Keefe climbed into a chair at a rectangular conference table in front of a small box of Lego building blocks that Barbara Rhue had given him to play with. He spread out the Legos and reached for the box of orange juice she had also provided.

Keefe started bouncing the juice box between his hands on the table.

"Be careful," Wilcox gently cautioned him. "You could poke a hole in it and spill it on yourself. You wouldn't want that to happen because you might have to go back into court and testify some more."

Keefe stopped playing with the juice and looked up. "I'll say Rob hurt me again," he said simply. His words hung in the air.

Aghast, Wilcox swallowed hard, but made no reply.

She knew that what the little boy just said could be very important to the case in the courtroom next door.

Just then, Barbara Rhue came through the door and said the judge had excused Keefe. He didn't have to go back into court. She picked up her Legos and escorted the boy out of the room as Wilcox stared after them.

Wilcox stood motionless for several minutes. She had only been with Keefe for a few minutes. Why couldn't he have just played quietly? Why did he have to say *that*?

Wilcox knew she had to do something about it. She decided to tell Herb Carlson. He would have to figure out what to do. Pale and shaken, she immediately went to search for him.

■CHAPTER TWENTY-TWO■

A Glimpse of Hope, A Glimpse of Despair

The jury got their first view of Schoenhorn's defense that afternoon, when two of his witnesses were taken out of order—Henry Hurvitz and Susan Blackwell, Keefe's pre-school teacher.

Though the prosecution had not completed its case, Carlson allowed the defense witnesses to testify because both were planning to leave the state for vacations during the next week.

Hurvitz testified about a series of letters on the custody dispute that he exchanged with John Clifford, Vicki's lawyer, during the divorce.

With disgust evident in his voice, he said a scheduled custody hearing on February 6, 1987 was canceled because Vicki told the police her son had been molested.

Susan Blackwell, Keefe's teacher who had expressed her sympathy and belief in Rob, made several telling points when Schoenhorn asked her if she remembered the boy.

"Yes," she said in a firm, distinct voice.

Schoenhorn inclined his head. "Is there a particular reason why you remember him after all this time, despite the number of children you've had?"

"Well, I have a fairly good memory for the children that I have had in my room, and I do remember K, because I recall this happening while he was in my room—the report being written in the newspaper of this alleged incident."

Schoenhorn zeroed in, "The report of Mr. McQueeney's arrest?"

"Yes," she said frowning.

"Do you remember approximately when that was—the report?"

"It would have been during February of 1987."

"It was after he was arrested, though?"

"Yes, yes." She nodded. "I read it in the paper, and that was how I found out about it."

"Did you have an opportunity to observe K on January 27th or January 28th, 1987?"

"He was present in my room at that time."

"Did you have an opportunity to observe him on February 3rd, February 4th, February 5th, and February 9th of 1987?"

"He was present in my room at that time."

"Did you notice any difference in his personality, appearance or emotional level from the end of January till that next week that we're talking about?"

"No, I didn't." She said nodding her head for emphasis.

Carlson stepped forward, "Objection, your Honor. Objection. Well, it doesn't make any difference with the answer, but it was a four-part question. That's what I aas going to object to, but I'll withdraw it, with the answer of 'nothing.' "

Mulcahy said "The answer may stand."

Schoenhorn gestured, "It saves some time, Your Honor, but I agree if—in the possibility of multiple answers."

Mulcahy held up his hand "Objection as to form."

Schoenhorn's eyes turned inquiringly to the witness, "So the answer is no to all those?"

"That's right," she smiled somberly.

"Did you notice any marks on K's face?"

"No, I did not."

"Did you see any signs that K had been abused in any way?"

"No, I . . ."

Again Carlson stepped forward, "Objection, your Honor. That is—because of what Mr. Schoenhorn said earlier about physical versus sexual abuse, I'd object to form, because I don't know which he might be talking about."

Mulcahy repeated firmly, "The objection is sustained as to form."

Schoenhorn frowned, "All right, I'll break it down." He swallowed hard.

"Did you see any physical—signs of any type of physical injury at all?"

"No, I did not," Susan insisted.

"Did you learn of any allegations of sexual abuse of any kind? From the child?"

"No, no, I did not, from the child," she said.

"Did the child say anything to you about injury caused by his father?"

"No, he did not," she said clearly.

After Blackwell's brief appearance on the witness stand, Barbara Barrett was scheduled to testify. But she could not be found.

Mulcahy asked Carlson about it.

The prosecutor stood up and said in a curt voice, "Mrs. Barrett never appeared in our office, and I don't know why she didn't, your Honor." She's not at her place of employment to-day. Her phone is not being answered at her home. So I just don't have an answer as to why she's not here . . . However, she isn't here."

Mulcahy adjourned court for the day.

The eight jurors reported, as ordered, to the court building Monday at eleven a.m., but were kept out of the courtroom.

Some were growing annoyed at the judge and the lawyers, suspicious of what was being done behind their backs. They felt they had a right—an obligation as jurors—to know everything that was happening related to the trial. But there was nothing they could do. They were captives of the system.

Emma didn't like idle time, and it became evident she and the others would have a lot of it. She had brought playing cards and games, Scrabble and Trivial Pursuit, with her to the court-house. They played the games hour after hour.

Emma also brought an album displaying porcelain objects she had painted and got one order for them. Lois Goodin, the legal secretary who worked for a prominent Hartford law firm, needed a present for a wedding.

Throughout the trial, Lois had been getting up before dawn so that she could put in a few hours of work at the law office before reporting to the courthouse. Dick Allison, the alternate juror who was a vice-president with Aetna Life & Casualty, had been doing the same. He had also been returning to his office late in the day before going home.

During the first week of the trial, Allison had spent most of his time in the jury deliberation room doing paperwork out of his briefcase. But even he joined the Trivial Pursuit game on Monday.

Paula did well at Trivial Pursuit, surprising Emma and Lois, who had pegged her as kind of an airhead. It was soon clear that somewhere under that red hair was a quick mind and a good memory.

The confinement, the frustration and the games brought the jurors closer together. Yet none knew what the others were thinking about the case they had to judge. And none dared ask.

After reporting to the courthouse Tuesday morning, the jury was again held for about an hour in the deliberation room. And, like Friday, when a sheriff finally led them through the door into the courtroom, someone was sitting in the witness chair.

It was a heavy set, fiftyish woman with a round face and short blond helmet-like hair.

"Good morning, ladies and gentlemen," said Mulcahy. "With reference to yesterday, I'm sorry that we did not present evidence to you. We thought we would be presenting evidence to you, and that's why I was holding you. However, we did proceed with certain matters in your absence. And after so proceeding with the full cooperation of counsel, it became apparent to the court that I was going to have to review certain matters and certain legal principals.

"So, in any event, thank you for your patience, and I'm sorry we had to hold you yesterday."

Mulcahy glanced down toward the woman sitting on the witness stand.

"We're prepared to proceed this morning, and the witness is Mrs. Barbara Barrett. The record will reflect, and I will indi-

257

cate to you, ladies and gentlemen now, that the witness has been previously sworn . . . Mr. Carlson?"

What the jurors didn't know was that Barrett had spent several hours on the witness stand Monday while they were playing Trivial Pursuit.

She had been pummeled by Schoenhorn, who had tried everything he could to bring out the inconsistencies in her testimony.

Schoenhorn told Mulcahy that Barrett had made false statements during her deposition and that she had shredded her notes in defiance of two subpoenas. He compared her act to a police officer destroying handwritten notes. However, Mulcahy overruled his objection.

Schoenhorn also tried to keep Barrett's video out of evidence, arguing again that doll demonstrations were unreliable and reminding the judge of Robson's expert testimony.

Mulcahy ruled against the defense and allowed both the video and the dolls.

The judge pointed out that Schoenhorn would have the opportunity to discredit Barrett and her methods on cross-examination.

Carlson took his usual post next to his desk, adjusted his glasses and began his direct examination of Barrett, establishing that she had been employed as a social worker in the Child Abuse Unit at the Langley Center for four to five years.

"And would you tell us what your educational background is, please," he asked.

"I have a Bachelor's in social work from Wheymore University Without Rooms, and a Master's from St. Marion's College in West Hartford."

"Okay," Carlson cleared his throat. "And what is the degree from St. Marion's College in?"

"It's a Master's of Art," she answered softly, "Master in Child Welfare."

"And would you tell us, please, what it is that the function of your particular unit at the Langley Center is?"

"We treat and assess children who have been alleged to have been abused."

Mulcahy interrupted. "Will you just try to keep your voice

up, because I have to hear you, they have to hear you," he said, motioning to the lawyers. "And of course, the ladies and gentlemen have to. Thank you."

"I'm sorry," Barrett apologized.

Carlson asked her about her sessions with Keefe. She said she first saw Vicki, Keefe and Wendy at an intake session February 5, 1987 and spent about ten minutes alone with Keefe that day. She testified she next saw Keefe and Wendy February 10 for a play session that lasted about an hour. The purpose of the session, she said, was to make the children feel comfortable with her and the center.

Then Carlson asked about the most important session.

"On February 19, 1987, whether or not you met with K?"

"Yes, I did," Barrett answered.

"And when you met with K, whether or not his mother was present in the building?"

"She was in the lobby. Yes sir."

"And was the sister, Wendy, present also?"

"Yes, she was."

"Alright," the prosecutor paused, looking up from his notes on the corner of his desk. "And can you tell us what the purpose of that time was, on February 19, 1987?"

"To make a videotape."

"All right. Then tell us how it is at the Langley Center that one goes about making a videotape."

"Within the playroom, there is a camera and microphones. The next room has the video equipment that one has to connect to the wall, turn it on, turn on the camera, and then record what is going on in that room."

"Alright." Another long pause. "And can you tell us, if you know, whose idea this was to videotape this particular session?"

"The mother had asked for a videotape."

Carlson offered the videotape as an exhibit.

Mulcahy asked Schoenhorn if he wanted to question the witness about the videotape.

"Just a few questions, your Honor," Schoenhorn replied as he stood, and walked to within two feet of the witness stand, looking directly into Barrett's eyes.

"The videotape does not show the entire session, does it?" he asked intimidatingly.

"No sir," Barrett answered meekly. "We had trouble with the equipment."

"Could you please speak up."

"We had trouble with the equipment," she repeated.

"So that it starts somewhere in the middle of the session. Correct?" Schoenhorn's lips tightened.

"There was a portion that did not record," she said. "I went out to check the recording, started the machine again, and we . . . came back into the room."

Schoenhorn was not about to give up. "But whatever happened beforehand doesn't exist at all on that tape?"

"Is not on that tape, right."

"At all?" Schoenhorn was looking to the jurors.

"Right."

"Now Mr. Carlson asked you at whose request was this tape made, and you said it was the mother's request. Is that right?"

"The mother asked us to . . . I . . ."

Schoenhorn interrupted.

"She was relating, as far as you knew—she was relating a request from the Terryville Police Department, wasn't she?"

"She asked for a tape that they could send to the police, yes."

"In other words," Schoenhorn's eyes swept the jury, "when you taped it, you understood that this was for the purpose of the police and prosecution. Correct?"

"For them to view it. Yes."

Schoenhorn returned to the defense desk. The judge accepted Barrett's videotape as an exhibit, and Carlson resumed his examination.

He asked her how much of the February 19 session was not on the videotape. Barrett said she could not estimate. During the portion that was not on tape, she said, she presented the anatomical dolls to Keefe and he undressed them.

Carlson said he was ready to play the videotape. A sheriff helped him set up the equipment. A television monitor was put on the rail of the jury box.

"Is the tape in?" asked the judge.

"Yes, sir," replied the prosecutor.

"All right," Mulcahy said to the sheriff. "Dim the lights."

The twenty-minute video was in black and white, shot from a stationary camera mounted high on a wall, looking down into the room. The picture quality was poor, like the closed-circuit shots of bank robbers in stocking masks shown on television news.

Keefe entered the room with Barrett, whose back was to the camera through most of the video. The dolls, undressed, were on a small table in the center of the room. The words were difficult to hear.

Barrett asked Keefe where the jumping game was played. On the floor, he said. She corrected him, saying he had told her it was played on the couch. It was one of many instances during the tape where after her corrections, he changed his answers and then she praised him.

The demonstration with the dolls was brief. When Keefe threw one doll on top of another, Barrett prompted him to "show me like you were doing the last time."

She asked him to show how the marshmallow game was played, and Keefe said he couldn't remember.

Wendy was shown coming into the room after a few minutes. She threw a doll after Barrett undressed it and gave it to her.

The rest of the video showed the children preparing a pretend meal and drawing. Barrett had Keefe describe his pictures. He drew a happy daddy and a rainbow.

When the tape ended, Mulcahy addressed the jury and gave them cautionary instructions regarding the exhibit and tape.

The videotape, Mulcahy further reminded the jurors, should not be considered as direct proof.

Carlson said he had no further questions.

It was Schoenhorn's turn.

"Mrs. Barrett," he began as he strode assertively toward the witness stand, his coat flapping. His first question was calculated to unnerve her. "You said that you received your Bachelor's from Wheymore's University-Without-Rooms program. Is that correct?"

"Yes sir."

He shrugged, "You never took any courses at Wheymore College, did you?"

"No sir."

He asked her about her degree from St. Marion's College. "You called it a Master's in Child Welfare. Is that right?"

"Right."

He shook his head, "In fact, it was a Master's of Social Work, was it not?"

"It's a Master's in Art, and you can use the Master's in child welfare."

Schoenhorn frowned, "Well, whether you can use it or not, isn't it true that the Master's of Child Welfare is not a recognized degree?"

She flushed, "It was a new degree, and I graduated in the second year of the program."

"Isn't it true that it's not recognized among mental health professionals as an authorized degree?"

"I don't know that it isn't, sir."

Schoenhorn waved a hand airily, "Now, when you took the Master's program at St. Marion's College, was there a course within the program offered concerning dealing with sexual abuse of children?"

"Yes sir."

"And what was your grade in that course?"

"I did not take that course."

Schoenhorn clapped a hand to his head in a theatrical gesture. He sauntered to the defense desk. He sifted through a stack of documents at the corner of the desk, slowly pulling one from the pile.

Carlson, anticipating what was to come, put his hands on the arms of his chair and started to stand. He was halfway up when Schoenhorn asked the next question.

"You are also a defendant, are you not, in a civil malpractice suit that has been filed against you by Mr. McQueeney and his parents. Isn't that correct?"

Carlson jumped to his feet. "I object to that," he bellowed. "I'd like to be heard on that."

Mulcahy raised his hand. "The jury may be excused," he said.

After the jurors filed out of the room, Carlson argued the malpractice lawsuit was irrelevant and immaterial.

"Anybody can sue anybody for almost anything these days, apparently," he said. "And the fact that someone chose to bring a civil action against her, I would suggest, does not in any way serve to impeach her believability."

Schoenhorn had already accomplished his objective of making the jury aware of the malpractice accusation. He cited three court decisions to buttress his position that he should be able to question Barrett about the lawsuit.

Carlson said he was not familiar with any of the cases.

"I would further note," said Schoenhorn, "throughout this trial a representative of this witness's law firm has been seated in the courtroom daily."

Mulcahy adjourned for the lunch recess to give Carlson time to review the cases Schoenhorn cited.

Outside the courthouse, vendors parked their carts and trucks by the curb to serve the lunch crowd.

Suspects, accused of all kinds of crimes, waited their turn with lawyers, sheriffs and jurors. The McQueeneys got in line at a large white catering truck known as "The Chuckwagon."

Schoenhorn had instructed Rob to be as visible as possible with his family. Even if the jurors went to a restaurant to eat, they would see the McQueeneys as they passed by.

Rob looked forward to lunch. He thought of it as a brief period of relief when he could be like everyone else, eating the same bacon-cheese melt as the sheriff, who seemed to Rob to scowl at him.

As the McQueeneys walked away from the truck to eat lunch, they noticed Barrett standing in line behind them. She was with Bruce Johnson.

Carlson had surprised Schoenhorn the previous afternoon when he told him that Bruce was going to testify.

When the trial resumed at two p.m., Mulcahy heard further arguments on Carlson's objection and issued his ruling. He had been persuaded that he should allow mention of the lawsuit, but he would not permit Schoenhorn to say "malpractice."

"I think 'malpractice,' even in terms of a pending lawsuit, where the issues haven't been resolved, perhaps is a bit strong for a jury," the judge said.

Schoenhorn agreed to rephrase the question.

The jury was brought back to the courtroom, and Schoenhorn resumed his cross examination of Barrett.

"Isn't it true that you are being sued by my client for your actions in dealing with his two children in your official capacity at Langley Center?"

"Yes sir."

"And that case is pending now. Is that right?"

"Yes sir."

"And in fact, during the course of this trial, a representative from your lawyer's office has been sitting in the courtroom, following the proceedings. Correct?"

"Yes sir."

Schoenhorn walked away from the witness stand to the far end of the jury box. Then slowly he turned back toward Barrett.

"Now," he said, pausing, his eyes glowering, "working in a center, you have to keep precise notes as to the things that the child says and things that you do. Correct?"

"Yes sir."

"And you know how important it is to be able to look at your notes and your reports, to be able to document events that happened a couple of years prior. Isn't that true?"

"Yes sir."

Rob quickly looked up from his note pad. Finally, he thought excitedly, the truth will come out. Shred her, Jon, he cheered to himself.

"Now," Schoenhorn went on, "you wrote a report in this case sometime in August of 1987. Correct?"

"Yes sir."

"And it purported to encompass all of your sessions with K, from February through sometime in the month of August of 1987. Correct?"

"Yes sir."

"And in order to write that report, you had your own personal notes. Correct?"

"Yes sir."

"And isn't it true that if there were specific quotations from a child that would be relevant to this kind of an allegation, that you would have been sure to include that in your report?"

"I would certainly have tried to, sir."

Schoenhorn had been inching back toward the witness stand with each question. Now he stood in front of it, towering over the witness.

"And isn't it true that through the time of your report in August of 1987, never do you say at *any time* that the child stated 'my father put his penis in my behind,' or 'my rectum,' or anything like that?"

"I do not state that in that report. No sir."

Schoenhorn paused, looking at the jurors, incredulous. The silence was like an exclamation point.

"Let me ask you this question," he resumed. "What did you do with all your personal notes that you used to write the August 1987 report?"

"As I explained to you before, sir, when I write a report I shred those notes. They're not personal clients, and therefore I don't keep them."

Schoenhorn voice grew dark and serious. He enunciated each word carefully, "I know you told me that outside the presence of the jury, but I have to ask it again in front of the jury."

"Okay. And that's what I'm telling you, sir."

"And you have a shredding machine. Correct?"

"Langley Center does. Yes sir."

"And you put the paper physically into the shredder, and it turns it into confetti, or whatever. Correct?" Schoenhorn's hands waved and his coat flapped as he demonstrated a shredding action.

"Yes sir."

Schoenhorn paused. He looked at each juror in turn. "Now prior to the time that you received . . . that you destroyed those records . . . did you receive a subpoena from our office, asking you to produce those notes."

"Yes sir."

His voice was thunderous. "And after receiving that subpoena, you destroyed those notes. Correct?"

"Yes sir." Barrett's voice had begun to tremble, and she was staring into her lap, where she was fidgeting with her hands.

Schoenhorn directed Barrett's attention to the February 19 session with Keefe, the portion that wasn't on the videotape.

"There must have been something that was different because I note from the videotape a number of occasions when you suggest that the child was doing something different than he did before. And you called his attention to that. Isn't that true?"

"I raised questions about what he had said."

"Don't you say something like 'I thought you said it happened here,' after the child gives you a different answer?"

"That's right, sir."

"At one point you asked K whether, when he played the game with his father, he was on his stomach or his back. And his answer is 'on his back.' Correct?"

"Yes sir."

"But from what I can see from the videotape, he places the doll on the stomach. Correct?"

"Yes sir."

"You testified—and correct me if I'm wrong—you said that the child undressed the dolls. Is that right?"

"Yes sir."

"Is that your standard practice?"

"Yes sir."

"Can you tell us, then, why it is that you undressed the doll for Wendy?"

"I don't know, sir."

"Now it is also my understanding that at no time during that session on February 19th or prior to that time, did you specifically ask K to differentiate between pretend and real. Is that correct?"

"Yes sir."

"And is it also my understanding that you didn't know at

266

the time of February 19th about a custody fight between Vicki, the mother, and Mr. McQueeney, the father?"

"I'm not sure when I learned that, sir."

"Isn't it true that you did not learn from Vicki McQueeney Johnson that K had told her that his father put his *finger* up his anus."

"I have no current recollection of that, sir."

"Wasn't it true, even back then, that you had no such information?"

"I have no current recollection of that, sir."

"Do you remember my asking that during a deposition in the divorce case? And do you agree that it came as a surprise to you when it was told to you at the deposition in October or November of 1987?"

"I do not have any current recollection of that, sir."

Barrett sounded like a broken record. Schoenhorn walked slowly back to his desk to retrieve a copy of her deposition. He handed it to her and asked her to read the pertinent section.

"Does that refresh your memory as to whether or not you knew about the finger in the anus allegation prior to February 19th of 1987?"

"No sir."

Schoenhorn glanced at the jury with a look of surprise: "Oh, it does not?"

"No sir."

"Isn't it important to know, for example, whether the child in his own mind differentiated between a finger and a penis?"

"That would be helpful, sir."

"You also did not know the results of the pediatrician's report from February 5th, 1987, did you?"

"I don't know when I learned that information. I did learn that there was nothing."

"Well, again, isn't that something that you first learned during the deposition that we took during the divorce case in October or November of 1987?"

"I'm not sure, sir."

"Do you have any recollection of Vicki Johnson, then Vicki McQueeney, telling you that the doctor found no evidence of any injury?"

"No."

Schoenhorn asked whether she had tried to talk to Keefe's father before the videotaping.

"No sir."

"Have you ever seen the movie *Ghostbusters*?"

"No sir."

"Did you ever try to familiarize yourself with the characters in that movie?"

"No sir."

Barrett's mouth barely moved as she spoke. Her answers were brief, but her voice was audibly shaking.

Schoenhorn walked to the clerk's desk and picked up the white Marshmallow Man doll. He held it up high for Barrett to see.

"Do you know what this is?" he asked.

"Looks like a toy, sir."

"Do you know what the name of this toy is?"

"No sir."

Schoenhorn asked Barrett about the daddy-picture Keefe was shown drawing on the videotape.

"You asked him whether or not the daddy was happy or sad. Is that right?"

"Yes sir."

"And what was is answer?"

"That he was happy, I believe, sir."

"Happy?" he repeated.

"Yes sir."

He asked Barrett about Susan Blackwell.

"Did you ever check with K's pre-school teacher about her findings with regard to K, during that crucial period around the time of the allegation?"

"No, I don't believe I spoke with her."

"You have no recollection now of having seen any reports from the pre-school teacher?"

"No sir."

"And I take it that you have no recollection of ever questioning the mother about the use of finger, applying it to the rectum, as opposed to penis. Is that right?"

"Right sir."

"And, other than to check on the correct terminology for certain body parts with the children, you did not seek, prior to February 19th, to explore the question of what kind of sex education K or Wendy had. Is that right?"

"Yes sir."

"And when you say 'yes sir,' you're agreeing with me, right?"

"Yes sir."

Barrett's head was bowed. She didn't meet Schoenhorn's eyes.

Schoenhorn walked to the defense desk and looked at his legal pad. He swung around and began to ask Barrett about the way Vicki left her husband.

"Were you aware that the mother literally disappeared one day, without so much as letting the father know that she was leaving with the children?"

"I don't believe I knew she disappeared, quote-unquote."

"And by that I mean packed up and left while Mr. Mc-Queeney was at work, and took the children with her without so much as a word or a note?"

"I don't believe that I knew that she . . ."

Schoenhorn stopped her.

"I'm sorry?" he asked.

"Specifically what you're saying. I don't know that I knew that. I don't remember that I knew that."

"And I take it also you didn't—again in this early period—expressly evaluate the relationship that K had with his new daddy?"

"Be more specific, sir."

"Okay. That you didn't specifically explore how he felt about Bruce?"

"No sir."

Schoenhorn asked the judge for a moment. He leaned down and conferred briefly with McQueeney. "I have no further questions," he told Mulcahy.

The judge called a recess.

When Barrett's testimony resumed, Carlson began his redirect examination. He brought out the fact that she had once attended a workshop on sexual abuse.

269

He asked her whether she knew, when she first saw Keefe on February 5, 1987, who was suspected of sexually abusing him?

"Yes sir."

"And who was it that you understood to be the suspected perpetrator?"

"I understood it to be K's biological father."

Carlson completed his questions in just a few more minutes. Then Mulcahy signaled Schoenhorn for further cross-examination.

"When Mr. Carlson just asked you about who the suspected perpetrator of something was on February 5th, that information came from the biological mother, did it not?"

"Yes sir."

"And isn't it also true that on February 19th, 1987—when that videotape was done—you did not ask the child to distinguish between his biological father or his new daddy?"

"In that videotape, no I do not."

"And you did not. Correct?"

"Yes sir."

"No further questions."

McQueeney smiled at Schoenhorn. His lawyer had done a masterful job of bringing out the truth. He had demolished Barrett's testimony. Rob looked to the jurors, trying to read their expressions. He saw nothing.

■CHAPTER TWENTY-THREE■

Bruce Johnson

Within minutes after Barrett was excused from the witness stand, Carlson escorted his surprise witness through the rear doors of the courtroom.

Bruce Johnson, looking big and muscular in a light-colored suit, pushed through the gate that separated the spectator section from the front of the courtroom and strode calmly to the chair between Mulcahy and the jurors.

Carlson had listed Johnson as a possible witness during voir dire, but hadn't told Schoenhorn he would definitely testify until the previous day.

Since Johnson had made no official statements to the police or anyone else, Schoenhorn had no reason to depose him back in 1987.

As Vicki's new husband gave his address and took the oath, Rob was thinking about the sequestration order. What a joke. Three of the prosecution's four witnesses lived in the same house in Glastonbury.

Johnson settled into the witness chair, a cool, self-assured look on his face.

His testimony centered on two points. One was the events of the evening of February 1, 1987.

"All right." Carlson said, "Can you tell us what it is that you heard K say?"

"Basically, I heard the words, 'you hurt me, you hurt me.' "

"How would you characterize the tone that K was using in his voice?"

"Fear, scared."

"I'm sorry," said the judge, leaning over the edge of his bench toward the witness stand, his hand to his ear, indicating that he had trouble hearing the answer.

"Fear, scared," Johnson repeated.

Carlson continued, "Now then, based upon what you heard, what if anything did you do?"

"Stood up. It was an L-shaped room, and I was at the far end of the L. I proceeded to the corner of the room, so I had some view of what was going on in the room."

"And then would you tell us what it is that you observed?"

"I observed Robert McQueeney bending over the child, and the child trying to pull away . . . And Robert McQueeney trying to pull the child closer to him."

"And would you tell us further what, if anything, you observed?"

"Well, basically, to my recollection, at that point it pretty much ended. The child broke loose and headed over towards Vicki. Robert McQueeney then stood up and explained something to the fact that the minor child had a rash, had discomfort in his bottom—his rear. And that was basically it. He once more said goodbye to the two children and left."

The second incident about which Carlson questioned him ostensibly happened in February on Cape Cod.

Schoenhorn, out of his chair, asked that the jury be excused, challenging Johnson's expected testimony as hearsay. Mulcahy excused the jurors and asked Carlson to proceed with his questioning before ruling on Schoenhorn's objection.

"Could you tell us what it is that K told you?" Carlson asked.

"He became more detailed, more exacting." Johnson paused, shifting slightly in his chair.

"Basically," Johnson said, "he had told me directly, with Vicki present, that Rob had hurt him; that he had placed his penis in the child's rectal . . . the anus area, causing the inflammation, and was told that he was not allowed to say 'penis' by Robert McQueeney. And that's why he had told us that he

272

had put his finger in there—because he was afraid of what would happen to him at that point in time . . . he had told us that he was in the living room area . . . was on the bottom. He was naked. Robert McQueeney was only partially clad, from his waist up, in a shirt. And that he had given him a bath earlier that morning and had put Wendy in a room. And he began chasing K . . ."

The judge leaned toward Johnson. "I didn't hear what you said. "I didn't hear that part of it. He had given him a bath earlier in the morning?"

Johnson turned and looked up toward Mulcahy. But he didn't look him in the eyes. He hadn't looked directly at anyone.

"He had given them a bath earlier in the morning, your Honor," he said. "He had placed Wendy, his sister, in her bedroom and then proceeded to chase the child around the room to the point . . . put him onto the floor in the living room, got on the child's back and placed his penis in his anal area."

There was no emotion in Johnson's voice, no expression on his face.

Carlson told the judge he had no further questions.

"Any objection?" Mulcahy asked Schoenhorn.

"Yes, your Honor." Schoenhorn stood up.

He argued forcefully that much of what Johnson said was inadmissable because it went beyond Keefe's testimony.

Whether Bruce Johnson would be allowed to get back in the witness stand wasn't decided until the next day.

When Judge Mulcahy issued his ruling, he said that Keefe's testimony was sufficient to show that the child, when he was four years old, had told his mother and Bruce Johnson what had happened to him. And, he said, the evidentiary value of Johnson's testimony outweighed any prejudicial effect it might have on McQueeney.

"I specifically overrule the objection," the judge declared.

Another setback for Schoenhorn—but also another potentially strong basis for appeal should McQueeney be convicted.

Before Johnson returned to the witness stand to testify in front of the jury about the Cape conversation, Schoenhorn made a final comment to Mulcahy:

"I'll just note, Your Honor, I doubt he said any of this."

Back on the hard spectator benches, Jackie was even more upset than she had been while Vicki was testifying. She couldn't believe Mulcahy was going to let the jury hear Johnson conveniently tie up all the loose ends in the prosecution's case. Couldn't he see this guy was nothing but a liar?

As she shifted in her seat, Jackie felt a kick. It must be eleven a.m., she said to herself as she turned to look at the courtroom clock. Each morning the baby started moving about the same time. And each day Jackie found it more difficult to get enough air into her lungs. Sitting on the hard benches was difficult when you were pregnant. And Mulcahy's ruling on Johnson hadn't helped her breathing.

Johnson, who was not in the courtroom while the judge was hearing arguments about his testimony, returned to the witness chair.

He was on the stand when the jurors—after enduring another long wait and yet another game of Trivial Pursuit in their deliberation room—were led back into court.

Carlson assumed his usual position at the corner of the prosecution desk next to the jury box.

He had Johnson repeat for the jury his account of what Keefe told him at Cape Cod.

Then Carlson asked him who had the idea of taking Keefe to Langley Center.

"I did."

"Can you tell us why it is that you suggested the Langley Center?"

"Yes sir," Johnson answered crisply. "Prior to that, I had been a member of the Board of Directors of the YMCA, Greenville. Another member was Philip Mercer, who is the Executive Director of Langley Center. I was familiar with Langley Center and their work and thought that would be a good spot to start finding out . . . and for help for the child. So I called Philip, and he referred us to David Marshall and Barbara Barrett."

After a few more questions, Carlson said, "Nothing further."

"Alright," said Mulcahy turning to the defense desk. "Mr. Schoenhorn?"

"Thank you, Your Honor," Schoenhorn replied as he

pushed back his chair. He looked directly at Johnson as he moved toward him. But Johnson's darting eyes wouldn't meet his.

Schoenhorn leaned on the rail of the jury box and asked his first question matter-of-factly.

"I didn't catch, Mr. Johnson, where you work now."

"Right now," Johnson gulped, "I do not, sir."

Schoenhorn looked up relishing the moment. Then he swung into action. He was on cross-examination, on a stage with a key witness who thought he was so smooth that nobody could touch him.

Schoenhorn turned to the jurors, eyebrows raised.

"You do not work at all? Is that right?"

"That's right, sir."

"You had worked prior to this as a deputy sheriff. Correct?"

"As a special deputy sheriff, sir."

"As a special deputy sheriff . . . Isn't it also true that you called yourself a lieutenant in the sheriff's department?"

"We were advised through . . .'"

"Yes or no," said Schoenhorn sternly.

"Yes, I did."

"And isn't it true there is no such title as lieutenant in the Hartford County Sheriff's Department?"

"No sir, there is."

"Oh, that's not true?"

"That is not true."

"Okay, so you had the official title of lieutenant. Is that true?"

Johnson said he was advised by one of his supervisors that he could call himself a lieutenant.

"And you wore bars at some point. Right?"

"Yes sir."

"And they were given to you by the Sheriff's Department. Correct?"

"No sir."

"You bought the bars yourself at a uniform store. Correct?"

"Yes sir."

Schoenhorn smiled, scanning the jurors.

"Just like I could go to that store, if I wanted to, to buy bars to put on my shoulders . . . Correct?"

"I assume you could, sir."

"And—correct me if I'm wrong—when you met Vicki and you first went out with her socially, whether with other people or alone—she was still married and still living with Rob Mc-Queeney . . . Correct?"

"I believe so."

"And approximately a month after she left Rob Mc-Queeney, you and she moved in together. Is that correct?"

"Longer than a month, I believe sir." Johnson lifted himself slightly out of the witness chair to shift his position.

"Well," Schoenhorn went on, "you said September of 1986. Correct?"

"Umm hmmm."

"And she's testified that she left him in August of 1986." Schoenhorn glanced thoughtfully toward the ceiling, as though he was straining to add a bunch of numbers. "So it's about a month. Right?"

"Could be," Johnson admitted.

Schoenhorn continued to question Johnson about his job and his relations with Vicki.

Then he turned to Johnson's testimony about Rob's son.

"After you heard the specific allegation from K, you, of course, called up the police. Is that right?"

"No sir."

Schoenhorn paused, resting his hands on the rail of the jury box.

"You didn't give a statement to the police about what you had heard?"

"No, I did not, sir."

"So you are telling us now that K told you a specific allegation concerning insertion of a male member into his rectum, which at least implies a sexual assault," Schoenhorn's voice was rising. "And you didn't see fit, either as a person, as a concerned boyfriend, or as a special deputy sheriff, to notify any police officials whatsoever concerning that allegation?"

"Vicki had," Johnson answered calmly.

"Oh . . . Vicki had?" Schoenhorn's voice was an echo now, his eyes on the jurors.

Schoenhorn paused for several minutes. He asked a few more questions on this subject and then turned to another.

"You gave a written statement to Langley Center?"

"No sir, a verbal statement."

Schoenhorn walked away from the witness stand along the front of the jury box and then swung back toward Johnson. "Did you ever refer to Rob as the Bemis Street Man?"

"No sir."

"Did you ever hear K refer to him as the Bemis Street Man?"

"Yes sir, I did."

"And you're saying you have no idea where he got that term?"

"No sir, I do not."

McQueeney swiveled toward his family with a look of disgust. Jackie and Ruth were directing their glare of hate towards Johnson. Jackie, leaning on the rail in front of her, looked like she was ready to jump out of her seat. Johnson hadn't acknowledged their stares.

After a few more queries, Schoenhorn was finished. He wearily walked back to the defense desk. "No further questions," he called back in a disgruntled tone.

Johnson, maintained a look of cool confidence as he walked out of the courtroom.

After excusing the jurors for lunch, Mulcahy turned to Carlson. "Is that substantially the State's case?" he asked.

"That's substantially the State's case," echoed the prosecutor.

"And I take it at two p.m., the State will very probably rest," continued Mulcahy.

"Most likely," Carlson answered. "Nothing brilliant came to me overnight, Your Honor."

On the ride home from court that evening, Jackie allowed herself—forced herself to think—for the first time about what could happen if her husband were found guilty.

The air-conditioned car provided relief from the oppressive July heat and humidity, but it did nothing to ease the torment of the seven days of the trial.

It seemed wrong for her to consider the possibility of a conviction. Rob was innocent.

Now that the State had completed its case, however, Jackie worried about how much the jurors had been manipulated. Would they be able to see Bruce Johnson for what he was? She and Rob tried to evaluate the evidence as though they were part of the jury, but they couldn't get past their own feelings. Jackie reached out to hold her husband's hand, desperately wanting some reassurance that the jury would see through the hoax and not convict her husband. His whole body betrayed his own fears and anguish as he squeezed her hand for a moment and then placed it back on the steering wheel.

That afternoon, Rob had asked his lawyer his opinion on how the case was going. Schoenhorn wouldn't speculate.

"We're doing our best to bring out the truth, but you can't guess what juries do," he had said. "I've seen other cases where I would have bet my life that there was no chance of conviction. And the jury came back with a guilty verdict."

But he added that he had also seen it the other way around.

"I don't know what will happen. I just do my best."

The trial would probably be over in a few days. Jackie figured it was time to prepare herself for the worst possible outcome.

Rob had turned off Interstate 84 onto Route 6, the exit for Bristol. They had taken Ruth home and were about fifteen minutes from their house. Rob was silent.

Jackie pulled the seat belt away from her bulging belly and shifted her position so she could face him.

"Rob," she said, "have you thought about what we'll do . . . what happens if the jury finds you guilty."

She felt guilty for raising the question.

"Not really." Rob's voice was curt, his eyes still on the two-lane road ahead.

Bruce Johnson

"I think we have to find out," she said. "I mean would you get to come home, or would they just take you off to jail? They couldn't do that, could they?"

"I don't know," Rob said after a moment. "I mean, I haven't thought about it. How can they convict me? I didn't do it."

"I know that," said Jackie, "and you know that, but you heard what Schoenhorn said . . . You just can't predict what a jury is going to do . . . I think we have to find out."

"Sure, I'll find out what they're going to do," Rob turned sarcastic. "I'll just call them up . . . by the way, my wife and I are a little anxious about this trial . . . could you tell us . . ."

"You know what I mean," Jackie cut him off. "I think you should ask Schoenhorn to tell you what happens if you're . . . if they come back guilty."

Rob took one hand off the steering wheel again and loosened his tie.

"You know what I'm afraid of," he said at last. "I'm afraid I'm going to jinx us . . . I'm afraid if I go up to Schoenhorn and ask 'What happens if they find me guilty?' if I use those words 'find me guilty' . . . it's going to jinx the trial . . . I don't want to say that word."

"But we have to know," said Jackie. "We need to know what we have to do."

"You're right," he said sighing, "I can say it another way. I'll talk to him in the morning."

"You know how I always think about what's the worst thing that could happen," she said. "Well, I've been trying to apply that logic here . . . Nobody's going to die. We'll all be alive, the baby will be born, and someday our lives will go on."

The car continued down Route 6, a strip of restaurants, car dealers and stop lights.

Rob didn't tell her but he was dreading something else—that the trial would end with a hung jury. And then the state would want to do it again. And, perhaps, again and again.

Life since the phone message from Schoenhorn's office had been surreal. Against the backdrop of the trial, the mundane tasks of everyday life still had to be done. Laundry, ironing, cleaning, doing dishes, paying the bills. All were necessary, but requiring real effort.

Grocery shopping was the worst. It had to be done in public. There hadn't been any newspaper or television coverage of the trial, but Jackie worried that someone might recognize the name when she wrote out a check. *McQueeney.* What would they say? What would she do?

When she waddled into the store Wednesday evening to pick up a few groceries, nobody showed any signs of recognition. Or, if they did, they didn't say anything.

When court reconvened, Schoenhorn told McQueeney that Carlson would ask for an increase in bail in the event of a guilty verdict. Schoenhorn advised him to carry a $2,000 cashier's check when the jury began deliberating, or to have the money available.

Rob found Jackie a few minutes later in front of the courthouse where the family gathered each morning, as Schoenhorn had instructed them to do. Jackie said she would call her father to provide the money.

As they talked, they saw Maurice Back, the retired engineer, walking to the courthouse entrance. As was his practice, he avoided them, walking briskly in a wide circle toward the doors. Rob shook his head trying to figure Back out. He had been watching the jurors closely—inside and outside the courthouse—searching for clues to what they were thinking.

Rob didn't want to think about good and bad omens but he couldn't help noticing that some other jurors had began to wave or say "good morning" as they passed by.

Rob had made eye contact during the last couple of days with one juror in particular, Lois Goodin. He was reluctant to read too much into it, but he couldn't help feeling she was on his side. He hoped he wasn't wrong.

Shaking off these thoughts for the moment, Jackie and Rob stepped inside the courthouse and faced another agonizing day.

■CHAPTER TWENTY-FOUR■

For The Defense

Schoenhorn began building the foundation of McQueeney's defense Wednesday afternoon, presenting two witnesses in quick succession.

The first was John Clifford, Vicki's lawyer in the divorce case. He testified about his exchange of letters with Hurvitz over the custody and visitation disputes.

The second witness was Dr. Ranjit Pandit, the Bristol pediatrician who had examined Keefe at the request of Langley Center.

Pandit, who received his basic medical degree in Bombay, India, spoke with a strong accent. He had done his pediatric residency training in the United States and had been practicing medicine in Bristol since 1985.

His answers to Schoenhorn were clear and responsive as he explained the findings of his medical examination of Keefe on February 5, 1987.

Schoenhorn inclined his head, "Did you examine K on that date?"

"Yes, I did."

"And specifically, did you examine the child's rectal area?"

"Yes, I did," the doctor raised his eyebrows.

"Did you—what was the result of your findings?"

He leaned forward, "When I examined the child, I did not find any specific injury, to the best of my recollection."

"Did you find any injury at all?"

"Well, I remember I did look over the other parts of the body, and I really did not see any signs of physical abuse."

"Referring specifically to the eye and ear area of the face, between the eye and the ear, did you see any injury at all?"

"To my best recollection, no."

"And with regard to specifically the rectal area, did you see any redness?"

Pandit's voice was deep and resonant, "No, I did not see any inflammation at all."

"Did you see any tearing?"

"No, I didn't see any tearing."

Schoenhorn continued pressing.

"Did you see any bleeding?"

"No, I did not see any bleeding."

"Did you see any swelling?"

"No, I did not see any swelling."

"Did you see any scabbing?"

"No, I did not see any scabbing."

"Did you indicate to the mother the results of that examination?"

Pandit nodded his head, "Yes, I think I did."

"Do you recall where she was during the examination?"

"During the examination, she was—I think she was right in the room."

"Thank you," Schoenhorn gestured that he was finished, "I have no further questions."

Judge Mulcahy announced, "All right, thank you. Cross-examination?"

Carlson stepped forward, his manner crusty. "How well do you remember this specific examination, Doctor?"

Pandit looked directly into his eyes, "Well, I remember one thing, that there was no signs of any injuries."

Moreover, Pandit said later in the cross-examination that signs of anal injury should have been visible if the boy had been abused a few days earlier, as his mother reported.

After a few more questions by Carlson, the witness was dismissed and Mulcahy adjourned court for the day.

For the first time since the trial had started, the jurors

didn't have to kill any time in their deliberation room on Thursday morning. They were escorted into the courtroom a few minutes after ten a.m.

"Thank you sheriff," said Mulcahy. "And good morning ladies and gentlemen." He looked toward the defense desk. "Mr. Schoenhorn, your next witness?"

"Yes, Your Honor," said Schoenhorn bouncing to his feet. "I'd like to call Robert Ledder."

The visits Ledder had supervised, back in August and September of 1987, were the last times Rob had been able to talk with his children. Ledder glanced over at Rob sympathetically.

"Do you know where Mr. McQueeney lived at that time? What street he lived on?" asked Schoenhorn a few minutes into Ledder's testimony.

"No."

"Do you recall any discussion concerning . . ."

"No wait," Ledder cut in. "Yeah. I believe . . . Now I remember. He lived on a street called Bemis Street. And I'm not even . . . I believe it's in Plainville. I'm not sure."

"In any event," Schoenhorn went on, "was there any discussion about Bemis Street from K?"

"One of the children—and I'm not sure whether it was K or Wendy—called me the Bemis Street Man. And I was . . ."

"Called *you* the Bemis Street Man?" Schoenhorn asked incredulously.

"And I was confused by this," Ledder continued, "and I didn't know what he or she meant."

"Was there any embellishment on the issue of the Bemis Street Man?" Schoenhorn prompted him.

Ledder thought for a moment. "It was coupled with: 'You're bad; you're the Bemis Street Man.' And I'm not sure if they said, 'you hurt us,' in that session or not."

Schoenhorn asked in turn about each of the four visits Ledder supervised.

During the second visit, Ledder said, a game was mentioned.

"Did the game have a name?" Schoenhorn asked.

"They called it Ghostbusters."

Schoenhorn asked him how Keefe described the game.

283

"K said his father would chase him and Wendy around the house, making believe that . . . Mr. McQueeney would make believe that he is the Marshmallow Man in the Ghostbusters movie and scare them."

"Did the child say what happened as a result of playing the game," Schoenhorn asked.

"He mentioned that he got hurt by it," Ledder said. "He said his shoulder was hurt or his father hurt his shoulder. And I said, 'Well, how did he do that?' He pushed on it. And I asked, 'Well show me how he did this; how hard was the push?' And K came over and showed me a push on the shoulder."

Schoenhorn had Ledder demonstrate *the push* for the jury —a one-armed press on his shoulder.

Then he asked Ledder whether Keefe told him when the game was played.

"He said that it had been played at least once after they had taken a bath, and they were chasing each other around the house . . . and at other times when they had clothes on."

"What else did he say about clothes?"

"I think part of the game was hiding the clothes and finding the clothes after the bath."

According to Ledder, the fourth session on September 9, 1987, was the most disruptive.

Schoenhorn asked whether there was any change in Keefe's story of the game in the fourth session.

"K came in and announced . . . I don't know the exact sequence, but: 'You're not my father; you're a bad person; you're going to jail; you stuck your penis in my butt.' "

"Did K say anything about neighborhood children?" Schoenhorn prompted him again.

"Yes. He said, 'You should move because you may hurt other children in the neighborhood.' "

"Now." Schoenhorn rested his hands on the rail of the jury box. "When he made the statement about 'penis in his butt,' what was his . . . would you describe the manner in which he said it? The tone?"

Ledder paused, his voice quizzical, "He said it very matter-of-factly. I was kind of taken back by the content of it. You know, hearing that from a five-year-old is kind of shocking. But he said it just as, 'Hey look, I have a new squirt gun; hey, look I did these good papers in school; you stuck your penis in my butt.' You know, it was kind of all in the same matter-of-fact kind of delivery, with very little emotional intensity coupled with it . . . very flatly."

On cross-examination, Carlson raised questions about Ledder's role at the visits. Ledder said he was supposed to act as a neutral party. Ledder explained that, "You get biased toward the people in the room . . . more involved, which was the result," he said, "of collecting more information."

Obviously annoyed by where Ledder's sympathy lay, Carlson asked him who got Keefe to talk about the details of the game.

"I'm not sure whether it was myself or Mr. McQueeney he paused, "because I was just curious. What is this game?"

Carlson's annoyance grew, he asked sharply, "Did you consider that part of your neutrality? To inquire about games?"

"Just collecting information, as I thought it might be . . ."

Carlson cut in. "For what purpose would you be collecting information?"

"So I can understand what was going on in the room a little bit better," Ledder said, his craggy face serious.

Alana Gayle, a lawyer who worked for the State Supreme Court and the State's appellate courts, was Schoenhorn's next witness.

Schoenhorn wanted to shed light on what he saw as Vicki and Bruce's heavy-handed methods of getting Rob out of the picture.

During the spring of 1987, Gayle testified, she had an encounter with Bruce Johnson and Vicki while she was employed as chief criminal clerk in Hartford Superior Court. The two of them came into her office one day.

Schoenhorn asked her how Johnson identified himself.

"As a Litchfield sheriff."

"And did he show you any kind of identification?"

"He had a badge."

"Did he show you that badge?"

"Yes."

"Did he at any time indicate to you any kind of personal relationship with the wife of Mr. McQueeney?"

"No, he didn't."

"Did he ever indicate to you that he was there on personal business?"

"No, he did not."

"And what did he indicate to you that he wanted?"

"He wanted to get some type of restraining order."

Since her court did not normally issue restraining orders, Gayle said, she went to see the presiding judge about the unusual request.

When informed that the judge would not sign a restraining order, Gayle said, Vicki and Bruce left the court.

Gayle completed her testimony just before the lunch recess.

When the trial resumed in the afternoon, Schoenhorn's next witness was Richard Dyer, the attractive, well-spoken Manchester lawyer who had been appointed to represent the interests of Keefe and Wendy during Rob and Vicki's divorce.

Dyer said he met the children once in May or June of 1987 and they talked about their plans to get a card for their dad.

Dyer gave a tight-lipped smile, "It piqued my interest, given the allegations against their natural father, that they would be going to do that," he testified. "And I thought that was a nice gesture, at least in terms of reunification of the family."

"However," Dyer said, "it turned out that the 'dad' they were talking about was Bruce Johnson."

"Did they have any term referred to for their natural father?" Schoenhorn asked.

"One of the children—I believe it was the boy that we're referring to here today as K—I believe it was he who initially said that they referred to their natural father as the Bemis—that's B-E-M-I-S—Street Man."

Dyer said he later spoke to Vicki about what Keefe had said.

286

"I sought to suggest to the mother that despite what I understood to be serious allegations, and also the real strain in the family, that the children should be encouraged to refer to their father, their natural father, as 'Dad.' And I made that suggestion to her."

Schoenhorn asked Dyer whether he made any comments at a court hearing in October of 1987 about the way the children were referring to their natural father.

"Yes, I did."

"And what were those comments?"

Dyer looked him directly in the eye, his voice deepening, "The comments were that I felt that the children were being splashed with the venom of the divorce . . ."

After these telling words Carlson objected. Then he and Schoenhorn sparred until the judge sustained the objection. But, nevertheless, the jury heard.

The courtroom clock read three-thirty p.m. when Dyer was excused from the stand—leaving enough time for Schoenhorn to set the stage for his big guns.

He announced that he was ready to call the first of three expert witnesses, Nancy Eiswirth, the Hartford psychologist.

Carlson wanted to know the purpose of Eiswirth's testimony before she was allowed to take the witness stand.

"The first purpose would be as an impeachment witness against one of the State's witnesses, in particular Barbara Barrett," responded Schoenhorn grimly.

Eiswirth, he said, would not offer opinions about whether Barrett's testimony was right or wrong. But, based on her review of the records, he said Eiswirth would be "pointing out things that Mrs. Barrett did, which were wrong as a professional."

Carlson said he was concerned that Schoenhorn's strategy was a "backdoor way of giving an opinion concerning the testimony of Barbara Barrett."

The debate over how to handle Schoenhorn's experts lasted more than a half hour.

Mulcahy summed up his position. "It would be my feeling," he said, "that the witness could indicate, assuming that she's properly qualified, assuming that she's familiar with the tape and all of the facts and circumstances that were apparently available to Mrs. Barrett . . . that this witness could testify as to what she would do under those circumstances and why she would do it."

Looking at the clock, Mulcahy said Eiswirth might not be able to complete her testimony before he adjourned court.

"It will be unlikely we'll finish, Your Honor," Schoenhorn said, "but I would like to get started."

The jurors were brought back to the courtroom and prepared to listen to their fourth witness of the day.

Eiswirth was an attractive woman with blonde, shoulder-length hair.

Schoenhorn liked Eiswirth's down-to-earth manner. He knew jurors could be turned off by experts who came across as self-important.

He walked up to the jury box as he introduced his witness.

"Would you please indicate to the members of the jury what your profession is?"

"I'm a clinical psychologist."

"And what is your educational background?"

"I have a Master's and a Doctorate in Clinical Psychology."

Schoenhorn asked her to tell the jury about her work with children.

"I work with children that are abused in a number of different areas, both by parental or physical abuse, emotional abuse, sexual abuse, neglect issues. I work closely with different agencies and schools in setting up special programs for these children . . . and performing extensive evaluations of what the consequences of the abuse, or what the alleged abuse, has been."

He had her list the papers she had written and professional organizations with which she was affiliated.

After several more minutes, Mulcahy ruled that Eiswirth qualified as an expert witness in the field of child mental health.

"Now specifically with regard to the case of State vs. Mc-Queeney," Schoenhorn asked, "would you please indicate what it is that you reviewed before today?"

"OK. I reviewed the clinical records of both the boy and his sister. I reviewed the depositions given by the mother in the case and the depositions given by the professional who interviewed the children. And I reviewed the videotape of the evaluation session performed by the clinician of the child. And I reviewed the *Ghostbusters* movie."

"I'm sorry?" said Schoenhorn.

"The *Ghostbusters* movie."

He let the answer hang in the air for a moment before asking about Barrett.

"What title did she use for herself?"

"She had a degree of M.C.W. after her name."

"Which stood for what, as far as you know?"

"Master's of Child Welfare."

"Now, other than seeing that after Barbara Barrett's name, in your professional career have you ever heard that title used for anyone?"

"No."

The clock was nearing five p.m.

"This might be a good time to stop," Schoenhorn suggested to the judge.

Mulcahy dismissed the jurors and adjourned court.

Eiswirth was back in the witness chair when the jurors filed into the courtroom Friday morning at ten a.m.

Schoenhorn directed her attention to Barrett's videotape and asked her what steps she would have taken before introducing the dolls to the child.

"One of the first steps to take is to have a thorough family history of the child and his family, including relationships among various family members, relationships to other important persons, a history of the marriage, a developmental history on this child . . ."

Schoenhorn cut in, asking why family relationships were important.

"When you're talking about sex abuse, you're talking about it occurring within the context of the family, which has been together for a number of years. And it is the family dynamics that usually lead up to the situations that could cause sexual abuse to occur."

Schoenhorn asked about the distinction between sexual abuse and alleged sex abuse.

"Because an allegation of sexual abuse has been made doesn't necessarily mean that sexual abuse has occurred. There are cases where allegations are made, and they are found not to be true."

"Is that one of the purposes of investigating background information about the family relationships?"

"Yes, it is."

Schoenhorn asked why it was important to understand the marital history before introducing anatomical dolls.

"So you don't take any information that the child gives you —in whatever manner he gives it to you—out of context."

He asked about divorce and custody disputes.

"Any changes, especially major changes such as divorce, custody, visitation, new parental relationships, could all be the cause of a behavior that you see within a therapy session . . . or an evaluation session."

Schoenhorn referred to the Langley Center records and asked Eiswirth what sort of investigation had been done.

"I had no indication that any family history was obtained," she answered.

"Were there other items that . . ."

"I had no indication that a thorough developmental history was taken either."

"Either?" Schoenhorn emphasized the point.

"Correct," she said. "One of the things that I would want to know is how the child was functioning prior to the alleged incident."

"What does that mean?"

"How the child was behaving, how he was acting, what his play was like, whether anyone noted any problems with him, whether he was what's called 'acting out,' which means usually being oppositional or disruptive or showing behavior problems, or management problems at home."

"Why is that important?"

"Because if those issues predate the alleged incident, then

you would look at whether something else was going on to cause the behavior."

"Would it include any statements the child might make?"

"It would include any statements that the child would make, or statements towards . . . about divorce issues, or custody issues or parents' separation . . . how he's reacted to those before."

"If there was evidence that another adult had moved in with one of the parents after separation, is that something you would want to explore?"

"I would consider that a major disruption in the child's life. And that would be something I would want to explore . . . a child may be able to take . . . or all of us can take . . . if one thing goes wrong in our lives, or there's one stress or one change, that's pretty easy to take. When you have five or six going on at the same time, that taxes anyone."

Schoenhorn asked whether she would do anything else before a session such as the one Barrett conducted on the videotape.

She said she would want to know how the suspicions of abuse arose.

"What do you mean by that?"

"What statements were made by the child, to whom, when they were made, why they were made."

"And why is that important?"

"Well," she paused, shifting in the chair so she could look directly at the jurors, "it's important to have the child's exact wording because I think all of us have been heightened in the last several years to sexually-abused children. Because an adult interprets something in one way does not necessarily mean that a child interprets it in the same way.

"Adults are used to thinking in sexual terms. Children aren't, at least in explicit sexual terms. Children are not used to making sexual interpretations. The issues surrounding what's called the disclosure—when a child may say something that leads to a suspicion—are usually important issues in understanding how this family functions."

Eiswirth also said she would want to know who prepared the child to be taken to the center and what was said.

"What do you mean, 'prepared?' " Schoenhorn asked.

"Prepared in terms of taught, or given instructions, or given messages that this is what this place is for . . . this is what this person's going to do, et cetera, so that the child . . . whether the child has some preconceived idea of how he should act or what he should say."

"Have you had occasions where that's occurred?"

"Yes."

Schoenhorn directed her attention to the videotape—the evidence he had tried so hard to keep out of the trial. He asked Eiswirth how she would have conducted the session differently.

"At the beginning of the session, the dolls are in the center of the room on the table. They're already undressed . . . when I use the dolls, I do not put them in the center of the room."

"Why?"

"Because the dolls are only one tool. And I would want to make sure that the child, if he's going to use the doll . . . is it something he has chosen to do . . . or the method that he has chosen to use to communicate something to me."

Schoenhorn asked what else she would have done differently.

"I would not have asked leading questions."

"Why?"

"Children are very sensitive to what adults say, or how adults act. And if you lead them into something, they will follow."

"Why would they do that?"

"Because they're kids . . . they want to please adults in their lives. And obviously, if you're interviewing with an adult that your mother has taken you to, or your parent has taken you to, this must be a very important adult. So it's very important to please that adult."

"Anything else with regard to the session itself?"

"I would not have directed the child to do certain things."

"What do you mean by that? Give an example."

"At certain points in the tape, the clinician asked the child or told the child that that is not what he told her before—and would tell him: 'No, go put the doll in the bed;' 'No, that's not what you said;' 'Now, go do this.' And the child did that."

"And what's wrong with that?"

"Your job as an evaluator," she said, "is to be as neutral as possible and not to have any preconceived ideas of what has happened or what didn't happen."

Eiswirth said she would have questioned the child once the dolls were used.

"At one point in the tape, the child dropped the adult male doll on top of the small boy doll . . . that to me is vague. I don't know if they're wrestling. I don't know if they're, you know, just playing around, whether it's sexual behavior, whether it's some other kind of game."

During the video session, Eiswirth said the child mentioned his father a number of times. "Those were not followed up by the clinician," she went on. "A couple of times, he brought him up in a very positive fashion."

"Can you give an example?"

"At one point," she answered, "he was playing with the ferris wheel . . . he made one of the dolls into a daddy, who was helping to run the ferris wheel—which is putting the father into a helpful role . . . At another point, they had set up an entire family situation for making a meal. There were the four dolls, representing the family with two children. That theme was not developed, about how the child felt about various family members, or, you know, who was doing what during the dinner."

As he was wrapping up his questions about the videotape, Schoenhorn remembered that neither he nor Eiswirth had addressed the issue of a medical examination.

Eiswirth said she would want a medical examination done as quickly as possible and would want to see reports on past examinations.

"And why would you want that before doing a session like that on the videotape?"

"Probably the only sure indicator of sexual abuse is some of the physical findings. No other information is really solid."

"And in your review of all the notes and the reports by the clinician from Langley Center, did you see any indication that she had any information from the pediatrician?"

"No."

Schoenhorn asked why she had watched the *Ghostbusters* movie while preparing her review.

"This was a movie that this child particularly liked. The games he talked about were directly taken from that movie."

Carlson's cross-examination was mild.

Carlson got Eiswirth to admit that in certain difficult situations she used anatomical dolls and leading questions, such as Barrett had used with Keefe.

But Eiswirth also told him that she took extensive notes during her sessions and always wrote down any leading questions that she used, so that she would have a record showing the information was not volunteered spontaneously.

Eiswirth was excused from the witness stand at mid-morning. McQueeney and Schoenhorn exchanged nods of approval. She had been an excellent witness, Rob thought. Now they would have to believe him. He looked to the jurors and again saw nothing.

The judge called a recess.

■CHAPTER TWENTY-FIVE■

A Matter of Honor

When the trial resumed after the Friday morning recess, Schoenhorn told Mulcahy he was going to call a witness out of order. He had planned to call her on Monday, but she was going on vacation.

"All right," said the judge. "Then we'll start."

He looked, waiting for some sign of movement from Schoenhorn. Seeing none after a minute, Mulcahy appeared annoyed. Finally, he asked, "You're calling this witness?"

"My next witness is present, Your Honor," Schoenhorn replied politely. "But I'd rather call her when the jury's here."

"All right . . . Of course. Yes," Mulcahy sputtered. "All right, sheriff, please bring in the jury."

Several minutes later, the jurors were escorted to their seats.

"All right," the judge tried again. "Next witness, Mr. Schoenhorn?"

"Noreen Wilcox," announced Schoenhorn.

The dark-haired woman looked nervous as she headed for the witness stand to Mulcahy's right. Her job was to aid victims and witnesses, not to testify. Wilcox had been subpoenaed to testify several times during her nine years as a police officer. But she had never had to actually get on a witness stand.

It was exactly one week ago, almost to the hour, that she sat with the little boy and warned him about the juice box. But she had hoped it wouldn't come to this when she reported Keefe's words to Carlson.

Carlson knew his duty and had made his decision without hesitation when Wilcox told him what Keefe had said. He immediately met with Mulcahy and Schoenhorn.

"I hope I'm not going to become a witness," Carlson had growled after he told them what had happened.

Schoenhorn couldn't believe his ears. He never would have believed that of Carlson. For some time he had respected Carlson for his decent, ethical approach to a tough job. But making the disclosure about Keefe was the most honorable thing Schoenhorn had ever heard of a prosecutor doing.

He thought back two years—to the months when he had constantly badgered Carlson, trying to convince him that the State did not have a case, pleading with him to talk to Vicki and Bruce. He remembered how Carlson—half-jokingly—told him to ease up or he would turn the case over to another prosecutor.

Had someone else prosecuted the case, Schoenhorn thought, Noreen Wilcox might not be taking the witness stand now.

Wilcox gave her address to the clerk—101 Lafayette Street —and sat down, stiff, tense.

Schoenhorn smiled, trying to put her at ease while he moved to the witness stand. "Although we probably know that address very well," he asked, "what city is it in?"

"Hartford," she answered softly, and than added, "sorry."

"Is that address this building?" Schoenhorn asked with a sweep of his arm.

"Yes."

"I'm going to ask you to keep your voice up so we can hear you."

"Oh."

"Would you please indicate to the members of the jury what your job is."

"I'm a victim advocate."

"And where is your office?"

"In the State's attorney's office, here in this building."

"And is that the office where Mr. Carlson also works?"

"Yes."

"And how long have you been in that position?"

"Approximately a year and a half."

"With regard to the case of State vs. Robert McQueeney that we're here for today, at some point were you asked to become involved to some extent?"

"Yes."

"And specifically, what were you asked to do?"

"Sit with a young child."

Schoenhorn showed her the exhibit picturing Keefe, and she identified him.

"Where was it that you were asked to sit with him?"

"In the room next door, in the hearing room."

"Was this before or after his testimony?"

"After."

"And during that time, what was the child doing?"

"Playing with Legos."

"Now, during the course of playing with the Legos, at any time did the child pick up anything else besides Legos?"

"He had a container of juice, a cardboard container of juice."

"And was it full or empty?"

"Full."

"And what was he doing with that carton?"

"He was banging it on the table."

"And at that point, did you say anything to him?"

"I said, 'Be careful, you may poke a hole in the container and spill it on yourself.' "

"And what did he . . . did he say anything in response to that?"

"Yes. I also said something else. Did you want me to complete my . . ."

"Please."

"Okay. I said, 'Be careful, you may spill it on yourself, and you may have to go back in and testify some more.' "

"And did he respond to that?"

She sighed, "He said, 'I'll say Rob hurt me again.' "

The words filled the courtroom and then there was complete silence.

Schoenhorn let the words hang in the air. Then he resumed.

"Did he specifically use the word 'again?' "

"Yes."

"Thank you," Schoenhorn nodded. "I have no further questions."

Carlson rose and took his post at the corner of the prosecution desk, next to the jury box. He, too, looked uncomfortable. He cleared his throat.

"What exactly is a victim witness . . . excuse me, witness advocate . . . or whatever it is you said you do?"

"Victim advocate. We work with crime victims in the court system, explaining the system and providing services."

He asked Wilcox whether she knew what Keefe meant by what he said.

"No, I don't."

"And did you pursue it any further, to inquire of K what it was that he meant by that?"

"No, I did not."

"Okay. Thank you." Carlson slumped into his chair.

Mulcahy excused Wilcox and the jury and prepared to adjourn court for the lunch recess.

Schoenhorn interrupted. He reminded the judge that he had not advised Wilcox that she could not talk with other witnesses in the case.

"Mr. Carlson," called the judge. "If she is down in your office, would you please advise her of the sequestration order and the terms thereof?"

Carlson looked up from his desk.

"I think she'd like to forget about the whole thing," he grumbled, "but I'll tell her."

■CHAPTER TWENTY-SIX■

The Defense Continues

As the second week of the trial neared an end, Kenneth Robson, the child psychiatrist who had already testified as an expert once outside the presence of the jury—in Schoenhorn's failed attempt to keep Barrett and her video out of the courtroom— was recalled.

This time Robson, wearing his signature bow tie, walked to the witness stand with the jurors watching. Mulcahy again qualified him as an expert.

He testified that his familiarity with the case was limited to a couple of brief discussions with Schoenhorn. Unlike Eiswirth, he had not reviewed the records, the videotape and the depositions. And unlike Eiswirth, he did not use anatomical dolls. He said he preferred other forms of information to evaluate suspicions of sexual abuse.

No responsible professional, he said, would use dolls in isolation—without the benefit of other information.

"What types of other forms of information would you deem necessary?" Schoenhorn asked.

Robson listed many of the items mentioned by Eiswirth, and stressed that he would want information about a divorce, if the parents were splitting up.

"Why is that important?" asked Schoenhorn.

"Because," said Robson, leaning toward the jury box,

"most false allegations of sexual abuse are made in the context of custodial disputes."

Schoenhorn paused to let the point sink in. McQueeney, working on his notes at the defense desk, wanted to pump his fist, but settled for a hard nod.

Schoenhorn examined Robson at length about his methods and about dolls. Then he got to one of his favorite questions regarding Barrett's qualifications. Robson said he had never heard of the title of Master's of Child Welfare.

"Or, MCW?"

"No."

"Have you ever heard of any degree of that sort?"

"No, I have not."

"Has anyone applied to work at the institute, that you've looked at a resume and it has such a statement or a listing of degrees after their name?"

"No."

"Thank you, doctor."

During his cross-examination, Robson stated that anatomical dolls could be beneficial in getting young children to demonstrate something they might not be able to put in words.

Schoenhorn zeroed in on that during redirect.

"You indicated to Mr. Carlson some of your beliefs as to the benefits of the dolls. Are there detriments or negative aspects to the dolls, as well?"

"Yes."

"And what are they? What are some of them?"

"I think the main hazard to the dolls clinically is that one can get a lot of false-positives."

"And what does that mean?" Schoenhorn asked. "That's a scientific term. Right?"

"Well, kind of," Robson leaned forward, becoming the college professor. "But it really means that one concludes from what one sees that an event has taken place, when in fact it hasn't. That's the biggest clinical hazard. The second hazard is that based on the data from those dolls, drastic decisions—that are irreversible, that will affect that family, that child—may be made."

Mulcahy excused Robson and the jury shortly after four p.m. and then turned his attention to scheduling for the final days of the trial.

"There's an expert who will be coming in from out of state, as I understand it," he said.

"It would be my intention, Your Honor, to have my client testify next in this matter," said Schoenhorn, getting out of his chair. "My only request, which Mr. Carlson has kindly agreed to, is that if we're not done with my client's testimony by the one p.m. recess, that we'll suspend and allow the expert to testify at two p.m., then continue with my client's testimony after the expert has departed."

McQueeney trembled at the mention of the witness stand.

"Then at this point in time," Mulcahy asked, "it's anticipated that Mr. McQueeney will be testifying in this case?"

"Yes, Your Honor."

"Well," Mulcahy looked at McQueeney, "Let me ask you, Mr. McQueeney, you've discussed that fully with Mr. Schoenhorn?"

Rob pushed back his chair and stumbled to his feet while trying to button his suit coat.

"Absolutely," he said, looking up.

"And you've been thoroughly advised of your rights to testify or not to testify. Is that correct?"

"Yes, I have, sir."

Mulcahy gave him a recitation of his rights, how the burden of proof was entirely on the State, how the defendant didn't have to prove anything and was under no obligation to testify. He warned McQueeney that if he did testify, the State would have the opportunity to cross-examine him. He reminded him that the jury could not draw any inference of guilt if he decided not to testify.

"Do you understand that, sir," the judge asked.

"Yes I do, sir."

"Has all of that been thoroughly explained to you?"

"Absolutely, and I wish to exercise my right to testify, Your Honor." McQueeney's voice was firm.

"Now what you said right now isn't any commitment or

anything of that nature," Mulcahy assured him. "So again, I understand at this point you've pretty much made a decision."

"That's correct," Rob answered. "And of my own volition, as well."

"Needless to say, you have the weekend now to further reflect on it," the judge advised him.

"Thank you, Your Honor," said McQueeney.

"Thank you, sir," said Schoenhorn.

During the drive home from court that evening, Rob popped a favorite cassette into the car stereo. It was U2's "Joshua Tree," release and his half hearted sing-along suddenly was halted during one song:

You have to cry without weeping,
Talk without speaking,
Scream without raising your voice . . .

The haunting lyrics brought home his frustrating role as the silenced defendant, the restrained accused. Now, his testifying would change that.

CHAPTER TWENTY-SEVEN

A Father's Fight

The judge's obligatory lecture didn't shake McQueeney's determination to testify.

For two and a half years he had been waiting to tell his story. No one had taken the time to hear him out. Barrett had never tried to talk to him. She just made a videotape and pronounced him guilty of raping his four-year-old son. Only once had anyone who accused him asked what he had to say—the cop who was getting ready to arrest him back in February of 1987.

Originally, Rob had figured he could quickly straighten out the whole misunderstanding by going down to the police station and telling the truth. Hurvitz and Schoenhorn wouldn't let him. They had said it wouldn't make any difference. Maybe they were right. They knew a lot more about criminal justice then Rob did. Two years had passed.

But it was Rob's turn now. He figured an innocent man had no choice.

"Are you kidding?" McQueeney had asked, his indignation flaring, when Schoenhorn first asked him what he thought about getting on the witness stand. "You just say the word. It's about time that I get to have my say."

Schoenhorn had tried to curb Rob's fervor. He wanted Rob to calmly, seriously think about the pros and cons of testifying. Rob felt he didn't have to. "I would certainly be scared," he quickly explained, "but I absolutely want to do it."

Early Monday morning, Rob got his final instructions for being a witness, "Be yourself, but be calm," Schoenhorn advised him. "Look at the jurors, talk to them. And, above all, don't give Carlson a hard time."

Schoenhorn didn't rehearse his witnesses, especially in this case where he was going to argue that the child had been rehearsed. He wanted McQueeney to be spontaneous.

He told Rob some of the general areas of questioning he would be covering. He also said he might want Rob to do his Marshmallow Man walk for the jury. At the same time, Schoenhorn said he would point out how much heavier McQueeney was back in the winter of 1987.

"Oh thanks, Jon," McQueeney had chuckled. "Thanks a lot."

McQueeney hadn't been able to sleep past two or three o'clock in the morning since the beginning of voir dire. Saturday and Sunday were not different. Once again, he woke up, his mind racing, unable to stop thinking about what he wanted to tell the jury.

He wanted to be more than an instrument of rebuttal. He wanted the jury to know the warm relationship he used to share with his children. He would tell them about the good times. He wanted to make them feel what Vicki and Johnson and Barrett had taken away from him. The agony he'd had to endure. The shock when he hadn't done anything wrong. When all he'd ever wanted was to be a good husband and father.

"Returning to 53031, State vs. McQueeney, are the parties ready to proceed?" asked Mulcahy as he opened court.

"Yes, Your Honor," answered Schoenhorn.

"All right," said the judge. "And as I understand it, Mr. McQueeney is going to take the stand today. Is that correct?"

"That's correct, Your Honor."

Mulcahy reminded McQueeney of the advice he gave him Friday afternoon. "Do you still wish to exercise your right to testify in your own behalf? Is that correct?"

Rob, standing next to his lawyer, took a deep breath. "That's correct, Your Honor," he said.

Mulcahy said he would instruct the jurors on credibility of testimony and would point out that they should weigh any interest a witness might have in the outcome of the trial. "Do you understand that?"

"Yes, I do sir," Rob answered forthrightly.

"All right. Thank you." Mulcahy turned to the sheriff. "The jury can be brought in."

Rob's stomach churned as the jurors filed into their seats.

"Mr. Schoenhorn," the judge said, "you may proceed."

"Your Honor, the defense will call Robert McQueeney."

Trembling and pale, Rob slowly made his way to the witness stand. It seemed farther now than it had looked.

Schoenhorn, his hands clasped in front of him, stood at the opposite end of the jury box from McQueeney so that Rob could face the jurors as he answered questions. He began by having Rob talk about his employment, then he asked about his family.

"Could you please indicate what your family consists of?"

"Well, I have a son, and a daughter, Wendy. K is six and a half, and Wendy is five. And my wife and I are expecting a baby girl in September."

"And just so we're clear, who are you referring to as your wife?"

"Jacqueline." Rob motioned toward Jackie, who was in the first row of the spectator section behind the defense desk, the same place she had been throughout the trial.

"Jacqueline McQueeney?" Schoenhorn asked.

"Yes."

"And she's in the courtroom right now?"

"Yes, she is."

"And when were you married?"

"November 6th . . . of last year."

Though he was nervous, Rob tried to talk to the jurors, as Schoenhorn had instructed, trying to meet their eyes. It was so hard, he thought, to keep all Schoenhorn's instructions about how to do it and all Rob wanted to say in his mind at the same time. He glanced over at Lois and made eye contact again. Red-haired Paula was leaning toward the witness stand, possibly straining to listen, her face contorted. Others appeared attentive, except for one. Maurice Back, the retired engineer, was staring off toward the ceiling. Did Back think he was guilty?

He began to tremble. What were the others thinking? Did they believe him? Schoenhorn's voice cut into his thoughts, "Now," said Schoenhorn, "I'm going to call your attention to the weekend of January 31st and February 1, 1987. I'm going to ask you specific questions, but first of all, at that time, who were you living with?"

"I was by myself."

"And how long had you been by yourself?"

Rob felt anger rise in his throat, he tried to keep his voice calm, it came out a bit stilted, "Vicki left July 31st of the previous year."

"Would you describe the circumstances under which she left?"

McQueeney told how he had returned home to find the note that had said simply: "The cat's outside. Vicki." Wondering where she and the children could be, he recalled how he had grown aggravated, then worried and finally desperate, and had called the police, giving them a description of the car he had bought five days earlier for Vicki.

He testified how he had spent the night in his car outside Vicki's mother's house and then had driven home after seeing no signs of anyone.

He rushed on, trying to patiently convey all the information, his mind flashing back to the terror he'd felt that day.

"And I believe mid-morning, I called my mother and was trying to piece together some semblance of what may have happened. Around ten o'clock, I saw a white Cadillac pull up my driveway, and I hung up the phone and went outside. I was served with the summons by a sheriff. That was August 1st."

"Just so we're clear. What summons are we talking about?"

"For divorce."

Angrily, Rob recounted his telephone call with Vicki's lawyer, John Clifford. "At that point my primary concern was where my children were, and I asked him to tell me where they were. And he would not. So I asked him if he knew where my son and daughter were."

"Why did you ask that?"

Rob's upper lip trembled, he said slowly, "I felt that at some . . . If I knew somebody knew where they were, that at least it wasn't that they had disappeared from the face of the earth. He indicated that he, in fact, knew where they were. And I had to take that as being enough."

Schoenhorn asked why, as the divorce proceedings went along, Rob wanted joint custody of the children.

"I certainly felt it was only right that I share in the future of the children . . . be able to share in the decision-making, about education and all the issues. And that was certainly something that I expected and never felt would ever be denied," Rob's face was somber, his voice flat.

Schoenhorn had him describe the arrangements for his weekend visits with his children. He asked about the games they played together.

"Well," Rob perked up and began to gesture, his words coming faster, "The most prevalent games that we played on a consistent basis were . . . we had a He-Man game, He-Man being a superhero in cartoons and movies. And my son had every He-Man toy imaginable, figures and castle. He also had a number of related cartoon figures, Thundercats. And my daughter had her own collection, which were not the superhero line, but they were Wuzzles and Popples and Care Bears. And . . ."

Schoenhorn cut in. "What's a Wuzzle?"

"A Wuzzle is a combination of animals. You might have an elephant with a bumble-bee body, or kind of a strange genetic crossbreed of animals."

"Are they stuffed animals?"

"No, figurines with the moveable arms and legs."

"Okay."

"And we would devise these very elaborate games—rescue type—rescuing Wuzzles from Skeletor . . ."

Schoenhorn stopped him again, frowning. "Who's Skeletor?"

Rob didn't know what was going on. Why did Schoenhorn keep stopping him. Wasn't he believable? What was he supposed to say so they'd all know he was telling the truth? He hadn't time to think it out, more words poured out.

"He's the antithesis of He-Man."

"In the cartoons and comic books?"

"In the cartoon. And we would play that for quite a while with the various cars and toys, and all surrounding the theme of good guys helping good guys. And so forth."

Schoenhorn, frowning again, asked about other games.

Rob explained in detail how he and the children would prepare elaborate multi-course meals using a play kitchen set.

"Any other games?" asked Schoenhorn.

"Well, we played the Marshmallow Man game."

"Why don't you tell us about the Marshmallow Man game?"

"Well, my son was very fond of *Ghostbusters*. And to my recollection, we had seen the movie three times. And somewhere along the line, I developed the idea of being . . . myself being the Marshmallow Man. And . . ."

"Let me interrupt for a second, if I may," Schoenhorn looked at his client with a sly grin. "Was your physique any different in the winter of 1987 than it is now?"

"Yes."

"Could you indicate in what way it was different?"

"Well, I was about thirty to thirty-five pounds heavier."

Schoenhorn asked him to describe the game.

"Welllll," for the first time Rob grinned, he shifted his position. "The Marshmallow Man is a character out of *Ghostbusters*. He's essentially a bad guy. And what I would do is I would take on this role. And I would never say, 'Okay, I'm going to be the Marshmallow Man.' I would just begin to . . . if there was maybe a little bit of a lull in the activity, or if we'd been wrestling or something, I would begin to be the Marshmallow Man.

"And the way I would do that would be to just start taking these hulking, lumbering steps. And as soon as they saw me, they would begin to scream and run. And as I . . . even though I was taking this very slow, lethargic pace and they were running at the speed of light, of course I always caught up to them —probably because they wanted to be caught up to. And they would scream, 'Run, run, it's the Marshmallow Man,' you know, as if they were warning the public. And my daughter was the echo. So whatever K would yell, she would be trying to verbalize herself, two steps behind him. So eventually I would catch up to them, to one of them. The child would immediately fall helpless to the floor, and I would sort of descend down onto whomever it was. And then get them so that I was on my hands and knees with them kind of caged beneath me. And at that point . . . now I would begin to verbalize. Although it's not how it's done in the movie, I took liberties. And I would begin to say that I was the Marshmallow Man, and they were my prisoner, and there's no escape.

"And that, of course, gave them the opportunity to shoot me with an imaginary raygun, which if they remembered, and usually they were so . . . trying to get away from the Marshmallow Man and laughing and giggling . . . that they would forget that they could blow me up with the imaginary raygun. But if they . . ."

He was rambling, Schoenhorn had to cut him off again. "Is that done in the movie, by the way? Is the Marshmallow Man blown up?"

"Yes."

"By a raygun?"

"Yes." Rob rambled on. "So Wendy never remembered to blow me up. But my son—it would occasionally dawn on him, and he'd try to shoot me. At some time, I would say: 'No; that wasn't the right gun; you have to have a different gun.' And, of course, that would really get them into a state of excitement. And if he did choose the right gun, and he shot me, then I would go into this mock explosion.

"It's kind of hard to imitate, exploding marshmallow. But I would do my best. And of course, then they would be free until I usually would then, you know, like regroup and made all the noises, whatever was necessary to make it as vivid to them as possible. And start the cycle all over again, usually then going for the other child. And that was about it."

Schoenhorn, standing patiently at the opposite end of the jury box, asked whether McQueeney ever pounced up and down on Keefe.

"Wellll," Rob went on in a loud voice—just telling the story

309

of the game brought out his extroverted nature for the first time. "The idea of being a Marshmallow Man, as you could have seen from the toy, was squashing your victim. I don't know what the technical term for this is, but you've got them on the floor, and you kind of squash them, you know, till you get them to do this vibrato in their voice. And so they're trying to—you know, they're trying to tell you that 'I'm strong, and I'm going to beat you, Marshmallow Man.' Or 'I've got this gun.' And you're not letting them be able to speak because you're giving them the shakes, and of course, they get silly. And that was part of it."

Rob said he and the kids played Marshmallow Man just about every weekend.

"Did you ever play it unclothed?" Schoenhorn asked.

"There were instances where after a bath—the children will often like to take a little streak through the house. And so there were times when the Marshmallow Man had to capture these fleeing children—to get their jammies on."

"And when you say 'jammies,' I assume you mean pajamas?"

"Yes. Pajamas."

"Did you or they ever hide the pajamas?"

"Well, they never hid them. But if they gave me a bad enough time about getting them on, I'd say, 'Fine, when you're ready, you're going to have to find them.' Usually I'd put them in the dryer. That would be one of the hiding spots. I never had a hundred hiding spots. It was no fun if they couldn't find them . . ."

Schoenhorn looked outwardly calm, but behind his dark mustache, his teeth were clenched. Schoenhorn feared Rob was coming across as smug.

Schoenhorn went on with the examination. He asked McQueeney to describe Sunday, February 1, 1987. Rob did it in excruciating detail, including what he prepared for the children at each meal. The highlight of the day was sledding.

"I started trying to get my son to come down by himself," McQueeney recalled. "He was afraid, and eventually he made the decision that he was going to do it. And he got on the toboggan by himself and came down by himself—eyes like dinner plates—but he did it by himself. It was a very warm experience."

After sledding, Rob said he took the kids back to the house and put them in a bath.

"Now did there come a time when you were washing K's behind?"

"I pretty much finished with Wendy, and I did my son's hair. I asked him to stand up so I could wash his genitals and his rear end. And he complained. He said, 'Ow,' when I was between his buttocks with the face cloth."

"Did you say anything to him at that point?"

"Yeah. I asked him what was wrong, and he says, 'It hurts.' So I figured well, there's something back there that the soap isn't being too kind to. And I immediately rinsed him back there with water out of the faucet. By this time now, I got Wendy out. She's toweling herself. And just finished up with K and got him out of the tub."

"And then what did you do?"

"Well, there was something obviously wrong. So I asked my son to turn away from me, and I got down on the floor. And I was trying to spread his cheeks apart to see if I could see something. But I was all scrunched down, and I couldn't see anything. So I put the lid on the toilet down, and I asked him to bend over. And I spread his cheeks apart, and I saw an inflammation."

"Would you describe that inflammation, please?"

Rob's voice had turned almost defiant, "Well, it was bright red, and it was almost perfectly round, around his anus, right up to the sphincter itself. The size was about three-quarters of a inch in diameter."

"Now, prior to that weekend, had Vicki told you that K was not doing a good job of wiping himself after going to the bathroom?"

"No, she did not."

"When you saw the inflammation, the redness, what did you do?"

Rob said he had some medicated powder in the bathroom which he knew had a cooling effect because he had used it himself.

"I got the powder," he continued. "I brought it back. With one hand, probably my left hand, I spread his cheeks apart. I sprinkled the powder on liberally, and then with the other hand, I applied the powder not only on the reddened area, but you know, all vertically thereabouts."

"And you applied it with what?"

"With my fingers."

"Did K respond while you were doing that in any way?"

"He at one point said, 'Ow,' and he also said it hurt. But he was being a good boy about being in that position and allowing me to do that."

Schoenhorn asked Rob to describe how he told Vicki about the inflammation when he took the children back to the house in Goshen where she and Bruce lived.

"I told her I didn't want to embarrass my son, but he had an inflammation on his butt. I said it was red, about the size of a quarter; told her I put on the powder and suggested that she take a look at it."

Schoenhorn asked about Keefe's expression as Rob prepared to leave after dropping the kids off.

"He had what I would call 'the look.' "

"All right, and would you describe what 'the look' was?"

"During the last weekends that my kids were visiting with me, my son began to voice his unhappiness with the living arrangements that he had."

"Can you be more specific."

"Yes, I can be very specific," Rob said his voice filled with the dislike he could not hide. "My son would say that I was alone and that he and his sister wanted to come stay with me."

"All right. Would you indicate how that manifested itself in a 'look?' "

"Eventually on those Sunday nights when I would bring them back to Goshen, there were several occasions where my son looked distraught that I was now dropping him off and I was going home. And he would almost be on the verge of crying. And on that particular evening, he gave me 'the look.' "

"And what did you do?"

"I knelt down in front of my son. And I just told him that I would see him next weekend and that I loved him and to take care of his sister. And I gave him a hug."

"Did he at any time that evening pull away from you?"

"No, he didn't."

"Or struggle to get free?"

"No."

"Or run over and stand next to his mother?"

"No, he did not."

"Did that ever happen when you were bringing the children back?"

"Never," Rob said flatly.

Schoenhorn asked whether McQueeney had ever heard his son use the word "penis?"

"To my recollection, I've never heard him use that word."

"Did you ever tell him he shouldn't use that word?"

"No," Rob paused, thinking. "That would follow. If I didn't hear him use it, then I would have no need to tell him not to."

"Did you ever stick your hand up K's rectum on January 31st or February 1st of 1987?"

"Absolutely not," Rob said angrily.

"Specifically, did you stick your hand up to your wrist up his rectum?"

He shook his head for emphasis, "No."

"Did you ever stick your finger up his behind, other than to put medicated powder on him that weekend?"

"No."

Schoenhorn asked why Rob had agreed to give Vicki legal custody of the children as part of the divorce settlement.

"Pending the outcome of the criminal charges," he replied, "there wasn't a whole lot of latitude to do anything but."

"And can you be more specific?"

Rob bit his lip and continued, "I don't have a great deal of strength as an alleged felon regarding any visitation or custody of my children."

"Have you given up on the possibility of having visitation with your children?"

"I have never given up on that," he said emphasizing each word.

Schoenhorn asked Rob whether he had seen the *Ghostbusters* movie since he last saw it with his children.

"Yes. Once."

"How recently?"

"Last week."

"Now at my request, did you make a copy of that film?"

"Yes, I did."

Schoenhorn walked to the defense desk and picked up a videocassette.

"Let me show you this item and ask you whether you could identify it?" He handed it to McQueeney.

"Yes. This is the copy requested."

Schoenhorn turned to the judge, holding out the movie. "Your Honor," he said, "I'm going to offer it."

Carlson was already out of his chair. "I'm going to object, Your Honor," he said. "I think it's probably something that should be argued out of the hearing of the jury."

"Yes," agreed Mulcahy. "That'll have to be outside the jury. All right, ladies and gentlemen, we'll excuse you."

When the jurors left the courtroom, Carlson asked the purpose of putting the movie into evidence.

The games that were discussed by Vicki, Keefe and Barrett all came directly from the movie, Schoenhorn said.

Carlson said he didn't remember anyone asking the child if he had made anything up based on *Ghostbusters*. Therefore, he said, the movie should not be admissable as evidence.

The judge said he would consider his ruling on the objection, and called a recess.

During the break, Carlson and Schoenhorn reached an agreement: Carlson would rent the movie, watch it that night and then meet with Schoenhorn in the morning to try to settle their disagreement, possibly by allowing certain portions of the movie into evidence.

McQueeney found Schoenhorn before he went off to lunch and took him aside.

"How am I doing?"

Schoenhorn shook his head, "Didn't you learn anything from watching Bruce?" Schoenhorn spoke softly, but his voice was shrill. "You seemed overbearing and smug."

McQueeney's mouth dropped open in disbelief.

"I'll guarantee you," Schoenhorn went on, "that Carlson's going to use that against you in closing arguments."

Rob couldn't understand what was wrong. He'd tried to be friendly, open, honest and at the same time firm and knowledgeable.

His face flushed with embarrassment. He couldn't believe anyone could think he was smug, not after all he'd been through.

When court reconvened at two p.m., Diane Schetky replaced McQueeney on the witness stand. She had come from Maine to testify as Schoenhorn's third expert witness.

Schoenhorn had talked with her many times on the phone, but today was the first time he had seen her.

"Doctor," Schoenhorn addressed her from his position at the far end of the jury box. "Good afternoon. Would you please indicate to the jury what your field of specialty is?"

"I'm a child psychiatrist, and I specialized in the area of child psychiatry and the law. This includes the interface of issues that affect child psychiatry and the courts, such as abuse, neglect and so forth."

"And how long have you been in that field?"

"Probably since about 1977."

Schetky's posture was unusual. She was a tall woman, and she leaned awkwardly to the side of the witness chair, fiddling with a chunky necklace she was wearing.

She estimated that she had testified as an expert in court proceedings around one hundred times.

Schoenhorn led her through her qualifications, and Mulcahy declared her an expert.

"Incidently, Doctor," Schoenhorn resumed his questioning, "are you familiar with the title of Master's of Child Welfare?"

"No, I'm not."

It had been more than a year since Schetky had produced her report for Schoenhorn, along with a suggestion that Langley Center could be sued for malpractice.

But when Schoenhorn asked what she would have done

differently in the session that Barrett videotaped for the police, Schetky's expertise showed through, "I think, first of all, she was very distant with the children, really wasn't interacting with them, except when they talked about sexual abuse. And then she'd get very interested, or draw them close to her. Her tone of voice would be more animated.

"A couple of times, she even reinforced the children's statements. When K said, 'It hurt,' she said, 'That's good, that's good.' Another time, K didn't recall something, apparently the way he had the previous time, as to where the alleged abuse had occurred. And you could sense the disappointment in her voice."

"What would you do in the same circumstances?" asked Schoenhorn.

Schetky stressed the importance of the therapists questions and actions remaining neutral. "You've got to be very neutral. Children are extremely eager to please an adult. So automatically, if she's conveying to this child what she wants to hear . . . another trap she fell into was using a lot of either/or questions, which implies to the child there are only one out of two possible answers—when in fact there may be others she hasn't mentioned. It also encourages the child to guess.

"Another problem was she got into using leading questions. And this is where you introduce information to the child that the child hasn't brought up yet—an example being, 'Did you tell him it hurts?' She introduced, 'hurts,' suggesting that it hurt before the child had used that term in the interview."

"What would you do in place of that?"

"How did it feel? How did you feel?"

Schetky said she was also troubled by Barrett's video, because so much weight was put on the child's play with the dolls without any real explanation from him about what he was demonstrating.

As Schoenhorn continued to question her, Schetky brought out a major discrepancy. She had noticed a contradiction in the videotape. When Barrett asked K what position he was in when his father jumped on him, the child said he was on his back.

"What she's reading in, is not what the boy is demonstrating," Schetky went on. "You don't sodomize a child with him lying on his back, usually."

Like Ledder, she also commented on Keefe's note-like presentation.

"I also noted, as he was demonstrating the father jumping on him, that he didn't display any particular anger towards the father at that time. Often, if children are re-enacting sexual abuse, it brings back all sort of memories and feelings—either of shame or anger or sadness. I didn't see this on the video. In fact, later on, he went on to draw a picture of his father smiling."

A chastened Rob McQueeney returned to the witness stand following the mid-afternoon recess.

Schoenhorn resumed by asking his client to tell the jury about the plot of *Ghostbusters*.

As Rob went on and on trying to describe the paranormal experience which led the characters into becoming Ghostbusters, Schoenhorn groaned to himself. Finally he asked, "Approximately how many times did you play a game based on the movie?"

"Dozens."

"Now Mr. McQueeney," Schoenhorn paused, looking at his client. "You were here, and you heard the testimony of your son. Right?"

"Yes." Rob braced for what he knew was coming.

"And let me ask you this question: Have you ever inserted your penis in your son's rectum?"

The question stung.

"No sir," Rob looked straight at the jury.

"Have you ever sexually molested either of your children?"

"No, I have not." Rob's voice was quiet, firm.

"Have you ever placed your penis against your child's rectum, in a sexual manner?"

"No sir." His final words, strong and determined, filled the courtroom.

"I have no further questions at this time."

Carlson stood, buttoned his dark suit coat, folded his arms

across his chest, tucked in his chin and began his cross examination with the He-Man and Ghostbusters games.

He asked McQueeney how his children would know he was beginning the Marshmallow Man game.

"It would be hard to verbalize," replied Rob.

"Well, I'm not going to ask you to demonstrate."

"Okay. I would be glad to, though, if you wish."

"Well," Carlson rocked back on his heels, putting his hand in his pockets. "If Mr. Schoenhorn wants you to, he may ask you. I'm not going to."

The prosecutor's questioning was mild. He explored Mc-Queeney's story in detail, but didn't push hard.

"Whether or not K was confined to his room at any point in time?" Carlson asked of the weekend of January 31 and February 1, 1987.

"Neither child was ever confined to their room," Rob answered decisively.

"I thought you had indicated that when a child didn't obey a particular rule, such as borrowed another child's toy, that the child would be sent to their room?"

"Correct."

"Is there a difference between 'sending to' and 'confining?' " Carlson asked.

"I think so," Rob said quietly.

"All right. What is it?"

"I think sending a child to their room can indicate a very brief stay, whereas confinement, I think, might indicate a more lengthy and punitive stay."

"Do you have a time-frame break off between those two that you use?" Carlson asked.

"I think," Rob said slowly, "if a child's going to be confined to their room, it would perhaps be for an afternoon."

"Whether or not during that weekend, K was sent to his room for some transgression?"

"I don't have any recollection whether he was or wasn't."

"And whether or not during that weekend K was confined to his room—as you define confined?"

"No," answered Rob. "He was not confined to the room."

318

Before Carlson was able to complete his questioning, Mulcahy adjourned court for the day.

News travels fast in a courthouse, where lawyers and sheriffs spend long hours trading stories between cases. Jack Ewing, the Hartford newspaper's Superior Court reporter, had heard about Schoenhorn's unusual move Monday.

The next morning Jackie had good reason for her paranoia that someone, somewhere might recognize her name and connect her with the ghastly affair going on in Hartford.

"DEFENSE SEEKS TO LINK SEX-ABUSE CHARGE WITH POPULAR MOVIE," screamed the headline prominently displayed on the cover of the Connecticut section of the *Hartford Courant*, the state's largest newspaper.

"A Hartford defense attorney is trying to introduce the movie *Ghostbusters* as evidence in a criminal trial, contending that a child's description of alleged sexual abuse was lifted from popular culture, not reality," Ewing's story began.

Later in the newspaper account, he wrote: "In what may go down in courtroom annals as the 'Ghostbusters defense,' Schoenhorn contends that the boy was just describing things— such as ghosts flying through the air—that he'd seen in the movie."

Ewing's description of the movie was much more succinct than the one McQueeney had delivered from the witness stand on Monday.

"The 1984 comedy-thriller, starring Bill Murray and Dan Aykroyd, concerns the efforts of a team of renegade scientists to defeat an epidemic of ghosts and demons in New York City," Ewing wrote. "The film culminates with the destruction of a giant, evil creature made of marshmallow."

When Mulcahy reconvened the trial on Tuesday, he pointed out the new development to Schoenhorn and Carlson.

"I understand there was a newspaper article in the paper this morning," the judge said. He paused, then added, "In fact, I know there was. I read it."

Mulcahy asked the lawyers whether he should question the jurors about it.

"It's up to you, Your Honor," replied Schoenhorn.

The story had quoted Schoenhorn at length about his defense and his contention that the child in the case had been coached by his mother to implicate McQueeney.

Mulcahy called for the jury to be brought to the courtroom.

"Ladies and gentlemen," he said, "It's been brought to my attention that there was a newspaper article in this morning's *Courant,* and I wish to inquire whether any of you have read that article?"

Maurice Back, the retired engineer, raised his hand.

The judge asked Back whether he had been influenced by the article.

"No. I did what you instructed. I set it aside," said Back in his strong Dutch accent.

Then Mulcahy asked another juror, James Stewart, about the article. Stewart hadn't read it but had been told about it. "It wouldn't affect me in any way," said Stewart, the white-haired video manager from Cigna.

The judge asked the lawyers whether they wanted to question the jurors further. Neither saw any need.

Mulcahy told Carlson he could resume his cross-examination of McQueeney, who had taken the witness stand before the jurors were brought into the courtroom.

Carlson reminded Rob of his description of *Ghostbusters.*

"You had indicated, I think yesterday, that these people were engaged in paranormal research, or parapsychological research?"

"Yes."

"Do you happen to know what that is?"

"Yes, I do."

"Ooookay," Carlson drew out the word, letting it hang. "Tell us how you know what it is."

"It's an interest of mine."

"All right." Carlson tucked his chin. "And what is it?"

"What is paranormal or . . ."

Mulcahy interrupted. "What's the other word, sir?"

"Parapsychological," answered Carlson.

The judge nodded for McQueeney to continue.

"It's a scientific study of things that go bump in the night," Rob answered.

"Do you want to tell us how it is that you came across this knowledge?" Carlson asked.

"Back in college," he said. "I belonged to a club that was interested in ESP, telekinesis . . . and things that go bump in the night—haunted houses, that type of thing."

When Carlson completed his cross-examination a few minutes later, Rob was surprised. He had expected to be hammered, pushed to a point where he might lose control. It hadn't happened. He breathed a heavy sigh of relief.

Schoenhorn's redirect examination lasted just a few more minutes.

"I know that Mr. Carlson declined to have you demonstrate how you lumbered along as the Marshmallow Man," he said. "But I'm going to take you up on that. I'm going to ask you right now to demonstrate that, here in front of the jury, if you would please."

Rob stepped down from the witness stand, spread his arms and legs, put on a menacing look and did his impression. His wide body swayed with each slow, hulking step, as though he had weights on his legs.

"Thank you sir," Mulcahy said as McQueeney completed a pass in front of the jury box. "You may resume the stand."

"I don't know the best way to describe it, your Honor," said Schoenhorn. "But let the record reflect that the witness walked along in a slow manner, with his arms outstretched and moved in a very slow, lumbering pace."

"Lumbering fashion," echoed the judge.

Schoenhorn went to the defense desk and picked up the copy of the *Ghostbusters* movie that Rob had made for him. "I'm going to offer it at this time," he told Mulcahy.

Carlson said he watched the movie at home Monday night and was withdrawing his objection.

"Then I take it there's nothing for me to rule on," observed Mulcahy. He excused McQueeney from the witness stand.

Jackie gave Rob a big smile as he returned to his swivel chair at the defense desk. He had done much better this morning. This was the Rob McQueeney she knew and loved. Tears came to her eyes. The jury had to know, as she did, that he was a good man.

"Now, we'll have to set up some equipment for the movie," Mulcahy said. "I did some research last night, ladies and gentlemen, and I ascertained that if the tape were admitted . . . my research indicated that I have to stay in here and watch it with you. So I looked for some legal authority to the contrary and couldn't find any. So in any event, we'll watch it together."

Introducing a note of levity, he went on.

"No popcorn or anything of that nature is available. So we'll just have to sit through it."

He excused the jury and called a recess while the courtroom was turned into a theater.

A television monitor was set up on the prosecution desk, facing the jury box about six feet away.

As the jurors filed back into the courtroom, the judge sounded like an usher.

"If you'd use the first four seats in each row," he asked. "Thank you. I think that perhaps it is the best viewing angle. Does the screen appear to be visible to everyone?"

The jurors nodded.

The lights dimmed and eerie instrumental music filled the courtroom.

The New York Public Library flashed onto the screen. A woman in glasses, presumably a librarian, was walking between tall stacks of books. Behind her, books began floating off the shelves through the air. Then drawers in a wooden card catalogue case opened by themselves and index cards flew everywhere. Startled, the librarian hurried back through the stacks. Suddenly she stopped. Her face, illuminated by a ghostly light, filled the screen. A look of confusion turned to horror. She screamed.

A drum beat erupted into the movie's theme song:
"If there's something strange
"in your neighborhood,

"who ya gonna call?
"Ghostbusters!
"If there's something weird
"and it don't look good,
"who ya gonna call?
"Ghostbusters!"

Jurors glanced at the judge. They didn't know how to act while watching a comedy in a courtroom. If Mulcahy laughed, then it would be all right to follow his lead. But the judge maintained his judicial face.

Everyone followed his example and kept their faces serious. The scene in the courtroom was as farcical as the movie—spectators swallowed their giggles.

Mulcahy had the movie stopped shortly before five p.m. The final twenty minutes would be played the next day.

As he had each afternoon, the judge quietly warned the jurors not to look at any media reports.

"Again, I caution you not to discuss the case among yourselves at this point," he said. "That's only appropriate after all of the evidence is in . . . Thank you so much for your attention today, and have a pleasant evening. Good night. You're excused until tomorrow morning."

That afternoon the McQueeneys sneaked out a rear exit of the courthouse.

Jackie walked back around the block to the parking lot entrance by the front of the courthouse. She slipped sideways past the gate, trying to make sure any reporters on the sidewalk in front of the courthouse could not see her face.

Rob and Ruth got in the car. As Jackie drove out, she passed in front of the building, turning her head toward the other side of the street. She glanced in the rearview mirror. Nobody following. She drove back around the block to the others and turned the wheel over to Rob.

He had to drive back by the courthouse on the way home. Ruth could see a television crew from the rear seat. She grimaced, glad they couldn't get to her to make her agony public.

That night, Ruth McQueeney felt better. She got a half-dozen telephone calls from close friends who had read the newspaper story and offered their support. One of the calls came from Cheryl, Rob's first wife.

CHAPTER TWENTY-EIGHT

Marshmallow Man

The inspiration for McQueeney's imitation of the Marshmallow Man materialized Wednesday morning when the trial—and the movie—resumed.

The Ghostbusters, warned by an evil spirit that they would choose the form of the demon that would destroy them and New York City, tried to empty their heads of any thoughts. But Dan Akroyd's character couldn't.

"I tried to think of the most harmless thing," he said, "something I loved through my childhood, something that could never, ever possibly destroy us . . . Mr. Stay-Puff."

He remembered how he and his buddies used to roast Stay-Puff marshmallows at camp.

Mr. Stay-Puff stood at least ten-stories high—puffy and white, with a gentle, smiling face, a blue cap and a blue sailor collar. The creature lumbered through the streets, crushing anything in its way.

"Roast him," shouted one of the Ghostbusters, and they blasted the creature with their rayguns. It caught fire and exploded, showering the city with marshmallow.

New York had been saved, and crowds cheered the Ghostbusters. For Rob, the movie brought back many happy memories of days with his children. For a moment he forgot he was on trial. Then he remembered, and tears filled his eyes.

The lights came on, and Mulcahy returned to his seat at the bench.

"At this time," Schoenhorn announced, "the defense rests."

The judge gave the jurors a long lunch while he and the lawyers prepared for summations, scheduled to begin at two p.m.

The trial had started July 18. It was now August 2.

One of the jurors, Emma Aceto, had missed one of her favorite annual events. Each year she and her husband rented a cottage at the beach in Old Lyme for two weeks. Traditionally, during the first week, they invited their grandchildren to stay with them. A couple of times during the trial, Emma had made the hour-long drive to the cottage so that she could spend a few hours with her family before returning to the courthouse the following morning.

She continued writing her notes from memory late at night, and her husband still hadn't discovered her secret. It wouldn't be long now before she would bring her notes to the courthouse. She was sure the dates would help the other jurors reconstruct the case.

Emma was anxious to find out what the other jurors were thinking. *Her* mind was made up. It had been for some time.

As she was escorted back into the courtroom after lunch, Emma was thinking past the summations to the moment the jury would no longer be muzzled.

"All right," said Mulcahy. "Ladies and gentlemen, we're now going to proceed with the summations of counsel. The format that we follow is this: The State, Mr. Carlson, begins with his initial summation; and then Mr. Schoenhorn delivers his summation to you; and then Mr. Carlson, since the State does have the burden of proof in a criminal case, is given an opportunity to address you in rebuttal."

Rob was troubled by the prospect of Carlson getting the last word. Rob took a deep breath, pulled his note pad toward him and got ready to write.

"Mr. Carlson, you may address the ladies and gentlemen of the jury."

Carlson pushed himself out of his chair and for the first time during the trial strayed a few feet from his desk. He walked in front of the jury box, folding his arms across his chest.

"Thank you, Your Honor." He turned to the jurors and tucked in his chin.

"As his Honor said, this is the time of the summations. This really means that the lawyers have the opportunity to point out to you certain items which they would both suggest to you had been proved, and to point out how it is that, if you agree that these items have been proved, as to how you can consider them. It's a time to argue the evidence, some law, and of course, point out to you how you might use your own general knowledge and experience.

"Sympathy and thoughts of potential punishment play no role whatsoever in jury deliberations. The judge will tell you about that at the end of the case. And, as in many cases which are presented to juries, the credibility of the witnesses who have been called is, of course, a very important function for you to perform—that is, the assessment of their credibility."

Carlson went over each of the three separate criminal charges that had been filed against McQueeney and talked about intent.

"This can't be something which was done accidently," he said. "It has to be an intentional act . . . although I suppose if one were really to think about it, the chances of having accidental sexual intercourse are pretty minimal. But I suppose it could happen."

Carlson seemed to be rambling.

"Really what you have to decide here is whether or not you believe the testimony of K, given here in the courtroom," Carlson said, gaining his focus again. "That is the key to the case, I suggest.

"And instead of me relating to you everything that he said —talking about being chased, being caught, being hit, being thrown onto the floor and then anally sexually assaulted—what I'm going to suggest that you do is, after the judge's instruction, if it's appropriate, tomorrow, if you think you need to, have it played back to you so you can listen to everything it is that K told you—because it was a week ago Friday that he came in and testified.

"And what I'm going to ask you particularly to do is when . . . if you decide to do this, listen to his tone of voice. And I'm going to suggest that if you listen to the way he spoke, this is going to help you a lot in making this determination."

He reminded the jurors of Barrett's videotape.

He argued that Keefe had never wavered in his allegation that his father sexually assaulted him—from the time he first told Bruce Johnson on Cape Cod in February of 1987.

"The only change that I suggest that occurred was the difference between finger and hand to penis," he went on. "And Bruce Johnson had indicated to you how that happened in his testimony."

Carlson listed some of the witnesses that testified for the defense.

"Now we have Dr. Pandit," he said. "In just a few seconds, according to Dr. Pandit, at two and a half feet—with a flashlight in one hand—he looks at K, and he doesn't see anything. What I'm going to suggest to you is that Vicki had already told you that she had cleared that up . . . there was nothing to find."

He brought up Noreen Wilcox and the child's spontaneous statement: "I'll say Rob hurt me again."

"But, what does that mean?" Carlson asked. "What was it in response to? She didn't pursue it. Again, I'm going to suggest to you that that really isn't dispositive of anything. I don't know the extent to what meaning you can put on that. That would be up to you."

Carlson checked his watch. "We each get an hour," he said. "I get the opportunity to split it up. I've done about a half an hour now. So that seems like a good time for me to sit down. But you certainly will be hearing from me again."

McQueeney put down his pen. That wasn't too bad, he said to himself.

After a brief recess, Schoenhorn got his last chance to tell the jury Rob's side. He walked slowly to the front of the jury box. He looked solemn as he began.

"There's no question, ladies and gentlemen, that K, as he's

been referred to in this case, is a victim." He let the word hang in the air for a moment.

"But does that mean he's a victim of sexual abuse? Or perhaps of something else? Is he perhaps a victim of a domineering and hysterical and somewhat manipulative mother? Is he perhaps the victim of a self-important, ex-lieutenant deputy sheriff, who not only controlled Vicki's entire life by telling her to quit her job, picking the center to send the child to, picking her divorce lawyer for her, but also in determining, to a large extent, her life?

"You'll recall, ladies and gentlemen, Vicki McQueeney picked up and left without any word whatsoever, except mentioning 'the cat is outside,' on July 31st, 1986. And took Rob McQueeney's two children and disappeared.

"Obviously, it's something that she had planned—because she had already been to the lawyer. Now, you've heard Bruce Johnson testify that he's the one who picked Attorney Clifford for her. So he was scheming with her even before she left.

"And, what's also of interest, ladies and gentlemen, is within three weeks of that date, three weeks of her disappearing with the children, they're already looking for a house together."

He pointed out that Bruce was a law enforcement officer who did not call the police about anything that he claimed Keefe told him.

"And, what's more interesting, ladies and gentlemen, is the difference between Bruce and Vicki . . . is that Vicki did not come in here and say that K made all these other allegations and supposedly explained the discrepancy about a finger or a hand, all the way up to the wrist. And that suddenly at some point became a penis. Vicki didn't mention the Cape.

"If, ladies and gentlemen, you're considering what needs to be believed and not be believed, do you believe that the mother wouldn't remember that significant event?"

Schoenhorn touched again on the victim theme.

"But who else is a victim here, ladies and gentlemen? Not only K, but Wendy is a victim as well, because Wendy has been deprived of not only her father, but that whole side of the family."

Then he focused on Keefe.

"K does not have to have lied about anything," he said. "We start, ladies and gentlemen, from the notion that K had a rash."

Schoenhorn reminded the jurors that Vicki testified the little boy regressed in his toilet training after she took him away from his father.

"Now I don't think we need to be doctors to know that in terms of hygiene, if you do not wipe yourself after having a bowel movement, and you don't do that for some period of time, a rash is likely to form around the anus."

He referred to the child's testimony during the trial.

"Mr. Carlson was asking him questions, and he said, 'Do you want to hear the story?' And you were all looking at him. And you may recall that he then looked up for a moment. And then he told a story, which went from beginning to end.

"Now he admitted later on that he had gone over the story once with Mr. Carlson. And at home with his parents. And, of course, his parents are not Rob and Vicki, but Vicki and Bruce, his 'new daddy.'"

Schoenhorn highlighted the testimony of some of his witnesses and then got to Barrett's videotape.

"Mr. Carlson has pointed out—here's the proof in the videotape—there are pictures of the child with two dolls.

"I ask you, and I submit, you show me where it shows a penis being inserted into an anus. All he shows is the doll . . . first he drops it a couple of times. Drops it. Then he goes . . . pounds up and down."

Schoenhorn was growing more passionate. His coat flapped as he moved back and forth in front of the jury box, waving his arms to demonstrate the doll action.

He reminded the jurors of the child's statement that he had a beltmark from his eye to his ear, where he claimed Rob hit him.

"Not even Vicki and the new daddy talked about that. So it's convenient just to forget that part of what K said. But when we're talking about fantasy—or rather, fabrication—it can be a combination of truth and fantasy.

"And I suggest, ladies and gentlemen, if a child wakes up in the middle of the night and has a nightmare, and feels that there was a monster under his bed, and he runs to his parents' room, and those parents calm him down and tell him: 'No, no, there's no problem; you can go back to the room; there's nothing there.' Then that child has had the true experience explained to him.

"But what if, ladies and gentlemen, what if any of us were to take a child when he runs in the room and says there's monsters under the bed . . . and, instead of telling the child it was only a dream, forget about it, everything's all right . . . instead you go, 'Yes, there's an awful monster under your bed, and it will eat you, it will kill you if you go back in there' . . . and you say this to that child over and over and over again, and repeat it to him—we also know that K was good at repeating things— then won't that child believe that?"

Schoenhorn brought up Barrett again and drew a parallel with the attempted Watergate coverup that led to Nixon's downfall.

"Note the way Barbara Barrett came across here in the courtroom, the shredding of documents, ladies and gentlemen after being subpoenaed . . . shades of another case, ladies and gentlemen, after certain records are requested that they get shredded. I won't mention what that case is, but I'm sure most of you are familiar with it."

He raised his arms and his voice rose resonantly as he reminded the jurors of Barrett's memory lapses on the stand. "I'll call it willful blindness that she's brought into a case by an acquaintance of the director."

Schoenhorn went back to the child's testimony.

"You'll notice the way he testified here. Was there any show of horror, emotion—like this was a horrible experience? Or did he tell it like this was his story that he had to tell?"

He mentioned Keefe's statement to Noreen Wilcox. "It's hard to believe that a now-six-year-old child could have a cavalier attitude about the court . . . but if it's instilled in him, if that's what's been told to him: 'Good boy, just keep saying Rob hurt you and you'll do fine.' "

Schoenhorn's voice deepened as he returned to the victim theme.

"I can only say, ladies and gentlemen, that whatever the

outcome of this case, there aren't any winners—because there are only losers, because no matter what, Rob McQueeney hasn't seen his children in two years. And there's no telling that even if he wins this, that he'll be able to get custody and visitation again.

"When we're talking about victims in this case, K and Wendy lost an entire half of their family . . . Why? Because of decisions made by Vicki Johnson and Bruce Johnson, with the assistance of a social worker who called herself some other title that no one's ever heard of . . . who's being sued."

Schoenhorn, checked the clock in the rear of the courtroom. "These accusations are so easy to make," he went on, "especially when there are other issues involved, such as custody and divorce . . .

"Vicki McQueeney Johnson is permitted to think what she wants. She's entitled to that. But when it comes to an issue of making you think the same thing, it's got to be by the standards of the law. And those standards are proof beyond a reasonable doubt, as to each element of each offense.

"Without that, ladies and gentlemen, it could make every one of us afraid to be with a small child, a grandchild, a niece, a cousin or a neighbor's child . . . That if there aren't witnesses and a camera watching your activities at all times, the child might say something to someone that can be misinterpreted.

"And once it's misinterpreted, it can snowball and become a case. And a person can be accused, can face prosecution—and the outcome and the penalties associated with that—simply on the basis of something that started off as simply an explanation of a game."

He paused, and then issued the jury a challenge.

"I suggest, ladies and gentlemen, that Rob McQueeney should be allowed to at least try to rebuild his family . . ." As Schoenhorn finished his last words of summation and walked back to his seat the hurt swelled up inside Rob and he swallowed hard to keep his own tears back.

The judge called another recess before Carlson got his last shot. He was brief, rapidly hitting a number of points.

On the expert witnesses, he said, "Simply because someone

who has an M.D. says that this is correct, doesn't necessarily make it so."

He urged the jurors to remember the way the experts presented their testimony, and then he singled out Schetky. "I'm going to suggest to you," he said, "that she was going to get her ideas across no matter what."

He brought up Barrett's videotape again: "I'm going to suggest to you the old adage, a picture is worth a thousand words."

Then he turned his attention to Rob, and his voice rose in intensity for the first time during the trial.

"Don't forget," he told the jurors, "that under certain circumstances, people can really say anything. He can say anything he wanted, really, about what happened that weekend.

"The defendant's attitude, I suggest, here in the courtroom and particularly when he testified, was that of smugness. Is that consistent with what Mr. Schoenhorn told you about him?

"You should very carefully consider the attitude that he has shown you in this courtroom—and particularly when he testified—in determining what really happened. I suggest to you that it's his attitude that is the real key to this case.

"Thank you very much."

McQueeney was dumbfounded. Carlson had been so emotionless throughout the trial. His cross-examinations had been quiet and contained. And then, out of nowhere, how could he suddenly turn so vicious?

What would the jury think of this last brutal shot by the prosecutor? Would it leave its mark in their minds. Would they believe Carlson or Rob?

A spasm of terror shook Rob's body, and his agonized face showed it. He looked toward the jury box. Several jurors were watching him, expressionless.

When they drove home Wednesday afternoon, the jurors knew that the next day would finally belong to them. During the past three weeks, they had come to know quite a bit about each other—and about Robert McQueeney. All of them were thirsting for the moment when they would finally be left alone to talk.

Mulcahy opened court Thursday morning with more questions about press reports of the trial. The "Ghostbusters" trial had made the television news broadcasts.

"I personally read the article in the *Courant*," the judge said. "And I did see one of the TV reports towards the end. But I do understand there were others. Now, does either counsel wish me to make some inquiry of the panel before we proceed?"

Neither lawyer thought it was necessary to question the jurors.

"All right," Mulcahy swung his chair toward the jury box. "Now, ladies and gentlemen, it becomes my duty as the trial judge to instruct you concerning the law which is applicable to the facts of this case. In doing so, it is necessary that I restate certain general principles.

"It is your function to decide what the facts are in this case, and in that respect you and you alone are the sole judges of what the facts are."

Mulcahy went on for two hours, interrupted once by a recess. He talked about the presumption of innocence, about the burden of proof being on the State, about the elements to consider in assessing credibility of witnesses, about how a guilty finding could be made only if the State proved its case beyond a reasonable doubt.

"A reasonable doubt means a doubt founded upon reason and common sense," he explained. "As the words imply, it is a doubt held by a reasonable person after all the evidence in the case is carefully analyzed, compared and weighed. A reasonable doubt may arise not only from the evidence produced, but also from the lack of evidence.

"Reasonable doubt is the kind of doubt upon which reasonable persons like yourselves, in the more serious and important affairs of your own lives, would hesitate to act.

"If, on all the evidence, you have a reasonable doubt as to the guilt of the defendant, you would find him not guilty."

Mulcahy went through each of the three charges against Robert McQueeney, explaining all the elements of each charge that the State had to prove in order for the jury to find McQueeney guilty. He explained the law on anal intercourse in detail.

Finally, shortly before one p.m., Mulcahy gave the jury

their last few instructions and told them they had to reach a verdict without passion, sympathy or sentiment. "The State does not want the conviction of innocent persons," he said. "The State is as much concerned with having an innocent person acquitted as having a guilty person convicted.

"But for the safety and well-being of society—including the safety and well-being of children of tender years—and for the protection of all members of our society, the State is concerned in securing the conviction of persons who have been proven by the evidence beyond a reasonable doubt to be guilty."

He told the jurors that any questions during deliberations should be written on paper and signed by the fore-person. They should then knock on their door and pass the paper to a sheriff, who would give it to the judge.

Since it was one p.m., Mulcahy gave the jury a lunch recess.

When the case reconvened at two p.m., he turned the case over to the six regular members of the jury.

The two alternates—Richard Allison and Jim Stewart—were asked to remain in the courtroom. They watched wistfully as their companions for the last three weeks disappeared through the door back to the room where they had spent so many long hours together.

Mulcahy praised them for their services in the case and said "You're excused. Have a nice balance of the summer."

Allison and Stewart walked out of the courtroom, but not out of the courthouse.

Allison, the Aetna vice president, did not consider returning to his office. There was only one thing that mattered at the moment. He and Stewart *had* to stay to hear the end—the jury's decision.

A bond had been created among eight people who would never have met had not their names been drawn for jury duty.

Allison and Stewart envied the other six: Paula, the lingerie clerk; Emma, the typesetter and porcelain artist; Lois, the legal secretary; Hillary, the young Sears manager; Bob Luff, the salesman; Maurice Back, the retired engineer.

Allison and Stewart went off to a corner of the third-floor

lobby in the courthouse. They had no idea what the others were thinking. But, at least now *they* could talk.

For Allison the trial had been painful, dredging up memories of his own divorce.

Stewart remembered an encounter in a men's room at a New York Giants football game a few years earlier. A little boy, who had trouble raising his zipper, had asked Stewart to help him. And he did. Now, he realized with a chill what someone else might have thought—walking into the men's room and seeing him with his hand on the little boy's pants.

The McQueeney family settled into a small conference room next to the courtroom. It had been four long weeks since they first came to court. Now, they had to endure a different kind of agony. They read the newspaper and talked about anything to keep their minds off the question nobody dared ask: What do you think they're going to do?

At three-forty-five p.m., Schoenhorn called Rob and his family back into the courtroom. Something had happened. Mulcahy was at his seat on the bench.

"As I indicated to counsel in chambers," he began, "the sheriff delivered to me a note from the jury. I will read it into the record. It reads: 'We would like to hear the testimony of K,' and it's signed Lois Goodin. And then under her signature, it states, 'Can we take notes during the replay?' "

Mulcahy passed the note to his clerk and asked that it be marked as an exhibit.

Allison and Stewart grinned at each other. So Lois had been elected fore-person. A good choice. God, they wished they were in there.

"With reference to the taking of notes," the judge announced, "I am not inclined to permit that. I'll hear counsel if they wish to be heard. However, I would tell the jury that certainly if there's any portion that they later request to be replayed, or anything—even if they want the entire testimony replayed at a subsequent time—that would be permitted. Does either counsel wish to be heard?"

Neither Carlson nor Schoenhorn had anything to say about the issue.

"All right sheriff," said Mulcahy, "would you bring in the

ladies and gentlemen of the jury? You can tell them they won't need any notepaper."

Allison and Stewart smiled at the other jurors as they took their seats with their usual blank expressions.

Emma noticed the alternates in their new seats in the spectator section. She wasn't surprised that they had stayed.

Mulcahy explained that the rules did not permit note-taking and gave the court monitor the go-ahead to replay the tape-recording of Keefe's testimony.

McQueeney sat at the defense desk with Schoenhorn, listening while his son once again told "the story." The jurors were doing exactly what Carlson had suggested they do.

Rob was pleased with the selection of Lois Goodin. He still couldn't help but feel the eye contact indicated she was on his side. But the memory of Carlson's closing shot was churning inside his mind.

When the replay was completed at four-forty-five p.m., Mulcahy adjourned court for the day. He cautioned the jurors not to watch news reports and not to discuss the case until they returned to their deliberation room Friday morning.

"Thank you and good night," said the judge.

Allison and Stewart were in the spectator section Friday morning when Mulcahy sent the jurors back to their deliberation room promptly at ten a.m. They were sitting on the prosecution side of the Courtroom 3A.

Less than an hour later, word buzzed through the lobby that Mulcahy was back on the bench.

"Returning to State vs. Robert McQueeney, CR 53031, as I reported to counsel in chambers, there has been a written communication received from the jury," Mulcahy announced. "And I did read it and show it to counsel."

Allison and Stewart looked at each other with anticipation as the judge prepared to read the note for the record.

"It says: 'We would like a short recess.' "

The two alternate jurors sunk back on their bench.

"That part of it has been taken care of," the judge continued. "And then it goes on: 'And upon returning, we would like to hear the testimony of Barbara Barrett again, regarding the dates of the visits.' And it's signed by Lois Goodin."

Mulcahy asked the clerk to mark the note as an exhibit. He had the jurors brought back into the courtroom, and portions of Barrett's testimony were replayed.

McQueeney was confused. He couldn't figure out why the jury wanted to know about dates. Why weren't they exploring how badly Barrett had blundered?

The jurors were excused to return to their deliberations.

The McQueeneys went back to their small conference room —to wait, and wonder.

What they didn't know was that the jury was split, five to one.

Several jurors had developed serious doubts about the validity of the evidence against McQueeney early in the trial—they hadn't believed the prosecution's first witness, Vicki. Barrett's pathetic performance reinforced their skepticism. And Bruce Johnson's wise-guy attitude further alienated them.

Some of the jurors were upset that the State had taken McQueeney through a trial with such a flimsy case.

The lone holdout was Maurice Back, the retired engineer.

Maurice thought that Keefe's testimony and demonstration with Barrett's dolls, was persuasive evidence of a sexual assault. Beyond that, Back didn't think that an engineer, someone who dealt with science and facts, should be intrigued by the supernatural or captivated by a movie like *Ghostbusters*. Maurice firmly believed that evil spirits should not be taken lightly.

Against that, Back was weighing the final testimony of Noreen Wilcox, the victim advocate who had revealed Keefe's startling conversation with her when she spent a few minutes alone with him. Her testimony had served as a reminder that Keefe was not infallible but a small child, and that he might have been coached. And that forced Maurice to consider whether he had enough reasonable doubt about McQueeney's guilt to vote for acquittal.

The other jurors, all of whom felt McQueeney was innocent, were trying to convince Maurice that the State's evidence didn't add up, that the charges against McQueeney had been concocted by Vicki or Bruce, or by both of them.

It was Emma who suggested the jury rehear Barrett's testimony. Emma had brought her home-written notes to the deliberation room. She wanted to go over the sequence of events, with an emphasis on reviewing Bruce's role in getting Keefe to the Langley Center.

Outside the empty courtroom, the wait went on . . . eleven o'clock . . . noon . . .

The clock was moving toward one p.m. when, out in the lobby, Allison and Stewart noticed movement. They looked up and saw Schoenhorn marching briskly toward Jackie who was coming from the other direction.

"Where is everybody?" he asked urgently. "The jury's in."

"I don't know," she said, her body tightening. She cradled the baby in her belly with her hands. "I think Rob's parents are downstairs getting something to eat. I don't know where Rob is."

"We've got to find him, *now*." Schoenhorn spun around and quickly strode back toward the courtroom. The sound of his heels hitting the floor echoed across the lobby.

McQueeney was in a panic in the elevator with Brian Kornbrath, an associate in Schoenhorn's law firm who had come to court for the verdict. Rob and Kornbrath were heading toward the first floor to get Jackie and his parents. They knew the verdict was in. Rob thought Jackie was in the parking lot, getting something out of the car.

McQueeney squeezed through the opening elevator doors at the first floor and spotted his parents through the glass doors. They were outside by The Chuckwagon.

"You get them, and I'll go look for Jackie."

"No." Kornbrath stopped him. "You get back upstairs, and I'll get them."

McQueeney turned around and ran back to the elevator. When he got to the third floor, he scanned the lobby for Jackie, but couldn't see her. She had gone to look for him.

The lobby, which had been empty a few minutes earlier, was now bustling with activity. McQueeney spotted Schoenhorn waving to him by the door to Courtroom 3A. His empty stomach clenched as Schoenhorn took him by the arm and led him back to the defense desk. He looked over his shoulder for Jackie, but saw nothing but a blur of blue.

More than a half-dozen uniformed sheriffs converged on the courtroom. Jack Bailey was behind them. McQueeney recognized his face from television.

McQueeney was in his swivel chair at the defense desk, watching the rear door of the courtroom, when he saw his family come inside. They looked as terror-stricken as he felt. Everything was happening so fast.

Ray and Ruth edged toward their seats, holding hands so tightly their knuckles were reddening. Jackie was behind them, holding her belly. She looked so helpless. She reached out longingly toward Rob. Her hand was shaking, but he couldn't go to her. And she couldn't get to him.

For the first time during the trial, Jackie didn't take her front-row seat. She squeezed into the second row of the spectator section, behind Ray and Ruth, and sank onto the bench, her face frozen with fear.

Across the aisle, Bailey took a place on the bench behind the prosecution desk, near Allison and Stewart. Eight sheriffs were in the courtroom now, most of them crowded around the rear door. Allison thought it looked like they were preparing for war.

The door next to the judge's bench opened, and Mulcahy walked in. He looked around the chamber and took his seat.

"All right. Thank you sheriff," he said. "The court did receive a further written communication from the sheriff . . . that is from the jury.

"And I did not call counsel into chambers for reasons which will become apparent when I read the communication into the record. And that is that it reads as follows: 'This is to advise the court that the jury has reached its verdict.' And it's signed by Lois J. Goodin. At this point it may be marked as a court's exhibit."

Mulcahy suggested the clerk show the note to the lawyers.

"All right," said Schoenhorn upon seeing it.

Carlson waved the clerk off. "That's okay," he said. "I believe it."

Mulcahy continued. "Now the manner in which we proceed, Mr. Clerk, in taking the verdict, first of all a roll call when they are brought in, and then you can proceed with the taking of the verdict.

"All right, sheriff. The jury may be brought back in."

McQueeney gripped the arms of his chair to try to stop the trembling in his hands. His face was pale.

"All right. Thank you very much, ladies and gentlemen," said Mulcahy. "Mr. Clerk, you can proceed."

Each member of the jury stood as the clerk called their names and then announced: "All present and accounted for, your honor."

"All right, ladies and gentlemen, you may be seated," Mulcahy said. "Mr. Clerk, you may proceed."

"Thank you, your honor." The clerk turned to face the jury box. "Would the fore-person please stand and identify himself or herself?"

Lois stood tall, her shoulders back. She, too, looked slightly pale. "Juror number 10767," she said. "Lois Goodin."

"Madam fore-person," the clerk continued, "has the jury reached a verdict? Please answer yes or no."

"Yes," she answered in a clear, firm voice.

The clerk turned his attention to the defense desk. "Will the accused, Robert McQueeney, please rise and remain standing. Now the fore-person will please face the accused."

McQueeney felt off-balance. He had trouble getting to his feet. He could feel the muscles in his face twitching. Then his whole body was shaking. He had never shaken like this, not even during the arrest.

He put his fingertips on the desk for support and looked at Lois. The two of them locked eyes, as they had done so many times during the trial.

Ruth McQueeney was crying loudly in the spectator section.

The clerk kept going:

"In file number 53031," said the clerk his voice ringing out, "State vs. Robert McQueeney, what say you madam foreperson, is he guilty or not guilty of the crime of sexual assault in the first degree in violation of Section 53a-70(a) of the General

Statutes of the State of Connecticut, which he stands charged in the first count?"

"Not guilty." Lois said in a strong voice, still looking into McQueeney's eyes, now wet with tears.

Rob's knees nearly buckled. He felt like he was falling. He gripped the desk for support.

Behind him, Ruth, was sobbing even louder. Jackie was crying quietly, but breathing hard. She edged forward and patted Ruth on the back. Ruth and Ray turned toward her and they exchanged brief but heartfelt hugs.

The clerk was continuing. "What say you madam fore-person . . ." Ruth, still sobbing, was gasping for air now, ". . . with which he stands charged in the second count?"

"Not guilty." Lois said firmly again, this time with a hint of a smile.

"Oooohhhhh," groaned Ray McQueeney. He slumped to his right, flat on the bench, overcome with emotion. Ruth, sobbing and gasping more desperately now, slumped onto the rail in front of her. Two of the sheriffs stationed by the back door, quickly moved forward.

The clerk was still reading. ". . . in the third count?"

"Not guilty." Lois had a full smile now, her eyes still locked on Rob's.

Ruth's breathing worsened. Her sobs echoed in the courtroom. Ray pulled himself off the bench and bent over her.

"Is she all right?" a sheriff whispered.

Ray shook his head, unable to speak. He stood up to hold Ruth, who was gasping for air. Each of the sheriffs took one arm and they half-carried her through the rear door.

McQueeney was conscious of the commotion behind him, but could do nothing about it. He stood still, almost rigid, his face and body frozen, unable for the moment to move or speak.

"Alright." It was Mulcahy's resonant voice this time with one of his familiar alrights.

"The verdicts may be accepted and are ordered recorded," the judge said.

McQueeney felt someone clasp his hand. It was Schoenhorn, smiling proudly. They patted each other on the back. Schoenhorn's legal pad was on the desk between them.

Scrawled on it in large, wobbly letters were two words: "NOT GUILTY."

Rob turned around. Jackie, tears streaming down her face, had moved up to the front bench. Rob stumbled back weakly. Their emotions mirrored in their eyes, they squeezed each other tightly over the rail. Oh, how McQueeney wanted to get out of this place.

"Thank you very much Mr. Clerk, and thank you Mrs. Goodin," Mulcahy said, maintaining judicial decorum. "You may be seated.

"Ladies and gentlemen, on behalf of the court, the parties in this matter, the State of Connecticut, the defense, the attorneys, Mr. Schoenhorn and Mr. Carlson, I wish to thank you very much for the valuable . . ."

"Whoosh . . . Whoosh . . . Whoosh" The sound of an oxygen tank intruded through the rear door of the courtroom.

". . . As I said I enjoyed very much working with you. I certainly hope that all of you—we'll let you return to your families now. And I hope that you have a very nice balance and remainder of the summer. Thank you so much. And you're excused."

McQueeney, exhausted, dropped back into his swivel chair, watching the jurors file out of the courtroom for the final time. He wanted to run after them and thank them one by one. But the door quickly closed behind them; he turned his attention to Mulcahy.

"Alright," said the judge. "I want to initially commend both counsel on a case—I might add a case, because of its subject matter that it was indeed a sensitive type of case—I want to commend both counsel on just an excellent trial of the case.

"And is there a motion to be made by the defense?"

"Yes, your honor," answered Schoenhorn. "I have two motions to make. I would first ask that the defendant be unconditionally discharged concerning the matter, and second, that the records in this matter, and all documentation concerning the matter, be officially ordered sealed by the court as an erased record."

There was no objection.

Mulcahy ruled that McQueeney was free. Rob whispered to Schoenhorn, "Now can I go?"

"Go out and see your mom," Schoenhorn whispered back. For the last time Rob pushed through the gate to the spectator section and put his arm around Jackie. Together, they walked out of the courtroom.

Ruth and Ray were in the small conference room just outside the door, surrounded by sheriffs. Ruth was slumped in a chair, still crying, an oxygen tank on the floor next to her. Her breathing was returning to normal. They all exchanged tear-stained hugs.

Schoenhorn joined them after a few minutes. Ruth reached for him, but couldn't get out of her chair. She wrapped her arm around his thigh. Then she pulled him down toward her.

"You're getting it right on the lips, pussycat," she said, kissing him. "We didn't like you at first. You know that. But I think you are absolutely one hell of a guy."

Schoenhorn's face reddened. With a shy, embarrassed look he excused himself so he could get downstairs to talk with the jurors, something he did after every trial.

With Ray's help, Ruth was able to stand a few minutes later.

The four McQueeneys, their arms around each other—as much for support as for affection—slowly made their way across the third-floor lobby and into the elevator.

Before the metal doors converged, Rob looked back for one long moment at the entrance to Courtroom 3A. The lobby was empty now, except for three blue-uniformed sheriffs, making arrangements for their next trial.

When the elevator opened at the first floor, the Mc-Queeneys stepped out and walked toward the front of the courthouse. Rob saw Schoenhorn outside on the sidewalk in the bright sunlight. He was surrounded by the jurors. It looked like all eight of them were there. Schoenhorn's arms were waving and his coat was flapping.

As Rob swept through the glass doors, some of the jurors hurried over quickly, embracing him.

A television news crew was standing off to the side, waiting for an interview.

Rob stared at his lawyer. On the pavement next to Schoenhorn was his dark, bulging briefcase. Stuffed inside were the remnants of the McQueeney trial, countless pieces of paper with thousands of words that couldn't begin to describe what it was like to be released from more than two years of torment.

■ CHAPTER TWENTY-NINE ■

Another Courtroom, Two Years Later

May 29, 1991

Rob McQueeney broke away from Henry Hurvitz and a huddle of lawyers. His suit was stained with sweat. He walked quickly across the crowded third-floor lobby of Hartford Superior Court toward Jackie and his mother.

"We're ready to go in," Rob told them purposefully, a steely edge to his voice. He strode forward a few paces, then turned to wait for his wife and mother to catch up. "It looks good. Let's go."

He put his arm around Jackie and guided her to the door of Courtroom 300, the place where family disputes are put on public display. Ruth followed. She looked like she was about to cry.

The heat and humidity were oppressive, even though it was just ten a.m. The windows of the old stone courthouse were open, but there was no breeze. It was days like these that made the new criminal courthouse across the street look good. At least it had air-conditioning.

McQueeney was all too familiar with both buildings. Two years after the trial, he was still a father fighting for justice. But now it was different. He was on the offensive—in court because he wanted to be there. His anger and determination were focused on his objective. He wanted to see his children.

Only one person stood in his way. Vicki.

Since the acquittal, McQueeney had been persistently trying one means after another to get his visitation rights restored,

346

but so far, Vicki had managed to thwart him. Before he could see his children, Rob was required to undergo a court-ordered psychiatric exam. He was on his second psychiatrist, because Vicki had refused to cooperate with the first one. She, too, was supposed to be examined.

The pursuit of justice continued to be expensive. The trial had cost McQueeney about $35,000, between lost wages and Schoenhorn's per-diem charges. Since then, he had paid out thousands more—to cover Hurvitz's legal fees and the cost of the psychiatrists. His and Jackie's house had a second mortgage. But he would not give up. Not now. Not ever.

Keefe was nearly nine and Wendy was seven. He wanted them to know their father loved them and was committed to being part of their lives.

Before coming to court that morning, Rob and Jackie left their daughter, Madeline, at a day-care center. Madeline, cute and blonde, just like her mother, had been born on October 11, 1989.

Up in the front of the cavernous courtroom, Judge Joseph L. Steinberg was calling cases. Off to the right side of the chamber, Bruce Johnson, looking important, took a seat by a side wall in a chair normally used by lawyers or sheriffs. He and Vicki were getting divorced. She had left him for another man.

On the opposite side of the courtroom, Hurvitz conferred with three lawyers: Joseph B. Burns, Vicki's lawyer for more than a year; Jacqueline A. Wilson, who represented Johnson; and Catherine P. Kligerman, who had been appointed by the court to represent the interests of Keefe and Wendy.

Vicki was not there. Nobody was sure where she was.

"Agreements?" called Judge Steinberg, looking toward the cluster of lawyers.

"We don't have an agreement, Your Honor," said Kligerman, stepping toward the bench. However, she told him the lawyers involved in the McQueeney matter were close to one.

"Oh really?" The judge perked up and called a recess to meet with them.

Steinberg, Hurvitz, Kligerman, Wilson and Burns disappeared through the door behind the judge's bench. From the spectator section, Rob and Jackie watched, and sweated.

Ruth McQueeney walked to the open windows, trying to get some fresh air. She looked outside toward the people on the sidewalk below and thought about the last four years since her son's arrest.

When the judge and the lawyers reappeared after twenty minutes, they got quickly to business.

"Let's deal with McQueeney, Number 173," said Steinberg, taking his seat on the bench.

Rob got up, gave Jackie a reassuring smile and walked to the front of the courtroom, taking a seat among the lawyers, who were lined up in a row of chairs behind two large tables in front of the judge. Johnson stayed on the sidelines.

Steinberg called for Dr. James C. Black, a child psychiatrist, to take the witness stand. Black was the second psychiatrist who had been hired to perform court-ordered evaluations of Rob, Vicki and Keefe.

Kligerman said she would do the questioning. She asked Black to describe his study of the McQueeney matter.

"It consisted of four and a half interviews with Mr. McQueeney, three interviews with Mrs. Johnson and two telephone calls with Mr. Johnson," said Black, a clean-cut, dark-haired man who seemed uneasy on the stand.

"Were you ever able to see the minor children?" asked Kligerman.

"I was not."

"Were they scheduled to visit with you?"

"Ahhh, Keefe was scheduled to visit with me," he said.

"Was that appointment kept?"

"It was not."

Black said he tried to reschedule the appointment, but was unable to reach Vicki by telephone. The first time he called, he said, he reached a man who agreed to give Vicki a message. When Black called again the following week, the man said he didn't know where Vicki was.

Kligerman asked Black to give his opinion on visitation.

"Well, I believe that given the proviso that I have not seen the children," he paused momentarily, "visitation for Mr. Mc-Queeney is in order."

"Do you have an opinion as to the time, the duration or the kind of visitation?" asked Kligerman.

"Well," said Black, "in light of the fact that he has not seen the children . . . more importantly, they have not seen him for approximately four years, I believe the frequency and duration of visitation needs to be keyed to their emotional state and receptivity."

"So," said Kligerman, "in essence, he should have visitation, and we should attempt to find out how the visitation is going to affect the children?"

"Correct. I think that it's important to ascertain in what emotional state the children are and what their attitude toward the father is, how well they recall him, and what their feelings are about him in order to determine the rate one should proceed."

Kligerman said she had no further questions.

Steinberg excused Black and turned his attention to a motion by Burns, who had asked to withdraw as Vicki's lawyer because he felt he had a conflict of interest, having once represented both Vicki and Bruce Johnson.

"Very well, I'm going to grant your motion to withdraw, sir," said the judge.

When Burns didn't move away from the table full of lawyers, Steinberg went on: "Which means, Mr. Burns, you're free to leave, sir."

As the courtroom doors closed behind Burns, the judge motioned for Hurvitz to proceed.

"We have discussed this with counsel for the minor children," Hurvitz began, "and we believe that it is in the best interests of the minor children that custody be changed.

"I believe that Ms. Wilson also believes that custody should be changed. And we would request, Your Honor, pending further order of the court, that custody be granted to Mr. McQueeney and Mr. Johnson jointly. Their purposes are to bring the children back to Connecticut to reside in a home that both Ms. Wilson and I and Ms. Kligerman shall determine to be a safe environment for them over the next period of time."

Steinberg asked Wilson for her position, as Bruce Johnson's lawyer.

"Your Honor," she said, "I have nothing to add. Certainly, I believe it's in the best interests of the children to grant an order of temporary custody to the father and stepfather at this point in time."

The judge asked Kligerman what she could add as a basis for ordering a change of custody.

"Your Honor," Kligerman stood up. "Dr. Black is the second expert that has attempted to do a custody . . . a visitation evaluation on this matter. The first expert started, and then Mrs. Johnson had problems with whether he was impartial, and refused to go. So we turned to Dr. Black."

She paused, checking her notes.

"This matter, I believe, has been going on since 1989. We were unable to get a complete evaluation done—only because Mrs. Johnson thwarts the investigation."

"What other basis might there be?" asked the judge.

"I believe that we could offer proof to the court that the children have been withdrawn from their school system," Kligerman went on. "We do not know, other than through her counsel, that they are, in fact, registered in another system in another state.

"We believe the children have been living, since March of this year, in more than one state . . . and have been living in a fleeing-type arrangement.

"There is a criminal proceeding at this point in time in court against Mrs. Johnson."

"What's the nature of the criminal charge?" asked Steinberg.

"It's possession of drugs, your honor . . . In addition to that, the Department of Children and Youth Services has begun an investigation in terms of seeking removal of her as a parent.

"As I see it," Kligerman went on, "Mrs. Johnson has so convoluted her life that it is unlikely that she will return to this jurisdiction without some pressure. And it is unlikely that these children are in a good, safe environment as she attempts to flee both Mr. McQueeney's efforts to see his children, and now Mr. Johnson, in his efforts."

Bruce Johnson had risen from his chair and was walking toward the tables where the lawyers were sitting.

"Your Honor," he called. "If I may make a short statement?"

"Yes sir," said Steinberg, turning toward him. "Who are you, sir?"

"My name is Bruce Johnson."

Wilson, a heavy woman, pushed herself out of her chair and hustled past the other lawyers toward her client.

"The children turned Mrs. Johnson into the authorities on the possession charge," said Bruce, as he continued to walk toward the lawyers' table. "It was on their . . ."

Wilson finally got to Johnson, cut him off and began pushing him back to his seat.

"Sir," called the judge, "if you're in a position to take the stand and testify . . ."

Wilson broke in. "Never mind, your honor," she said over her shoulder as she put Johnson back in his chair.

Steinberg waited for Wilson to return to her seat.

The judge then announced, "Based upon a finding of the best interests of the children, Keefe and Wendy, the court will order custody be modified and be entrusted to Bruce Johnson and Robert McQueeney, jointly."

Grabbing each other, Rob and Jackie hugged so tightly each gasped for breath. They could hardly contain their elation or believe what they had just heard. This was a huge victory that had seemed totally out of reach until today. A stunned Ruth followed Rob and Jackie out of the courtroom murmuring, "What happened? What did they do?"

Jackie paused. It was a moment to be savored.

"They gave us joint custody," Jackie said softly.

■ Afterword ■

Of the 328,000 cases of child sexual abuse reported in 1986, 195,000 were determined to be unfounded by child protection agencies, after the suspected molester was investigated. According to the authors of the most comprehensive study on the subject, completed in 1988, 70,000 to 90,000 accused molestors of the remaining 133,000—where the police and/or child protection agencies decided abuse had occurred and began criminal and/or juvenile court proceedings—were probably falsely accused too.*

The number of these cases which arose during divorce or custody disputes is unknown.

---

* The 1986 statistics cited are from the American Humane Association's "Highlights of Official Child Neglect and House Reporting," 1986. The other data is calculated from percentages of actual abuse obtained from Wakefield, Holida and Underwager's *Accusations of Child Sexual Abuse*, Springfield, Illinois: Charles C. Thomas, 1988.